FINDING FERNANDA
Two Mothers, One Child,
and a Cross-Border Search for Truth

Erin Elizabeth Siegal

CATHEXIS PRESS

Oakland, California
2011

CATHEXIS PRESS, LLC
4096 Piedmont Avenue, Suite 111, Oakland CA 94611, USA

Copyright © 2011 Cathexis Press
All rights reserved
Distributed in the United States by Ingram

LIBRARY OF CONGRESS CATALOGING IN PUBLICATION DATA
Library of Congress Control Number: 2011919066
Finding Fernanda: Two Mothers, One Child, and a Cross-Border Search for Truth / Erin
Siegal
Includes bibliographical references.
ISBN 0-98388-450-1
1. International adoption. 2. Guatemala. 3. Organized Crime.

Printed in the United States of America

Cover design by Bob Kosturko
Cover photograph by Erin Siegal
Interior layout by Julie Csizmadia
All photographs by Erin Siegal unless otherwise noted

Cathexis Press books may be purchased for educational, business, or sales promotional use.
For information, please write: Special Markets Department, Cathexis Press LLC, 4096
Piedmont Avenue, Suite 111, Oakland, California, 94611.

FOR JAMES L. McINTYRE

CONTENTS

Preface   8
Notes on Sources   11
Dramatis Personae   15

I.

   1. Choices   16
   2. Please Say Yes   31
   3. Beginnings   46
   4. The Last Emanuel   59
   5. A Pretty Little Girl   71

II.

   6. David and Goliath   82
   7. "Are We Ready for a Fall?"   94
   8. Risk Versus Reward   108
   9. Gone   129
   10. Dealing with the Devil   147
   11. Fundación Sobrevivientes   165

III.

   12. Revelation   185
   13. Two Mothers, No Answers   199
   14. Hogar Luz de María   218
   15. Custody   235
   16. The Perfect Crime   250
   17. Moving Forward   266

Epilogue   278
Acknowledgments   284
Additional Notes on Sources   287
References   298

*". . . oír un nombre que no es el nuestro,
pensar en cosas que no son nuestras . . ."*

*". . . to hear a name that is not ours,
to think of things that are not ours . . ."*

— Miguel Ángel Asturias
from his poem "Litany of the Banished"
(Guatemalan, 1899–1974)

PREFACE

The first time I set foot in Guatemala was in December 2007. My sister and I were visiting the country as tourists, wandering to the usual places of interest: the teeming markets of Chichicastenango, Antigua's famous cathedral, and the National Palace. At the trip's end, we waited for our flight home in Guatemala City's gleaming, modern airport, surrounded by over a dozen American couples. Each pair was leaving the country with a Guatemalan child.

As a photojournalist, I found the image arresting. Back in New York, I began skimming through press clippings about adoption, trying to find a compelling story angle that would enable me to return to Guatemala to photograph an adoption story. I imagined a human-interest piece touching on cultural blending, or the love and generosity that seemed intrinsic to adoption.

Instead, the news articles I found were anything but uplifting. Many were downright shocking. In June 2000, nearly a decade earlier, the *Miami Herald* had reported that Guatemala was "the fourth-largest exporter of children in the world, a ranking sustained by often ruthless means." The piece noted, "Child robbery is extraordinarily commonplace here" and described the experience of a young, poorly educated woman from the countryside who had been tricked into giving her baby up for adoption after a C-section. A year later, in 2001, the *LA Times* published a substantial feature by Juanita Darling entitled "Little Bundles of Cash," which said Guatemalan children "have become a major export. . . . There is growing evidence that the profits and demand for babies have become high enough to foster child-trafficking rings." Darling mentioned that the rings relied on various kinds of intimidation and financial incentives to induce impoverished women to give up their children. "Law enforcement officials believe that demand has become so intense," she wrote, "that some traffickers are stealing babies from their mothers."

Certainly, I thought, trafficking and kidnapping problems from almost a decade earlier would be cleaned up by now. But as I continued reading press clips from 2006 and 2007, the same transgressions kept popping up. Babies were taken, by force or coercion. Birth mothers, largely disempowered, were tricked or paid.

By 2007, the Associated Press was reporting that Americans were adopting around one in every one hundred babies born in Guatemala each year. Other articles referred to Guatemala's international adoption program as "unregulated, profit-driven, and much-criticized" (Cox News Service) and "believed to be rife with corruption" (*The New York Times*).

Photographing a straightforward human-interest piece no longer seemed appropriate. In fact, the issue felt better suited to detective work than to visual storytelling. In spring 2008, I applied to the Stabile Center for Investigative Reporting at Columbia University's Graduate School of Journalism, pitching an examination of adoption fraud in Guatemala as a potential thesis topic. By August 2008, I was one of a dozen Stabile fellows receiving specialized training in investigative reporting. Some of the reporting contained in this book began at Columbia under the guidance of Stabile Center director Sheila Coronel and veteran investigative journalist Wayne Barrett, who was my advisor. At first, the project seemed to be a dry kind of historical documentation, tracking legislative evolution and lobbying efforts. I wasn't sure how my own reporting would effectively serve the public interest, since I couldn't imagine anyone being interested enough to actually read through such dense subject material. I asked Wayne repeatedly if I should change subjects. He told me to keep digging, and I did.

On December 8, 2008, I found an email that had been written a month before by a woman named Betsy Emanuel. I'd been reading the archives of a popular public email listserve, the Adoption Agency Review List (AARG), learning about how different American adoption agencies operated and how clients compared and contrasted them. In her email, Betsy offered stark advice to a list member who'd asked how to choose an agency.

"Ask strong questions about exactly who any agency is dealing with in-country," she instructed. "If you get ANY feeling that you are annoying the agency with these types of questions, then dig deeper and DO NOT ignore your feelings. These measures would have helped me if I had known to do this. . . ."

I was instantly curious. That same afternoon, I sent Betsy an email explaining that I was a grad student researching adoption and asking if she'd feel comfortable sharing her experience with me. She responded vaguely, saying she'd had four great adoptions and then a "nightmare" with a Florida agency that she "would not recommend." She didn't provide additional details.

I asked if we could set up a time to speak on the phone.

"I don't have a lot of spare time," she responded. "But if I can help you, I'll try. I have a daughter who'll be in grad school soon..." She mentioned that she knew it was hard to get people to "take the time to share information." I expected a brief, ten-minute phone call.

Our conversation the next day lasted for three hours. Betsy summarized what amounted to a decade of adoption experiences as I tried to wrap my head around the fact that this down-to-earth, honey-voiced Southern woman had eight children. At that time, I didn't understand how adoption hooked some families — and not just celebrities like the Jolie-Pitts. In a piece published in *Good Housekeeping* in 2000, journalist and mother of nine Melissa Fay Greene recounted her first adoption experience and ". . . the feeling I can't save all the children, but I can save this one." After adopting four more times, in 2011, she told *Publishers Weekly* that "it wasn't a humanitarian act. We simply wanted more children, and the children needed families."

That day, when Betsy Emanuel first recounted her experience with the Florida-based adoption agency Celebrate Children International to me, the story seemed too strange to be true. Afterwards, Betsy emailed me a few articles from Guatemalan newspapers that supported her account, involving a young woman named Mildred Alvarado and her children.

A week later after our first conversation, I left the U.S. on the first of what would be multiple month long reporting trips to Guatemala City. Although I planned to do general research, speaking to a variety of diverse sources, Betsy's complicated story remained in the back of my mind. I decided that I'd start looking into what had really transpired if, and only if, I could find Mildred Alvarado without too much work.

I found her within days.

NOTES ON SOURCES

The information in this book is based on interviews, informal conversations, and interactions with sources that took place from August 2008 until August 2011. While working in Guatemala, I reported side-by-side with a local journalist, using a buddy system for safety, to ensure accurate comprehension while immersed in a foreign culture, and to make sure my interviews were accurately translated. I was fortunate that Associated Press Guatemala City correspondent Juan Carlos Llorca was willing and able to help.

Various people and institutions in Guatemala provided me with information, including sources from the U.S. Embassy in Guatemala, the Comicíon Internacional contra la Impunidad en Guatemala (CICIG), the Ministerio Público (Ministry of Justice), the Procuraduría General de la Nación (PGN), independent investigators, lawyers, adoption facilitators, *hogar* directors, foster mothers, birth mothers, cab drivers, the Archivo General de Protocolos (General Protocols Archive), judges, nonprofit organizations, and many others. Sources have emailed me spreadsheets and databases, handed me photocopies of legal depositions, and allowed me to photograph stacks of court documents that include email, lab results, and more.

In the United States, I've spoken with officials from the Council on Accreditation, the Office of Children's Issues, the Adoption Unit at the State Department, adoptive parents, adoption agency staffers and former staffers, social workers, nonprofit organizations, advocacy organizations including the Congressional Coalition on Adoption Institute, GuatAdopt, and the Joint Council on International Children's Services (JCICS), journalists, doctors, and many others. I've also attended adoption events that include the 2009 Adoptive Parents Committee conference in NYC and the 2009 Adoption Law and Policy Conference at New York Law School.

I've filed over 40 federal public records requests in the United States, including to the FBI, the U.S. Embassy, the Department of Homeland Security, and the United States Citizenship and Immigration Services. I've also filed numerous public records requests with the Archivo General de Protocolos, and the Ministerio Público in Guatemala and with various agencies in the state of Florida.

Detailed endnote citations are available online at the project website for this book, http://findingfernanda.com, along with email, hundreds of government documents, video clips, interview transcripts, and other relevant material about this story and the larger issue of international adoption corruption. A general outline of chapter sourcing can be found in the book's end material, along with a chronology of events.

Sue Hedberg, executive director of the adoption agency Celebrate Children International, declined my requests for interviews, as well as requests for clarification and response to the accounts and allegations contained in this book. Hedberg's former business partner Marvin Josué Bran Galindo also declined requests for interviews. In order to try to understand their actions and motivations, I spoke to people closely associated with them, including Hedberg's husband, employees, former employees, clients, and adoption industry colleagues. Several former clients also provided me with email to and from Hedberg and Bran. I interviewed Bran Galindo's mother, Lilia Consuelo Galindo Ovalle de Bran (Coni Galindo Bran) twice in person, as well as Galindo Bran's former lawyer, current lawyer, and several business partners who worked with the Galindo Bran organization. I also spoke with Americans who had adopted "Marvin Bran babies" through Sue Hedberg's agency and with various Guatemalan government investigators and legal analysts who have investigated or are currently investigating the Galindo Bran organization.

The recollections, feelings, and memories of Mildred Alvarado and Betsy Emanuel, as offered to me directly over the last two years of reporting, are at times single-sourced. Interviews with both Betsy and Mildred were conducted between December 2009 and August 2010. A diverse and lengthy document trail, some of which is available on the book's website, supports the accounts of both women.

Certain names have been changed in this book to protect the confidentiality of sources that agreed to speak under the condition of anonymity. Others requested the use of pseudonyms out of fear of reprisal or to protect their children's privacy. All such instances are clearly footnoted.

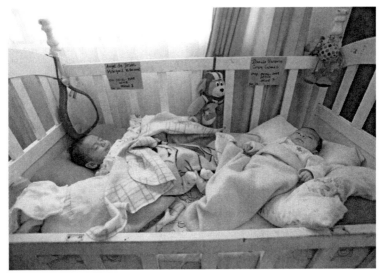

Babies sleep two to a crib at Hogar Luz de María, January 19, 2009.

DRAMATIS PERSONAE

ELIZABETH AND LESLIE EMANUEL
Betsy and Leslie Emanuel live in Gallatin, Tennessee, and are the parents
of eight children: three biological and five through international adoption.

MILDRED NAVEL ALVARADO YAC
Mildred Alvarado, born November 13, 1978, lives in Villa Nueva,
Guatemala, with her family and her sister Patricia. She is the mother of
Maria Fernanda (Fernanda) and Ana Cristina Alvarado Yac.

MIRNA PATRICIA ALVARADO YAC
Patricia Alvarado is Mildred Alvarado's younger sister and best friend.

JENNIFER YASMIN VELÁSQUEZ LOPÉZ
Jennifer Velásquez Lopéz is a Guatemalan child who was offered as an
adoptable orphan to American families in 2005 and 2006.

SUSAN ZELEK HEDBERG (SUE HEDBERG)
Sue Hedberg is CEO and executive director of Celebrate Children
International (CCI), a Christian international adoption agency based in
Oviedo, Florida. She has worked in international adoption for over ten
years.

MIRLA SABRINA DONIS HERNÁNDEZ
Sabrina Donis lives in Mixco, Guatemala, with her boyfriend, Rony Cruz
de Bautista.

LILIA CONSUELO "CONI" GALINDO OVALLE DE BRAN
Coni Galindo Bran and her son Marvin live on the same block in Mixco,
Guatemala, in the gated community of San José Las Rosas. The Bran
Galindo family found and offered Guatemalan children for placement in
adoptive families.

NORMA ANGELICA CRUZ CORDOVA (NORMA CRUZ)
Norma Cruz is a human-rights advocate and founder of the nonprofit
Fundación Sobrevivientes (Survivors' Foundation) in Guatemala City.

MARVIN JOSUÉ BRAN GALINDO
Marvin Bran, the son of Coni Galindo Bran, worked as an adoption
facilitator in Guatemala for Celebrate Children International.

1. CHOICES

May 2006–August 2006

The summer of 2006 was shaping up to be the most difficult of Mildred Alvarado's life. In just a few months, her living situation had crumbled: Her husband had left, she had no job, and her three young children were growing hungrier with each passing day. In Villalobos, the Guatemalan neighborhood she had recently moved to, most houses were fashioned from garbage. Walls and roofs were patched together from sheets of plastic and scrap metal. Gang graffiti defaced the sides of houses and even roadside waste like broken concrete slabs. The stagnant creek splitting the suburban slum in half seemed to contain more empty Coke bottles and waste than water. Feral urban pigs, their thin bodies caked with sewage, picked their way through the dry riverbed.

Stray dogs and chickens ambled alongside children in the dirt streets, and the hot stench of the ravine drifted over the rooftops. When it rained, the creek flooded, threatening makeshift homes along the embankments. *It is not a good life, but it is a dignified life,* Mildred told herself. It was temporary.

The crime that plagued Guatemala City's metropolitan areas routinely washed through Villalobos, leaving bloodstained streets and corpses strewn in its wake. The atmosphere throughout Guatemala was heavy with dread. Drug cartels and crime syndicates had organized the country's economy and political landscape and reigned with impunity. Crowded areas like Villalobos were more dangerous than they had been even at the peak of Guatemala's civil war, when over 200,000 civilians were killed. Back then, most of the violence had taken place in the countryside. Now it was largely an urban problem.

The estimated 140,000 people associated with gangs battled nightly and extorted the public bus drivers daily, killing those who got in their way. Commuters, too, were robbed, and hundreds were killed each year. Mildred's neighbors eyed each other carefully, keeping both conversation and family members quiet and close. An academic survey from two years before showed that 44 percent of Guatemalans believed that "few to no people are trustworthy."

Mildred was used to such silence. Guatemala's 36-year civil war had affected her family, as it had most, but the details weren't discussed. Instead, like most Guatemalans, the Alvarados had buried the gruesome facts and terror of their collective national history. At twenty-eight years old, Mildred had always lived as a member of the nation's vast underclass, born poor with no hope of upward mobility. Of the country's 13 million inhabitants, 6.5 million lived at or below the poverty line, and millions supported themselves on less than two dollars a day. Mildred's education had ended with the fourth grade. Many others like her were fortunate to land work in low-paying factory and assembly-line jobs that those from the developed world considered sweatshop labor. Mildred had been able to work for the wealthy, caring for children, cooking food, cleaning homes.

Her life had been good, simple but satisfying, until recently, when she had discovered that her common-law husband, Romelio Perez Argueta, had been cheating. The couple had been together for almost a decade, and they had three children. Romelio had been seeing another woman on the side, and rumor had it that she was pregnant. Mildred had felt her heart seize. She, too, was pregnant again by Romelio.

The couple shared a cheerful yellow apartment together in Villa Nueva, the second-largest city in Guatemala. Romelio worked a steady job for a construction company, and Mildred had worked at a car parts shop. Between them, they eked out a decent living, solidly working-class by Guatemalan standards. Villa Nueva was an impoverished, crime-ridden area twenty minutes outside the capital, with the sadly ironic nickname *La Ciudad de Paz* (City of Peace). About a million people, or one-twelfth of Guatemala's total population, lived in the teeming slums there. Seventy percent of residents were, like Mildred and Romelio, under the age of thirty.

The couple lived with their three children and Mildred's younger sister, Patricia. Their apartment was on a block of cookie-cutter duplexes, in a low-income gated complex. Each building had its own tiny patch of yard, and the community boasted a few shared amenities, like a dirt basketball court the neighborhood kids used as a soccer field. The family kept mostly to themselves.

Although Romelio was gone much of the time working on construction sites, Mildred was happy living with her sister and her children. Susana, the lanky oldest, was a natural athlete, outrunning many boys her age. She was seven. Mario, the most timid and serious of the three, assumed responsibility for looking after little Fernanda, the baby of the family. The four-year-old carried his little sister around and kept her entertained. Mario doted on Fernanda, doing anything he could to provoke the child's bright smile. Though she was the smallest, Fernanda, age two, had the most spunk. She was unusually beautiful, the kind of pretty child that made strangers stop dead in the street and bend down to her, cooing.

Proudly, Mildred believed she'd proved her father wrong. He'd said she would never have a nice home or amount to anything, and that no man would ever take her seriously. She had believed him: As a girl, Mildred had been sexually abused by an older brother. She had considered herself ruined. After meeting Romelio, for the first time in her life, Mildred was able to imagine having a relationship. But Romelio treated her kindly, and she felt like an equal. Life in Villa Nueva was humble, but good.

Now things had fallen apart. Mildred didn't tell Romelio that she was pregnant again, and she kicked him out. Her pride was wounded, and she couldn't stand the added disgrace of telling him about the coming baby.

The monthly rent of five hundred *quetzales* (approximately seventy dollars) for the yellow duplex quickly became unmanageable. With her sister's help, Mildred sold off most of the family's belongings, pawning everything that wasn't necessary to live, like their kitchen table. They adjusted to eating meals while seated on the ground. Mildred spent her meager savings and still couldn't catch up. The children were perpetually hungry, and she was, too. At times, the family subsisted on tortillas alone.

When a room became available for rent in Amplificación Solano, a rural part of Villalobos, Mildred seized the opportunity to relocate. She was in her fifth month of pregnancy. The new neighborhood, about twenty minutes away from her old one, was less populated. There would be enough space to raise chickens, Mildred imagined.

Selling eggs would help feed the kids, as would the chickens themselves. The vacant room offered by Marjorie Ariola Tomás, a young woman who sold homemade food by the highway, cost 200Q ($25) each month. It was near the Villalobos ravine, had been fashioned from sheet metal, and sat in a dirt yard surrounded by a chain-link fence. Mildred planned to find a job as soon as the new baby arrived.

Shyly, Mildred asked her new landlady, Marjorie, if she could help her sell food along the highway. Both women were in their late twenties and had young children. The arrangement pleased Marjorie, and she quickly realized that Mildred was an asset. Like her, Mildred minded her own business and didn't gossip like so many other women in their neighborhood. She'd found not only a tenant and business partner, but a friend. Mildred offered to help without being asked. They made a strong team.

As the days passed, the pair fell into a routine, patting out tortillas and chatting. On Mondays, they sold *rellenitos*, fried plantains stuffed with bean paste. Wednesdays were *revocados*, pig insides, which repulsed Mildred. She let Marjorie deal with those. Thursdays were *chiles rellenos*, Mildred's specialty. On Tuesdays and Thursdays, the women subtracted their business expenses and divided their profits.

Mildred had previously worked at Repuestos San Carlos, an auto parts shop. There she had cleaned the office, run errands, cooked, and done miscellaneous chores. Her natural timidity and obedience, along with a tenacious work ethic imparted by her iron-fisted father, had ingratiated her to her boss. She had always tried to be the first to arrive, waking up at six in the morning to cook food that could be sold as breakfast to her co-workers. Each day, Mildred made lunch for the bosses in the auto shop's kitchen. She was proud that they trusted her with petty cash for trips to the market, and she made a habit of walking back to save the company the cost of cab fare. She memorized the bosses' favorite meats and painstakingly prepared them for lunch, the main meal of the day. Some weekends, Mildred even worked as a maid for one of them, when his usual maid had the day off.

The other employees at the auto shop had noticed her willingness to please and teased her. *Arrastrada*, they hissed. It was a spiteful slur, insinuating that she was trying to get ahead in sneaky ways, like a snake. Instead of defending herself, Mildred would cast her eyes downward, feigning nonchalance while her insides burned.

She remained at Repuestos San Carlos for about a year and a half, until she heard about another position offering to pay almost a hundred quetzales more per week. The raise would be substantial, more money than Mildred had ever made. She imagined being able to buy another bed for her family. She and her sister Patricia slept curled together on a single mattress.

Later, Mildred realized the pay had always seemed too good to be true. At the time, she had chosen to swallow her doubt in the service of hope. While still in the application process, Mildred learned that the new job, selling perfume from a telephone call center, required each job seeker to make an investment of cash up front. Even if the scheme had been legit, she had nothing to offer.

It was a silly mistake undertaken with the best of intentions. Mildred regretted quitting the auto parts shop but was too embarrassed to ask for her old job back. There was no way she could have faced her co-workers. Mildred swallowed her shame long enough to place a call to one of her former bosses, the one whose house she'd sometimes cleaned on the weekend. She asked for a loan of 200Q (about $25). To her surprise, her old boss refused. *I have to pay for my children's tuition,* the woman said. Mildred thought about the times she'd left her own children at home on the weekend so that she could wash the woman's floors and tend to her laundry. The amount of money she had requested wasn't much to the woman, whose husband owned six other shops like the one Mildred had worked in. She felt humiliated for asking.

During their days together selling food by the highway, Marjorie began teaching Mildred about Christianity. She attended a small evangelical church, one of thousands that had popped up in Guatemala's poor neighborhoods. One aspect of the religion seemed sharply relevant: following Jesus Christ made for well-behaved kids. Marjorie's children regularly attended services at church with her, and her boys were remarkably well-mannered — a change, she told Mildred, from how wild they'd been before.

In the few months since moving to Villalobos, Mildred's oldest, Susana, had begun to rebel. She was running in the streets with a tough crowd of boys. It wasn't ladylike. When Mildred herself was small, she had never played with boys, with the exception of her own brothers. One day, as Mildred was cooking, Susana came home from a soccer match and thrust her hand straight into the pot. The child didn't ask, or even hesitate. Mildred gave her a good swatting. From then on, the Alvarado family went to church.

Church seemed like a better solution than the talks Mildred usually tried to have with her children when they misbehaved. She just couldn't hit them, save for the occasional spanking. Now Susana didn't just have to beg for her mother's forgiveness — she had to beg for God's, too. To Mildred's surprise, Mario and Fernanda loved attending church, Mario in particular. The little boy took religion to heart and led the family in prayers before meals. Fernanda, his sidekick, followed suit.

Making ends meet remained difficult. Patricia kept working at El Pulpo, a *cevichería* [1] in their old neighborhood. But even with Mildred's contributions, they began falling behind on the rent. Mildred felt like hanging her head in shame the second month she told Marjorie they were short. Her father's words about being a failure and never having a good life haunted her. For a while, back in Villa Nueva, she had proven him wrong. Now she wasn't so sure.

One day, after an afternoon of selling food by the highway, Mildred got a call from a woman named Karina. She had been a neighbor back in Villa Nueva. Patricia had washed clothes for Karina and had confided in her about the family's problems with money, Romelio's infidelity, and her sister's latest pregnancy. Karina told Patricia she could help and prodded her to pass along Mildred's phone number. When she called, Karina told Mildred she could help. She asked to meet in person.

It took a few more calls before Mildred, ferociously private and annoyed that her sister had given her phone number to a stranger, finally agreed to talk to Karina in person. In late July, they arranged to meet at the Pio Lindo pedestrian walkway, a narrow greenish

---

[1] *Ceviche* is a seafood dish made from raw fish, chilies, and lime juice, popular throughout Central and South America. A *cevichería* is a restaurant that serves ceviche.

footbridge that stretched high above the highway, connecting the Villalobos slum to a large chicken packaging plant across the way.

Three people waited for Mildred on the footbridge. She climbed the steps of the bridge, feeling slightly winded in what she guessed was her sixth month of pregnancy. Below her feet, a steady stream of cars and buses rushed by. She eyed the strangers. Karina looked to be about thirty-five, and she introduced her younger sister, Sabrina Hernández Donis. Sabrina was in her twenties and had a plain face with surprisingly thick, pillowy lips. Her eyebrows had been plucked into two razor-thin lines, and her clothing looked new. Sabrina's boyfriend, Rony Cruz de Bautista, stood near her. He was small and thin, no more than a few inches taller than Mildred, who stood under five feet tall. Rony's jeans looked as if they were a size too large, sagged in the popular urban fashion.

"I know what it's like to be a single mother," Mildred remembers Karina telling her. "I've been there. Some days you eat, some days you don't."

Sabrina explained that she was a Christian, a good Samaritan of sorts. She owned a house in Villa Canales, and Mildred and her family were welcome to stay there at no cost until the new baby arrived and the family was back on its feet. It would be a privilege if Mildred accepted her charity, she said.

Mildred listened skeptically. Lately, in an attempt to cling to the remains of her tattered pride, she'd taken to praying every night, only to awaken each morning resigned to the tedium of daily survival. *Maybe this is God's doing*, she thought, bewildered. She'd been attending church for only a few weeks and wasn't sure that prayers could be answered so fast.

"I can tell you work hard," Sabrina said kindly. "I know you're trustworthy."

Mildred softened. She *was* a hard worker. Her father's severe work ethic was imprinted on her core. *Mildred, she's an upright woman*, Marjorie always said. *She's derecha* — correct, a woman of values and morals. *Not like everyone else around here.*

Still, Mildred didn't allow herself to smile at Sabrina, or Rony, or even Karina. Solemnly, she said she would consider their offer, thanking them and saying she'd be in touch. At home, Marjorie was instantly doubtful. "Why would you go live with strangers?" she asked. "You can't just trust someone because they're nice. I think I saw someone follow you home."

Mildred brushed off her friend's apprehension, chalking it up to the mistrust everyone in Villalobos felt towards one another. She thought about a temporary move and failed to see a downside. After all, Marjorie, too, had been a stranger at first. Plus, the longer Mildred and her family stayed in Villalobos, the more their debt would grow. Her little *pollitos* hadn't turned out to be the meal ticket she'd hoped for, as the hens seemed to be happier cavorting in the streets than nesting and laying eggs. Selling food along the highway with Marjorie was decent work, but it wasn't very profitable. Patricia's earnings remained inconsistent, as the restaurant changed her hours every week.

A few weeks passed, and Karina called to check in, asking if Mildred needed anything. "No, we have enough to eat today," Mildred replied. Nevertheless, Karina stopped by days later, dropping off a bag of rice and some cooking oil. It was a nice gesture. Mildred decided she'd accept their offer if she spoke to either woman again. It seemed like the right thing to do.

It was a cool night in mid-July when one of Marjorie's sons burst into the seven o'clock Villalobos church service. He told Mildred to come home. She had visitors.

Sabrina was waiting outside Marjorie's rickety front gate, flanked by a *flatero* (a moving man with a flat-bed pickup). She was there to move them. When Marjorie arrived home, Sabrina handed her money for Mildred's rent.

Marjorie nervously pulled Mildred aside, out of Sabrina's earshot. "Are you sure about this?" she questioned her friend. "You don't know these people. Are you sure this is ok?"

Mildred nodded. She'd made up her mind. In a few minutes, her possessions, children, and sister were loaded on the truck and were on their way to Villa Canales, prepared to move into a single upstairs room in the back of a hot-pink house they thought belonged to Sabrina Donis.

The neighborhood of Villa Canales was similar in feel to Villa Nueva, where Mildred and the children had lived with Romelio in their sunny duplex. To a Westerner, it might look poverty-stricken, but to most Guatemalans, it was a middle-class neighborhood. Sabrina's house was next to railroad tracks that been abandoned for so long that residents had constructed cinder-block homes directly on top of the rails. Every hour or so, a loud public bus barreled down the street in front of the house, flashing chrome and belching smog.

Sabrina's home was a two-story concrete structure that looked like any other on the block, with peeling paint and a roof that looked to be crumbling in places. When the front door opened, a pungent odor hit Mildred head-on. A Siberian husky roamed around freely. It wasn't housebroken.

Inside, the walls were bright green, and there were the same kitchen appliances, like a refrigerator, that Mildred had seen in the homes of her old bosses. Yet despite the apparent wealth, the house smelled worse than the sewage-filled ravine in Villalobos.

A little girl sat amid the squalor. Her name was Kaylee, and she was the daughter of Sabrina and her boyfriend, Rony. Though her mother wore new jeans and shiny patent leather kitten-heels, the one-year-old was dirty and apparently neglected. An angry rash covered part of her face.

The mess repulsed the Alvarado sisters. Although they'd never had money, Mildred and Patricia had always kept their living space immaculate, as their mother had done. Remorsefully, Mildred thought of her time by the highway with Marjorie, questioning her decision. Even her children were disgusted, especially Susana. "It's just until the new baby comes," Mildred tried to reassure them. "We have no money. These people took us in. It's just for a little while."

After the initial shock passed, Mildred set about cleaning, hoping to bring the house up to livable standards. She scrubbed the floors and walls and attacked the bedroom with oversize black garbage bags. Judging from the trash strewn about, Mildred imagined Sabrina and Rony lived on fast food, candy, and soda. Smashed French fries turned up in the young couple's bed, along with dark stains Mildred chose to believe were ketchup. Crumpled McDonald's and Pollo Campero packaging had coalesced into what looked like a nearly solid block under the bed.

The neighbors around them seemed wary. At the market, whenever Mildred mentioned that she lived with Sabrina and Rony, people would clam up, sliding away and averting their eyes. Rony's name especially seemed to inspire silence, though Mildred found him to be courteous and polite, gentlemanly even. People seemed to harbor a kind of low-grade fear of him. It was disconcerting. Sure, Rony looked tough, with his slicked back hair, chain necklace, and forearm tattoo of a floating head. Rony claimed it was a portrait of his mother, but the head was too blurred to look like anyone, let alone someone specific. When he came home and saw the three black trash bags Mildred had stuffed with garbage, he cordially thanked her. Sabrina hadn't.

"You deserve to live in a clean home," he told her. "Not like this." He gestured towards Sabrina, who ignored the barb. "All she cares about is wearing nice dresses and going dancing, then comes back here like a lazy slob."

Sabrina never reacted to his insults, and Mildred pretended not to hear them. She wasn't about to get involved. As the days turned into weeks, she learned more about Sabrina, who'd ran away from home as a teenager and had worked in Guatemala City bars as a dancing girl. She was the daughter of a washerwoman, raised in poverty. Now she delighted in parties and money, spending it on others as well as herself. She kept trying to buy new clothes for Mildred, but Mildred refused. Not paying rent was all the charity her pride could handle. Still, she didn't have the heart to say no when Sabrina came home with new shoes for Susana, Mario, and Fernanda.

At first, Sabrina was kind. She seemed worldly and wise, like someone who'd lived well beyond her years. She gave Mildred money to spend on groceries and encouraged Patricia to quit her job at the restaurant, El Pulpo, back in Villa Nueva. Since Patricia had to commute, the bus fare ate away about half of her pay. "There are other restuarants close to here," Sabrina told her. "I know people. I'll help you get a new job."

Mildred felt twinges of sympathy for her. Sabrina was slovenly, but there was an air of sadness around her. Rony usually treated her with a simmering contempt, but when he drank, he beat her badly. Kaylee, their daughter, got into the habit of sleeping upstairs with the Alvarados. Mildred figured the girl was drawn to the way she called her *mi amor,* as if Kaylee were one of her own children. From what she could see, Sabrina and Rony largely ignored the girl.

Neither Mildred nor Patricia understood where Sabrina's money came from. She always seemed to have a fresh supply of 100Q ($13) bills. Mildred didn't have the audacity to ask about it. As time passed, Sabrina grew distant and started acting cagey. Whenever she noticed that Mildred or Patricia had taken on a side job for extra money, like washing clothes for a neighbor, she'd refuse to buy groceries.

As July rolled towards August, Mildred realized she'd become a live-in maid for Sabrina and Rony. The cleaning had started as an earnest attempt to show gratitude to the young couple. Now it was expected. Sabrina began to insist that doing the housework on top of looking after three kids was too hard on Mildred, in her eighth month of pregnancy. Sabrina hinted gradually, and then more force-fully, that she had a church friend who could babysit for Fernanda. The friend, *Doña* (Mrs.) Coni, was an older woman who'd never been blessed with children of her own.

One of Rony's cousins routinely dropped by to visit, and when he was around, he snapped pictures of Fernanda on his cell phone. He didn't seem interested in Mario or Susana. "She's just so cute," he told Mildred when she asked him why he was photographing her daughter. "What fate, for such a beautiful girl to end up so poor!" It wasn't the first time that Mildred had heard such a sentiment, but still, it never failed to sting. Indeed, her girl was undeniably beautiful.

Fernanda had inherited Mildred's straight black hair and unflin-ching gaze, but her complexion was a few shades lighter than her mother's, a pale tone many Guatemalans associated with wealth and beauty. She was a spunky child, almost coy, as if fully aware of her beauty.

Sabrina wouldn't drop the subject of Doña Coni, but Mildred politely declined, again and again. She reminded herself that God had given Fernanda to her, not to someone else. There was no way she'd separate from her beloved girl. Yet Sabrina's insinuations of maternal failure rang in her ears: *Fernanda is too pure, she is too much girl for you. She deserves a family with money, a family that can take care of her. She's so much better than you ever could be.*

Sabrina switched tactics and began dropping hints that the Alvarados owed her money for food and rent. Letting Doña Coni care for the toddler would be a goodwill gesture, in the same vein as the charity Sabrina herself had demonstrated towards Mildred. Furthermore, Sabrina added, Doña Coni was a good Christian. Taking care of Fernanda would give the older woman the taste of motherhood she'd always longed for. Even better, it would be beneficial for all involved, a pure act of love.

Pangs of guilt pricked at Mildred's conscience. She tried to understand her gut reluctance about the seemingly benign request, but couldn't. Feelings of shame took hold of her. Sabrina was doing so much for her, and the last thing she wanted was to appear ungrateful. She agreed to let Doña Coni take care of Fernanda, just for a little while.

Days later, Mildred found herself sitting in the back seat of a blue Toyota Tercel parked outside at the Bosque de San Nicólas shopping center in Mixco, Guatemala. The car was either Rony's or Sabrina's, as far as she knew. It was an expansive parking lot, teeming with people who came to visit the modern big-box stores. A *Chica Fresa* (Strawberry Girl) air freshener filled the car with a sickeningly sweet aroma. Fernanda squirmed on Mildred's lap, wearing new sneakers Sabrina had bought her two weeks before. A white Nissan pickup truck pulled up. Inside sat Lilia Consuelo "Coni" Galindo Ovalle de Bran. Her husband, Oscar Bran Herrera, was in the driver's seat.

They got out of the car. The woman Sabrina had said was a church friend spoke in rapid-fire Spanish. Coni handed Mildred a small stack of twelve blank papers, coolly telling her to sign each one. Though she was literate, having attended school until the fourth grade, Mildred hadn't read or written much as an adult. When she signed her name, the letters slanted unevenly.

"You don't deserve a girl like this," Coni said. She had a plain, scowling face, and her neat clothes disclosed an upper-middle class background. Coni was the kind of woman who might employ Mildred to clean her house or cook her meals. "Don't worry about anything," Coni continued. Her words held no reassurance. "I'll take very good care of her."

Mildred didn't understand the blank sheets, and she summoned the courage to ask why she'd had to sign them. The cops are nosy, Coni explained hurriedly. They're always rounding people up. A signature would keep them from poking around and asking questions. She also wanted to see Mildred's *cédula,* or national ID card. Mildred asked if she would be able to visit Fernanda each week, and was told that it would be too difficult to arrange. Coni's short hair and thick build were imposing, and it struck Mildred that the only thing feminine about the older woman was the small gold chain laced around her ankle. Although her tone had initially been amicable, after being questions, Coni no longer seemed as friendly. The older woman spoke with clear, sharp enunciation. Her voice signified wealth. Mildred felt stupid. Bewildered, she started to cry.

Her thoughts scattered as the tears strained her ability to think logically. She recalled Sabrina's initial appearance, seemingly accidental and steeped in good intentions. Who else but a true Christian would take a stranger into their home? It was only natural to ask to be paid back for living expenses. Collecting herself, Mildred began slowly printing her name in shaky block letters across the bottom of the blank sheets. Doña Coni and Sabrina chatted. Mildred glanced again at each woman, hesitating. Each seemed matter-of-fact, as if nothing was out of the ordinary.

Mildred blinked hard, telling herself not to be silly. She lifted Fernanda and passed her to Doña Coni, getting back into the Tercel. Doña Coni handed the child an expensive-looking doll. It thrilled Fernanda. The two-year-old began chirping with delight.

Mildred's pulse raced as she got back into the Toyota. "No, wait," she said, tapping Sabrina's shoulder from the back seat. "Wait. I don't want to do this."

She watched as Coni shut one of the four doors of the pickup's extended cab.

Sabrina turned to face her.

"Don't be stupid," she said bluntly. "This is the best for everyone. If you make a stink here, the police will come over, and they'll drag everyone to jail. Including you."

Mildred remained silent. Tears rolled down her face. She watched as the city traffic swallowed the white pickup, and Fernanda along with it.

"Everything is fine," Sabrina said. Her tone softened. "It's only temporary, a month or so. It's no big deal."

During the ride home, no one spoke. Mildred tried to take comfort in the fact that she'd helped another person, but she still felt queasy. The car passed over the rutted city streets. The *Chica Fresa* air freshener swung back and forth wildly.

Leslie and Betsy Emanuel, 2008.
Photograph courtesy Betsy Emanuel.

2. PLEASE SAY YES

December 2005–August 2006

Golden afternoon light streamed in through the sheer curtains in Betsy Emanuel's downstairs bathroom, transforming the plain beige room into a lovely warm yellow. It was December 2005, with less than a week until Christmas. The forecast for Gallatin, Tennessee, a rural town thirty minutes from Nashville, predicted a slim chance of snow. The Emanuel kids, ranging in age from 17 months to 19 years, were excited to distraction. Even Steve Irwin, the Crocodile Hunter himself, couldn't hold anyone's interest. Usually, Irwin's TV show commanded rapt attention from all members of the household, even Betsy, who prided herself on being a fun, down-to-earth mother. Still, for the kids, the vicarious thrill of hunting crocodiles paled in comparison with the approach of Christmas.

Betsy sat down on the bathroom floor, bracing one foot against the door for insurance. She was sure one of the kids would try to barge in. From her bunker, the clamor of the household was pleasantly muffled, and it was hard to tell shrieks of joy from those of annoyance. Lately, Betsy had gotten in the habit of locking herself in the bathroom for a quick five-minute time-out whenever possible. She cherished the breaks.

Pulling out a cabinet drawer, she placed her old Dell laptop on the makeshift desktop and booted up. For six months, Betsy had been visiting the website Precious.org at least once a day, if not more. The Christian site was the biggest orphan-listing website in the United States, featuring children from around the world. The site published hundreds of tiny headshots of children listed as available for adoption. They were searchable by age, gender, agency, and location. Precious.org and Rainbowkids.com, a similar site, served as clearinghouses for those interested in international adoption, so you could simply check them instead of visiting what might amount to hundreds of individual adoption agency sites to look at child listings.

The Emanuels were ready to add one last child to their family, yet the search for an older child to adopt hadn't been easy. The majority of children listed on sites like Precious.org and Rainbowkids.com were babies. As the Emanuel family already had seven kids — four of whom were adopted — they were ineligible to adopt from certain countries, including China, Haiti, the Philippines, Thailand, and South Korea. Some countries, like Colombia and India, didn't have hard restrictions but preferred to place orphans with childless families.

The obvious option was Guatemala. The Latin American country seemed to have a surplus of children, as evidenced by the new listings cropping up on Precious.org. The small nation had no stipulations regarding existing family size, and Guatemala's popularity as a "sending country" for adoption had increased steadily. The number of Guatemalan children adopted by Americans was expected to exceed 4,000 in 2006.

"When it comes to red tape, Guatemala is one of the easiest places to adopt a child in the world," Sara Miller Llana wrote in the *Christian Science Monitor* in September 2007. In Guatemala, an adoption could be finalized in as little as four months. Aside from not having limits on existing family size, the country also put no age restrictions on adoptive parents. Singles, too, were allowed to adopt. Medical records of doctor's visits and monthly growth reports were usually available. Another draw was that Guatemalan children usually lived in foster care rather than orphanages, which greatly reduced the risk of developmental delays. In general, older children who languished in institutional care for months or years were more likely to suffer serious psychological and behavioral issues. They were also more likely to have been physically or sexually abused. For many interested in adopting an orphan, the risks associated with older children were simply too great. Babies were safer.

Yet an older child was exactly what Betsy Emanuel wanted. Neither she nor her husband, Leslie, a corporate controller, felt they had the energy to wrangle a baby. They were already in their mid-forties. Betsy considered herself to be a practical woman, a down-to-earth mother who wasn't easily shocked or surprised. If the child slated to become their last adopted daughter had issues, so be it. She'd take on the challenge with love, patience, and determination, the same way she'd dealt with the medical issues of the three special-needs children the Emanuels had adopted from Asia. Still, after six months of searching for an older child to adopt, Betsy felt discouraged. She hadn't expected it would be so difficult.

She crossed her legs, pushed her dirty-blond hair behind her ears, and continued clicking through the latest listings on Precious. org. The site was run by a company called Precious In HIS Sight LLC and claimed to be the largest and oldest photo-listing site on the web. Since its inception in 1994, the site had listed over 26,000 orphans and updated the listings hourly. Jason Damkoehler, who had purchased the site in 2005, was a pastor at an Illinois church that helped parents become "equipped . . . to fulfill their God-given responsibility to disciple their children" and to "train men and women to thrive in their biblical roles" via literal Bible interpretations. His church extolled divine healing through prayer and an evangelist world view of Christianity in which husbands "lead" their wives. The attitude reflected that of many Christians concerned with the unborn: Every adoption was an abortion deterred.

As Betsy scrolled through the latest listings, a new child caught her eye. Jennifer Yasmin Velásquez López was eight years old, and she was Guatemalan. Jennifer's steady gaze transmitted an air of maturity and grace. The adoption agency Celebrate Children International (CCI) had listed the girl. Betsy had never heard of CCI. For each of their three previous international adoptions, the Emanuels had used big, well-known agencies, including Holt International and Dillon. Still, Betsy liked the agency's name, enjoying the idea of adoption as celebration. Celebrate Children. It had a nice ring to it.

Jennifer was one of twenty-five Guatemalan children that CCI was advertising on Precious.org. "Alexis is oh, so cute!" one listing read. "Oscar is sad because he heard that it might be difficult to find a new home for him since he is a boy," another declared. Some ads were written in capital letters, lending an air of urgency. "THIS IS A CHARMING LITTLE BOY!" Franklin's description announced. "PLEASE SAY YES TO HIM!" Infant Norvin was described as "still puffy from birth." Javier's listing said "Here is your chance at a very young baby!" Many of the listings had a pleading tone, imploring visitors to "open their hearts" or to give a child a future.

Jennifer looked healthy, with a sturdy build. *Maybe she'd bond with Trigger,* Betsy thought hopefully. *Maybe Trigger could ease her transition.* The Emanuels' old family pony seemed perfectly sized for an eight-year-old. Her oldest daughter, Lee, loved horses and competed in local horse shows. She imagined her three daughters teaching their new sister how to pick out hooves, muck stalls, and clean tack in the paddocks surrounding the family's airy white Colonial.

The adoption agency's website, celebratechildren.org, had a deep purple background spangled with shooting stars. CCI's mission statement reflected a commitment to faith. "As disciples of Jesus Christ," the site announced, "we are committed to going into the world to serve others. . . ." Celebrate Children International seemed to serve various countries, listing not only Guatemala but Bulgaria, Cambodia, China, Ethiopia, Haiti, Kazakhstan, Taiwan, Ukraine, and Vietnam as options to adopt from. Orphans were described as "foreign treasures with limitless value and potential." Site visitors were encouraged to "browse" through the children and "prayerfully consider" adopting them. Some were offered exclusively to evangelical homes.

On the humanitarian-aid page, various projects were showcased. Potential donors could choose from options that included "ongoing support" to Nicaraguan, Guatemalan, and Dominican orphanages. None of the orphanages were named. Another program, "Celebration Gifts," collected Christian books, socks, and toys to be distributed to poor children at Christmas. A wish list of desired material donations contained everything from industrial-size washing machines to pajamas, high chairs, lice shampoo, and leather sofas. Some items were specific, like two Sony DVD reproducers, 400 student desks, and thirty Royal or Olivetti typewriters. The website assured visitors that 100 percent of contributions went directly towards purchasing items for children. The adoption agency was also involved in organizing mission trips to bring items including underwear and bibles to children in developing countries.

Sue Hedberg, the director of Celebrate Children International, smiled out from the top of the agency's staff page. A heavyset woman who looked to be in her 40s, Sue was pictured alongside her husband

and three children in a department store–style family portrait. All five Hedbergs had blond hair and blue eyes, and all were modestly dressed in button-up shirts. The picture had a glowing pink backdrop that complemented Sue's own pale-pink blouse. Below the image, a brief bio stated that Sue had been "involved with international Christian ministry for most of her life" and had facilitated adoptions for over 600 Guatemalan children. She'd also "brought home" twenty-five Cambodian children and had escorted twelve Korean children into the U.S. With her husband, Dave, Sue also found the time to volunteer, ministering to international students visiting Florida. Below the Hedbergs, a dozen other CCI staff members were listed, most with family photos. All were Christian, and many were adoptive parents themselves.

Betsy was impressed. It wasn't easy, she knew, to run a business while raising children. She'd managed her own home business, Bay Bounce Party Rentals, for years, shuttling two inflatable castles and the family's four-legged lawn ornaments, Trigger and Bonnie, from birthday party to birthday party. There was no shortage of lawns in rural Tennessee for the ponies to circle obligingly, but running the business while keeping her kids in check was exhausting. Even with her older children helping out, she'd had to make the difficult decision to shut down.

The fact that Sue Hedberg was dedicated to the church, managing a staff of twelve, and raising three teenagers awed Betsy. It was a serious, if not divine, responsibility to create families. She imagined the workload to be incredible, and she was right. Though she didn't know it, Celebrate Children International's 2005 net revenue totaled $4.5 million.

In February, Betsy placed a quick call to the adoption agency, eager to see if Jennifer had been matched to an adoptive family yet. She hadn't. The receptionist explained that Sue Hedberg was very familiar with the girl's case. When Sue spoke to Betsy, she wasted no time peppering her with questions. She said she knew Jennifer well and needed to see if the Emanuel family would be a good match for her. The child's mother, an HIV-positive prostitute, had given her up only recently. Jennifer's little sister, Dulce, had recently come to the United States in an adoption also facilitated by CCI. Sue explained that the relationship between the girls had been maternal and that Jennifer had looked after Dulce. *No wonder she looks so mature,* Betsy thought. Dulce's departure was very hard for her, Sue said, and Jennifer was grieving. She missed her sister terribly.

The country fee for the adoption would be an estimated $19,000. Betsy's heart plummeted. She'd hoped that adopting an older child would be more inexpensive, since most adoptive families wanted babies. Sue told her that a number of organizations donated adoption money to Christians, and that one in particular offered grants specifically to her CCI clients.

The agency director's direct manner struck Betsy as unsentimental and straightforward. It inspired trust. Sue seemed kind, authoritative, and devout, making frequent references to faith in conversation. When she hung up from the call, Betsy felt relieved. Her intuition had been right; it seemed Jennifer was fated to join her family. Sue had listened closely as she'd detailed her previous adoption experiences. They'd find a way to raise the funds. God's hand is always present, Betsy thought. Like Sue said, it was His will.

When she called Leslie at work, he teased her. "Celebrate Children International?" he joked. "Why not just call it the Acme Adoption Company?"

A few days later, a package from Celebrate Children International arrived in the mail. It was an unmarked DVD containing video clips of four Guatemalan girls. Sue was featured in each video, interviewing the children in accented Spanish.

When Jennifer's clip began to play, Betsy again felt drawn to the eight-year-old. She was beautiful, with dark, shoulder-length hair parted in the middle. Jennifer sat poised on a sofa next to Sue, her hands folded neatly on her lap. A lone dog barked incessantly in the background. Off-camera, a baby wailed. Betsy strained to make out the child's soft words.

After some of Sue's questions, Jennifer paused to gaze skyward. It was as if she were deep in thought, searching for the answer that was exactly right. When she finally spoke, her words were slow, carefully chosen, and meticulously enunciated. She exuded a quiet confidence.

After each answer, the eight-year-old flashed a proud smile, as if she knew her answers were correct.

"How long have you lived with Doña Mayra?" Sue asked. "Two months?"

Jennifer nodded.

"Do you understand what adoption is?"

Again, the child nodded. Slower, this time.

At first, Betsy was taken aback by Sue's direct line of questioning. It seemed cruel, almost, to be so blunt about the little girl's situation, to prod her so callously about the relinquishment. Yet Jennifer handled each question with a dignity that belied her eight years. Sue translated some of the conversation into English.

"What is your favorite color?" Sue asked towards the end of the clip.

Jennifer paused. Then she replied quietly, "I like all of the colors."

"You don't have a favorite? Pink? Or blue?"

"Blue," she said agreeably, smiling sideways at Sue for approval. When asked about her favorite food, Jennifer answered, "Cornflakes."

To Betsy, the girls in the other videos seemed more hesitant, almost unwilling to engage with Sue and her questions. One child who looked to be the same age as Jennifer broke down in tears, covering her face with her hands and mumbling in Spanish that she didn't want a new home. A third video showed two girls, seated side-by-side on a couch. Neither was smiling. Towards the end, a camera flash popped repeatedly as Sue snapped about a dozen photos while continuing to roll tape on the children. Betsy thought Jennifer's earnest answers and easy smile made her the picture of grace in comparison with the others.

She's the bravest little girl I've ever seen, Betsy thought. She replayed the disc five times.

Over the next few days, the Emanuels received more photographs of Jennifer from Celebrate Children International. One set of images was supposedly from the child's relinquishment day. Betsy thought Jennifer looked distraught, aware of what was unfolding in the lawyer's office. The little girl wore an orange T-shirt with a small Tweety bird on the front, and navy pants that looked to be part of a school uniform. The tops of her lacy white socks were carefully folded down above black Mary Janes. A small black garbage bag and a leather satchel lay at her feet. *Are those her possessions?* Betsy wondered. She couldn't decide if the eight-year-old seemed more sad or angry. The time stamp at the bottom of the pictures read December 19, 2005.

Jennifer's mother, Maria Josefa Velásquez López, was in two of the photographs. She wore a bright-turquoise T-shirt and cheerful lipstick. Betsy thought she looked despondent. Mother and daughter shared the same small, straight nose. The first image showed Maria Josefa sitting alone, staring dead-on into the camera. It was an uncomfortable image. The second showed Jennifer sitting on her mother's lap. Maria Josefa had wrapped her arms around her daughter's waist, and her hands were clasped across Jennifer's belly, fingers interlaced. Jennifer, looking doubtful, had placed her own small hands on top of her mother's. She'd woven her fingers together, too.

In another set of images Betsy received, taken later, Jennifer was alone in a doctor's office. She gazed directly into the camera with a raised chin, looking vaguely defiant. Her new foster mother, Mayra Estrada, was in one frame, a pudgy, middle-aged woman with thick glasses and a blank expression. Sue told Betsy that the newly orphaned child had been a handful and was struggling to come to terms with her situation. Jennifer was refusing to eat, she said, pushing away her breakfast cereal, and Mayra was getting frustrated. The child's demand was for her little sister to be returned to Guatemala.

Sue asked Betsy yet again if she was certain she wanted to move forward with the adoption. Betsy was positive. Every new detail that Sue revealed about Jennifer, no matter how tragic, amplified her desire.

Jennifer's younger sister, Dulce, had arrived in Pennsylvania a few months before, in January 2006, one of twenty-two children adopted from Guatemala into the United States by Celebrate Children International that month. Betsy asked Sue if she could contact Dulce's adoptive mother, and Sue provided a phone number.

At first, Mary McGraw,[2] a pediatrician from Pennsylvania, was hesitant to talk. Mary said Dulce's adoption process had taken six months from start to finish. She hadn't known that Dulce had a sister

[2.] The name has been changed to protect confidentiality.

who was also available for adoption, she said, until Sue Hedberg mentioned it a week before Dulce's adoption was finalized.

During her flight to Guatemala, Mary wrestled with the idea of bringing not one but two children into her home. It was overwhelming. She already had an adopted daughter at home, and adopting both Dulce and Jennifer meant that her daughter would be sandwiched in age between biological sisters. She didn't want to risk making her feel like an outsider.

The thought of separating the two sisters troubled Mary, but she couldn't afford two adoptions. She'd already negotiated for Dulce; after seeing the five-year-old listed on Rainbowkids.com, Mary had bartered with Sue Hedberg over adoption fees. In exchange for a break on the price, Mary had arranged an introduction between Celebrate Children International and Love Basket, the adoption agency she'd previously used. Love Basket worked in India, a country where CCI didn't have an adoption program.

When Mary arrived in Guatemala, Sue offered to have Jennifer brought to her hotel room along with Dulce. Mary fretted over the decision, ultimately declining. Wouldn't that complicate an already-difficult situation? Break Jennifer's heart all the more? As Mary relayed her experience to Betsy, Betsy detected strains of remorse in the other woman's voice. Now that Dulce was home, Mary told her, she'd never once mentioned a sister. She'd never said anything about Jennifer.

Well, that's odd, Betsy thought. She asked Mary if the two children could meet after Jennifer came to the U.S. After all, Pennsylvania wasn't far from Tennessee — maybe a full day by car, she calculated quickly.

But Mary insisted it wasn't a good idea for the biological sisters to remain in contact. A reunion might traumatize Dulce, she said, repeating that the child had never mentioned Jennifer or having a sister at all. Betsy pressed harder. She was certain that Jennifer would need to see her beloved Dulce with her own eyes — even just once, to understand she was safe. Yet Mary was firm. She just didn't believe there was a connection between the girls. Surely, Dulce would have said something.

With the cost of adopting a Guatemalan child ranging from $15,000 to upwards of $50,000, a contract with an international adoption agency defined a serious financial transaction. Many who hoped to adopt had already lost tens of thousands of dollars to infertility treatments. Couples regularly depleted their savings, took out second mortgages, or cashed out retirement accounts to finance the adoption of a son or daughter.

Through the spring and summer of 2006, the U.S. State Department says, the average time frame for adopting a child from Guatemala was approximately nine months. Like most agencies, Celebrate Children International refused to guarantee how long an adoption would take, but noted on their website that the average Guatemalan adoption process took between four and nine months. Among the online adoption community, CCI had a blossoming reputation for quick adoptions from Guatemala. Many parents-to-be viewed both speed and ease in an adoption as a testament to an adoption agency's professionalism and work ethic.

In 2006, when the Emanuel family began the adoption process with Celebrate Children International, the agency's online program guide listed the total cost of a Guatemalan adoption as $24,000–$26,000, including travel expenses incurred bringing the adopted child into the U.S. Of that, $4,250 went directly to the agency and $19,000–$20,000 went to "contacts" and lawyers in Guatemala. The agency's program description said referrals were typically provided within one to two months after a prospective family sent in its completed adoption paperwork. "Most available children are infants," the description stated, but young toddlers could be "requested." Special-needs children were available "on request" and were discounted. Some were as little as half the total adoption cost of a healthy baby.

The money given to in-country business partners was referred to as a "country fee," a catch-all phrase that could be slightly misleading. In her book *Successful Adoption: A Guide for Christian Families*, Nicole Nichols Gillepsie writes about country fees under the subheading "Foreign Government Fees." She lists no fees from the Guatemalan government; most of the money distributed in Guatemala by American adoption agencies goes directly to private, for-profit lawyers. According to various Guatemalan adoption lawyers, U.S.

agencies typically send a lump sum to a particular lawyer or contact, who then passes money down a chain of command. "Guatemala in-country fees range from $15,000 to $19,000," Gillespie writes, "including all legal fees and attorney costs, permits, registration, foster care, medical exams, DNA testing, translation, and other fees." In 2006, most American adoption agencies also advertised the cost of a Guatemalan adoption as being about $20,000. A 2009 memo from the U.S. Embassy in Guatemala, published by Wikileaks in August 2011, said that ". . . typically notaries plus the agencies were paid around USD$50,000 for their services."

In Guatemala, where the average annual salary in 2008 was $2,680 per capita, adoption was a profitable industry. Aside from the country fees, adoptive Americans usually paid for other expenses, such as an agency application fee. Celebrate Children International required their clients to pay a $500 "Humanitarian Aid" fee.

Many adoption contracts left adoptive parents with little legal recourse if something strange happened in their adoption. Celebrate Children International asked clients to sign liability waivers releasing the agency from responsibility for providing wrong or incomplete information about the children they offered for adoption. When clients signed CCI's waivers, they were releasing CCI from having to provide accurate information about medical conditions like HIV, mental retardation, and sexual abuse. The waivers also absolved the adoption agency from responsibility for any adoption delays, cost increases, or "complications caused by factors outside its control." CCI did, however, assure clients that they used "best good-faith efforts" to obtain information.

Still, if an adoption fell through, many adoptive parents risked losing the money they'd invested. In general, adoption agencies had trouble recouping fees paid to lawyers or "finders" on the ground in a foreign country. CCI stated that their own fees were "generally . . . nonrefundable" but that extenuating situations could result in a refund on a case-by-case basis.

Most adoptive parents willingly signed away basic legal rights and protections for the chance to become parents. CCI's contract was similar to, if not better than, those provided by other agencies. Some agencies required clients to sign additional papers such as "Internet confidentiality agreements," which prohibited sharing adoption information like costs and experiences, good or bad, online.

CCI did, however, prohibit clients from contacting "foreign entities" in their potential child's country of origin. Any such communication, if discovered, could be considered a breach of contract. Permission was required for CCI clients to contact anyone in Guatemala about their adoptions. Other agencies, like Holt International, also asked adoptive families to "refrain from unauthorized foreign contact." A clause at the end of CCI's adoption contract warned clients about the risk of a failed adoption. A child's coming to the United States was not guaranteed.

The Tennessee summer of 2006 stretched long and hot. The Emanuel kids stayed busy with basketball practice, motocross, and horseback riding lessons. Sue told them that Jennifer might be ready to leave Guatemala at any time and to be prepared if her adoption moved quickly. Though only three months had passed since the Emanuels had found the money required to officially start the adoption, Betsy had been thinking of Jennifer as her own daughter since January. Now that it was August, she was itching for good news.

Betsy's daughter Hannah, who was the same age as Jennifer, was particularly excited about her new sister's arrival. The girls were going to share a room, and the Emanuels had already redecorated, moving another twin bed in. Although Hannah adored shoes, she had been born with a birth defect that resulted in her having uniquely shaped feet. Most shoes didn't fit her. During one trip to Wal-Mart, she carefully picked out a pair of sparkly red flip-flops for Jennifer. She hoped that her future sister would love them as much as she did.

By summer's end, Betsy was thinking about going to Guatemala to meet Jennifer. She wanted to start bonding with the girl as soon as possible, and she emailed CCI to inquire about a visit trip. Visit trips were common among adoptive parents, and the client section of CCI's website had a page devoted solely to travel details, etiquette, and rules. Though CCI didn't prohibit visiting Guatemala before an adoption's culmination, they also didn't necessarily encourage it. They asked clients to relay trip details, including flight dates, arrival times, and hotel information.

Most Americans adopting from Guatemala stayed in big hotels like the Westin or the Marriott in Guatemala City, where entire floors catered to them. Gift shops at the chain hotels were stocked with diapers, bottles, and formula. Sue encouraged CCI clients to stay at the Radisson, where they received discounts on rooms. Certain staff there knew Sue by her Guatemalan nickname, Susana, and she'd arranged to have a green suitcase filled with supplies like baby wipes, diaper rash ointment, and infant Tylenol kept in one of the hotel's storage rooms. "If you need one of these items, just ask one of the bellboys (Henry, Rubin, Carlos) to bring you the suitcase," the instructions on the agency's website said.

During a typical visit, children would be dropped off at the hotel to visit with their potential parents for anywhere from a few hours to a few days. It was a convenient arrangement, one that allowed visiting Americans the comfort of never having to leave the hotel. At the end of the visit, someone, often a *cuidadora* (foster mother), would return to the hotel to pick the child up.

By early August, Jennifer's adoption had been received formal pre-approval from the U.S. Embassy, meaning that a DNA test had verified that the woman relinquishing Jennifer was in fact her biological mother. Visit trips were commonly planned only after the Embassy had issued pre-approval, in case the DNA test failed.

When Betsy brought up the idea of visiting, Sue discouraged her. A visit could endanger Jennifer, putting the whole adoption at risk. Adoptions had started to get a bad rap in the Guatemalan press, where stories touching on corruption and fraud had surfaced. Native Guatemalans didn't like seeing their nation's children in the arms of Americans, she implied brusquely. It might cause a scene. The local police were known to seize children from the arms of foster mothers on the street, and "anti-adoption" organizations like UNICEF had created a frenzied climate. If the police took Jennifer, Sue said, her own hands would be tied. The girl's future would be up to the Lord.

Betsy quietly thought it over. She'd read rumors on various adoption-related blogs and websites about UNICEF advocacy, which claimed that the organization favored keeping foreign children in their countries of origin, even if it meant that they lived in perpetual poverty instead of with adoptive parents. "While there are one hundred million orphans in the world," Guatemalan adoption lawyer

Susana Luarca declared on the website GuatAdopt.com in 2005, "UNICEF spends millions of dollars to convince the Guatemalan authorities to pass laws that would make adoptions impossible. . . ."

Betsy had seen other adoptive parents she'd met on message boards and online forums leaving every day on visit trips. They filled their blogs with beaming stories and happy snapshots of Guatemalan children floating in the clear aqua swimming pools of the expensive hotels. She asked Sue again, and again was told that visiting could harm Jennifer.

That summer, stories about adoption fraud had surfaced in both the American and the international press, as the number of Guatemalan children adopted by Americans steadily increased. On July 29, 2006, Guatemala City Associated Press correspondent Juan Carlos Llorca published an article called "Couples Rush for Guatemalan Adoptions," detailing a litany of corrupt practices and noting that the Guatemalan government had brought "30 criminal cases against notaries for falsifying paperwork, allegedly providing false birth certificates, and even creating false identities to avoid having to involve the birth father or the parents of underage birth mothers." The article noted that adoptions in Guatemala were handled by "notaries who act as baby brokers."

A story in Guatemala's oldest and most respected newspaper, *Prensa Libre*, published on July 9, 2006, called the country an "adoption paradise." The adoption industry, the article said, grossed between $150 million and $200 million annually and was subject to minimal oversight. In 2006 alone, according to the newspaper, Guatemalan police had recovered more than twenty stolen children. Sue Hedberg told her clients, many of whom were politically conservative Christians like the Emanuels, that the liberal media was anti-adoption and sensationalized allegations of corruption. *Prensa Libre*, she claimed, was Guatemala's version of the *National Enquirer*.

Nine months has passed since the day Betsy had first seen Jennifer listed on Precious.org, and the Emanuels had already paid $13,500 to Celebrate Children International. The family had waited all summer, wondering what was happening with her case. They received monthly "medicals," emails from a Dr. Pinto attesting to Jennifer's growth and development. Each medical said the child was healthy and happy. The Emanuels had gotten more snapshots, of Jennifer smiling in her school uniform, Jennifer staring into the distance. What was she thinking? How was she doing? Betsy's heart twisted into a knot, imagining the eight-year-old left alone, without her loving sister or her sick mother. She still had no idea how long it would take for the adoption to finish. Sue's disapproval about visiting seemed overly cautious. Other children got visit trips and the love and gifts that came with them. Why not Jennifer? It didn't seem fair.

She decided to take matters into her own hands. Replacing her flickering doubts with action, Betsy booked a round-trip plane ticket to Guatemala City on August 19, 2006. *One little visit can't be such a big deal,* she thought. *Really, what's the worst that could happen?*

3 . BEGINNINGS

December 2005–August 2006

A t first, Mayra Estrada wasn't sure what to think about Jennifer Yasmin Velásquez López. When the eight-year-old came to live with her in late December 2005, Mayra's house was already filled with her own three kids plus a baby being adopted out to the United States. Jennifer was the oldest child she'd ever been asked to care for. The girl was painfully aware of what was happening and seemed devastated and confused. She missed her mother. The relinquishment surprised Mayra, an experienced cuidadora, or caretaker, who was paid to provide foster care to children leaving Guatemala as adoptees.

Yet Jennifer was helpful and well behaved, cooperative. She was so sweet that Mayra went out of her way to enroll Jennifer in the same private school as her own daughters. In Mayra's eight years of work as a cuidadora, her wards had almost always been newborns. She'd gotten her start when a lawyer friend offered her a job after hearing she was out of work. A few years passed. Mayra began taking care of children for her boss's brother, a pediatrician who also worked adoptions. Then she started working for the pediatrician's lawyer, Alfonso Close, one of the busiest adoption lawyers in Guatemala. Mayra knew she was part of a larger network.

Over the years, more than forty children had passed through Mayra's household on their way to the United States. Long ago, she'd even breastfed one newborn girl, as her own daughter and the foster baby had been the same age. Children usually stayed from three to eight months before moving on to permanent homes abroad, almost always in the United States.

Sometimes babies were dropped off at Mayra's home just days after birth. Her boss supplied diapers, milk, and some clothing. Other cuidadoras who worked for cheaper lawyers were forced to use the most inexpensive formula and diapers they could find, paying for their foster children's expenses out of pocket. Mayra felt lucky to work for a good boss.

When the adopting Americans came to visit, Mayra would drop the baby off at their hotel. After a few days, sometimes even a week, she'd return to pick the child up. It usually seemed difficult for the adoptive parents to hand "their" son or daughter back, but the children generally were happy to see Mayra's familiar face. She loved her job and believed the babies knew how much she cared for them.

Certain visiting families greeted Mayra warmly, asking questions and trying out newly learned Spanish expressions. She wasn't supposed to interact with them, according to her boss's orders, but sometimes she did anyway. A few American families emailed her updates long after their Guatemalan-born children had "come home," as they described it, to the U.S. Some sent her Christmas cards, and a few even friended her on Facebook, tagging her in pictures of their adopted sons or daughters. One couple even asked Mayra to be their adopted son's godmother. She'd proudly accepted. It made her happy to see the kids enveloped by love. The Facebook images of the children, wearing new American clothes and playing in houses that looked like mansions, reinforced her convictions. Adoption was a beautiful institution.

Parts of the process, though, were always hard. Usually, an adoption began when a mother brought her son or daughter directly to Close's office. The woman would be videotaped relinquishing custody of her child to Close or one of his business partners. Witnesses were present. Later on, the video would be filed away and saved. It would be used as proof in court if the relinquishing mother tried to back out of the adoption agreement, for example, or was trying to extort money from the lawyer involved in the transaction. Baby-selling was common, and women sometimes sold the same child repeatedly by claiming they had changed their minds about the adoption. After recovering the child, they would re-relinquish him or her, to a different lawyer.

When one of Mayra's foster children left for their new home country, she'd usually visit Close's office to pick up a new one. At first, it was difficult watching a mother say goodbye to her child. After a while, though, it was just standard procedure. Mayra would leave the office with the newly minted "orphan" baby in her arms, and the child's mother would fade into the past.

Once in a while, a birth mother would remain in touch, visiting Mayra's home to check on a son or daughter. Those were the women who really loved their children, Mayra imagined. Others didn't seem to care. They were probably bad mothers anyway, she thought. She didn't know much about what happened on the U.S. side of things, but she knew that Americans loved the babies enough to pay small fortunes for them. Children typically left Guatemala within a year.

That's what was supposed to have happened with Jennifer.

Mayra first met Maria Josefa, Jennifer's mother, in Close's office on December 19, 2005. Close took a small portable video camera out of his desk and trained it on the young woman. She looked to be in her mid-twenties. Like hundreds of women who'd sat in the office before her, Maria Josefa followed instructions, stating that she was voluntarily choosing to give up her daughter. Mayra remembers that the young woman signed papers.

Mayra was told that Maria Josefa suffered from AIDS, although the young mother looked perfectly healthy to her. She wasn't emaciated the way Mayra imagined AIDS victims to be. Jennifer didn't know about the illness and had been told only that her mother suffered from stomach pains. To Mayra, the relinquishment seemed like *un acto de humanidad,* an act of kindness. In her head, she created a sympathetic narrative for poor Maria Josefa: The twenty-something knew she was dying and wanted to make sure that her daughter would be cared for. Adoption guaranteed a bright future for the child, almost certainly in the United States.

Eight months later, in early August 2006, Close called and abruptly instructed Mayra to drop the girl off at Fundaniñas, an all-girls orphanage in Guatemala City. It wasn't clear what had transpired, but the adoption was no longer going smoothly. Close told Mayra that Maria Josefa had refused to sign adoption documents, saying that his office hadn't delivered what they'd promised to her. He mentioned that Maria Josefa was unhappy with the quality of care her daughter was receiving. The allegation stung Mayra.

Threats had been made, Mayra understood, and Close implied that situation was serious. *Maybe someone is giving this woman bad advice,* she thought, wondering about Maria Josefa's motives. *Maybe she's being brainwashed or is trying to extort the lawyers for money. Maybe such illogical thinking is a side effect of AIDS.* Mayra never questioned her boss, though. The last thing she wanted was to be mixed up in legal trouble.

A judge would now have to decide whether Maria Josefa would regain custody of Jennifer or if Close would retain it. The lawyer could argue that Maria Josefa was an unfit mother and try to keep the adoption moving forward as an abandonment proceeding instead of a direct relinquishment. In the meantime, Alfonso wanted Jennifer at Fundaniñas.

The day Mayra left her, Jennifer was clutching a stuffed pony that had been sent by the American woman, Betsy, who was slated to become the child's new mother. Initially, Jennifer had wanted nothing to do with the adoption. She missed her mom and her brother. Mayra and her own teenage daughter, Adriana, had taken pains to shape the child's perspective, thrilling her with tales of her future big house in the green American countryside, her new brothers and sisters, and of course her new American mother, the pretty blond with the kind smile. They told Jennifer how lucky she was, explaining that the opportunity to live in the United States was a blessing. After a few months, the little girl, tentatively, grew excited. She started speaking proudly and openly about her real-life pony-to-be, Trigger.

It was hard for Mayra to leave her, confused and alone, at Fundaniñas. Less than a week later, Jennifer called Mayra. She had snuck into the orphanage office and dialed the number on the desk phone. The child's tone was hushed and nervous. She wasn't used to breaking rules. Her possessions had been taken away, Jennifer said, including her stuffed pony. She told Mayra that she missed her.

"What's going to happen to me?" Jennifer asked quietly.

Mayra didn't know what to say.

In 2006, Guatemala became the second-largest supplier of children for international adoption in the world. The country sent 4,135 children to the U.S. that year, or about eleven per day. China was the only nation in the world sending more children to the United States. According to the Associated Press, which had crunched census data against the numbers of orphan visas, by 2006 one out of every hundred children born in Guatemala left in adoption.

It hadn't always been that way. Before 1977, the guidelines that governed adoption in Guatemala had been patched together from different pieces of legislation, and a judge's signature was required to affirm a child's orphan status. On November 3, 1977, a new law created a loophole in the country's adoption policy. The Ley Reguladora de la Tramitación Notarial de Asuntos de Jurisdicción Voluntaria eliminated judicial approval of the adoptions of relinquished children, instead granting oversight to private lawyers and notaries. Besides lightening the workload for Guatemala's overtaxed, stumbling judicial system, the privatization meant that private attorneys had more power than ever before regarding adoptable children.

In 1987, another legislative breakthrough occurred. A new law granted civil registrars in provinces across the country the authority to create authentic replacement identification documents such as birth certificates. The duplicates would serve the same purpose as originals. The law was intended to help Guatemalans whose papers and national identification cards, or *cédulas,* had been destroyed during wartime. Yet the new rule also provided an opportunity for corruption: Some civil registrars took bribes in exchange for the creation of fraudulent documents that would be taken as authentic. Years later, newly created documentation papers would be used to launder identities for children in adoption processes.

In the 1980s and early 1990s, only a handful of Guatemalan children left the country in adoption. The country's civil war, which began in 1960 and lasted thirty-six years, resulted in 34,000 refugees and one million internally displaced persons, more than half of whom were children. The violence peaked in 1982 under the rule of Efraín Rios Montt, the self-proclaimed "President of the Republic." He was the former chief of staff of the Guatemalan Army and a graduate of the School of the Americas, a U.S. institution in Georgia that provided special training to over fifteen hundred Guatalaman troops between 1946 and 1995. Rios Montt instated himself as President via coup d'état and quickly became one of the most notorious military dictators in the Western hemisphere, known for a brutal scorched-earth campaign against leftist insurgents and rural peasants. He proceeded to annul the country's constitution, dissolve Congress, suspend rival political parties, and cancel electoral law.

"It became a fad among Army ranks to take care of three- or four-year-old children who were lost in the mountains," reported the Human Rights Office of the Archbishopric (ODHA) in its catalogue of war crimes, "Guatemala, Nunca Más" ("Guatemala, Never Again"), also known as the Recovery of Historical Memory Project, or REMHI report. "Guatemala Nunca Más" took a decade to complete and remains the most definitive chronicle of the conflict. It mentions the cases of two young girls who survived the infamous 1992 Dos Erres massacre in Petén province and were subsequently adopted by soldiers who'd participated in the killings of their families. Soldiers brought another three-year-old, whose relatives had been massacred in San Gaspar, Quiché, to the capital. There the child was given to an evangelical organization that arranged for her international adoption.

Guatemala's National Commission for the Search for Missing Children estimated that close to 5,000 of the country's children were "disappeared"[3] or separated from their families during the 1980s. In 2003, the Commission documented the cases of 1,084 children, half of whom were under the age of one, who had been kidnapped and then adopted. In some cases, children were adopted by the people accused of killing their families.

Part of the Guatemalan state's counterinsurgency methodology during wartime was to break up and "re-educate" families. The children of guerrillas and/or peasants were sometimes seized by the Army and the police and placed in government-run orphanages. In September 2009, a report published by Guatemala's Peace Archives attempted to detail the country's adoption history from 1977 through 1989. Researchers had gone through thousands of pages of classified police and military documents dug out of Guatemala's National Police Archives, a trove of government information that had been opened in 2007. They found evidence that at least 333 children, and possibly thousands more, had been seized by the Guatemalan Army and placed in government-run homes and orphanages. The

---

[3.] They were covertly taken and/or inexplicably went missing.

director of the Peace Archives, Marco Tulio Alvarez, said that most had probably been adopted by families in the United States and Europe, using false papers and identities. "A second report will be coming out," he said. "And then a third."

It was the beginning of a highly lucrative industry in a poor country. By the time United Nations–brokered peace accords formally ended the war in 1996, six million children made up half of Guatemala's national population. The small country had become one of the largest sources of adoptable orphans in the world.

Celebrate Children International was intended to be a fresh start. Back in late 2002, a group of adoption workers had left Tedi Bear Adoptions, a nonprofit agency based in northern Florida, after the state of Florida had threatened to revoke the agency's operating license. Agency director Tedi Hedstrom had closed up shop voluntarily. Cheraya Bor, a former Tedi Bear facilitator, used a loan from her husband to open up her own new agency, Celebrate Children International (CCI).

The new business established two locations: one in a tidy, three-story office building in downtown Celebration, Florida, and one along highway A1A in Ponte Vedra Beach, Florida, close to where Tedi Bear Adoptions had been based. The first Celebrate Children International website was simple, consisting of a few pages. Like Tedi Bear Adoptions, CCI self-defined as a "Christian organization, committed to improving the lives of children and families through promotion of traditional family values, provision of humanitarian aid, and celebrating families through adoption." On June 26, 2003, CCI received its first operating license from the state of Florida. Sue Hedberg, who had been working in adoption for years, began working with CCI as a Guatemala case manager not long afterward.

For Sue Hedberg, Celebrate Children International was a new opportunity., She'd previously worked for two other adoption agencies. Laura Beauvais-Godwin, the director of Carolina Hope Christian Adoptions, remembers her as being "aggressive." To her, Sue seemed careless, making promises to clients that she couldn't always make good on. "In all fairness, I think that she's competent, but I don't think she's honest," Beauvais-Godwin says. She started questioning Sue's ethics after discovering that she'd lied to a family about the availability of a child at the Guatemalan nursery El Jardín. Then she found that the same thing had happened to another client trying to adopt a different child. "She would tell a family something about a child," Beauvais-Godwin said, "and it simply would not be true."

The relationship between Carolina Hope and Sue Hedberg unraveled after about two and a half years. Laura Beauvais-Godwin says that she let Sue go because of an innocuous yet illegal technicality: Sue had been living in Florida while working for Carolina Hope. According to Florida law, if a Florida resident was working for an out-of-state adoption agency, that agency must apply for and obtain a Florida operating license. Carolina Hope had a single license, from South Carolina.

"My opinion is that Sue built the Guatemalan adoption program for Carolina Hope and was very, very successful, and then they decided, well, we don't need her anymore because we've got this great program," says Mike Bius, an adoptive parent of four Guatemalan children, all of whose adoptions were handled by Sue Hedberg. Bius worked with her at Carolina Hope, and later at the two other agencies she worked with, Florida Home Studies and Adoption and Celebrate Children International.

When Sue left Carolina Hope, she brought her Rolodex of Guatemalan contacts and loyal American clients to her new agency, Florida Home Studies and Adoption. Many of her contacts, including lawyer Alfonso Close, were personal friends as well as business partners. Close and his wife, Elsa, sometimes vacationed in Florida and stayed at the Hedbergs' home.

After eight months, Sue's relationship with Florida Home Studies and Adoption fell apart. Susan Ham, the director of the Florida agency, refuses to speak publicly about Sue Hedberg. Ham's office manager, Debbie Mignemi, says her boss can't talk because of a gag order and lawsuit related to Sue Hedberg's dismissal.

When Laura Beauvais-Godwin heard Sue had stopped working with Florida Home Studies and Adoption, she contacted Susan Ham. After comparing their experiences with Sue Hedberg, the two agency directors felt compelled to send a public email to the greater adoption community. Together, the two agency directors penned an email, signed it, and sent it to the popular Guatemala-Adopt listserve on May 20, 2003.

Established in 1996, the list, known in the Guatemalan adoption community as "the big list," was read by hundreds. "Dear Families," Beauvais-Godwin and Ham wrote. ". . . It has become apparent that the issues that led to the termination of the independent contract with Sue Hedberg with Florida Home Studies and Adoption Agency are similar to the issues that were experienced by Carolina Hope. . . ." Their letter went on to point out that facilitating adoptions independently, without working for an agency that holds a license, is a crime in the state of Florida. It insinuated that Sue Hedberg had been working as a free agent.

The Christian values of Celebrate Children International dovetailed perfectly with Sue Hedberg's own beliefs. She commonly closed her business email with the signature "IN HIS SERVICE," or sometimes "Serving HIS Children." After earning a bachelor's degree in occupational therapy from the University of Central Arkansas in 1982, Sue enrolled at Columbia International University (CIU), an evangelical bible college in South Carolina, for post-graduate work. The college was dedicated to a mission of "victorious Christian living and world evangelization."

At CIU, God came before grades. Academics were undertaken with the sole purpose of equipping students for a life of service to Jesus Christ, in order to help "His global cause." Students were expected to take the Bible literally and to adhere to scriptural principles. Immodest clothing like shorts was banned, and R-rated films, alcohol, and tobacco were forbidden.

While earning her master's degree, Sue met fellow CIU student Dave Hedberg. The couple was married on July 25, 1987. They went on to work as missionaries together in Venezuela, then spent time in Costa Rica studying Spanish. When the Hedbergs came back to the U.S., they bought a modest two-story home in Oviedo, Florida. Dave worked for a branch of a national evangelical organization with the goal of converting foreign students in the U.S. to Christianity. Each of the Hedbergs' three family cars had Florida plates emblazoned with the slogan "Choose Life."

When Sue began working with Celebrate Children International in 2003, the new business was in trouble. Founder Cheraya Bor and her husband, Alexis, filed for Chapter 13 bankruptcy in that year, only months after opening. On December 27, 2003, they told their local licensing agency, the Florida Department of Children and Families, that Sue Hedberg would be taking over as executive director. The adoption agency's offices were relocated to a rented space not far from Sue's home, nestled in a strip mall among other Oviedo businesses, including Domino's Pizza and Sew 'n' Tell Alterations.

Under Cheraya's command, CCI had net revenue totaling $32,775 in 2002. By the end of 2004, with Sue in control, the agency's net revenue climbed to just under $2.5 million. Sue received a salary of $209,750, telling the International Revenue Service that she worked an average of seventy-five hours each week. CCI's taxes that year noted that the business had no paid employees besides Sue, though their website listed a staff of six, including an office manager, a financial manager, a program coordinator, a humanitarian aid coordinator, and a computer specialist.

The Celebrate Children International website was updated, and it migrated from the URL cc-intl.org to celebratechildren.org. Soothing guitar music greeted visitors to the site, and an animated widget on the home page showed the Oviedo, Florida, weather forecast beside a colorful rainbow. A new password-protected client area was installed, along with a Yahoo listserve for families adopting from Guatemala. CCI clients were asked to share their adoption experiences on CCI's website, such as how God "has brought this child into your life" and how "you knew this child was meant to be yours." The agency retained the motto it had had from the start: "Reaching for the Stars."

". . . As disciples of Jesus Christ," CCI's mission statement read, "we are committed to going into the world to serve others. . . ." Under the headline "Professional Integrity," the agency noted that it was committed to "reflect Christ in all we do." A sparkling treasure chest sat on the left side of the home page, beneath a banner that announced, "Click Here to view some of our Foreign Treasures." The banner linked to a page of children's listings, where some of the descriptions were worded to mimic the voice of the child being advertised. "Oh! You startled me!!" one listing read. "Since you're here, though, can I introduce myself? My name is Bryan and I was born in October, so I am still a tiny baby."

Others played on Christian references. "Just like Moses from the Bible, this little Moises is needing a new home!" one description read. "Yes, this really is his name!" "Angel Gabriel is heaven-sent," another said. At the bottom of each listing, visitors were asked to pray for the child's well-being.

Some children had been taped, and the video clips were embedded in their listings. Babies were shown gurgling, cooing, and waving their arms. Older children were shown in conversation with Sue, who asked questions like "What do you like to eat?" Though CCI offered seven different countries to adopt from (two of these, Romania and Vietnam, were said to be on hold), almost all of the children listed were Guatemalan.

Only one of CCI's five listed staffers, Jessie "JT" Crowder, was listed as an adoption facilitator. The rest worked on the administrative side of things. Crowder's bio said he'd worked in over a dozen places in the former Soviet Union. "The matching of unfortunate children with loving forever families," the bio read, "is for him a Biblical response to a terrible yet exciting need in the world, one where the rewards can be worth any effort."

Sue was the contact for all other countries. By mid-2004, CCI was advertising adoption programs in both China and Russia. CCI clients were told that a new program had been started in Taiwan. Cambodia was also listed on CCI's website, although in 2001 the U.S. government had established a moratorium on American citizens' adopting from Cambodia. The ban had been put in place, *The New York Times* reported in June 2002, because of suspicions that adopted children "were being bought or stolen from their parents and put into orphanages with false paperwork in order to feed the growing American demand for babies." To get around the ban without breaking U.S. law, Celebrate Children International offered Cambodian children to those outside the U.S., like missionary families.

By December 2005, CCI listed twelve staff members on their website and boasted adoption programs in Bulgaria, China, Ethiopia, Guatemala, Haiti, Kazakhstan, Taiwan, Ukraine, and Vietnam. Sue continued establishing relationships with orphanages, visiting Guangzhou and Beijing, China, in summer 2005. Company profits increased every year. By 2006, Sue's salary was over a quarter of a million dollars, and CCI's total annual revenue was $4,570,558. Still, to many adopting families, Sue Hedberg seemed more like a devout woman of faith than the exacting CEO of a multimillion dollar company.

The entrance to Finca San Juan Bosco in Escuintla, Guatemala in August 2010.

4. THE LAST EMANUEL

1970–2006

Like many born in wartime, Mildred Navel Alvarado Yac had a childhood that was tense and troubled. Her family lived and worked on Finca San Juan Bosco in Escuintla, a sprawling gated plantation with miles and miles of open land. Mildred's father, Porfirio Alvarado, was a cowboy and tended to cattle and fields of sugarcane. He drank heavily and beat his wife and children often. The family was poor, and they lived in a small two-room shack provided by the owner. The seven Alvarado kids kept to themselves and grew up highly isolated. Mildred was the fourth-oldest, close only to her younger sister Patricia. In lieu of human friends, Mildred befriended the livestock, passing hours lying on the backs of cattle and playing with the goats.

Her brothers tormented her, and she constantly sought out new ways to escape their flying fists. The plantation's many banana trees offered respite in their branches. With an old rope, Mildred would shimmy up their trunks and tie herself, by the waist, to their thick, stalky branches. That way, she felt safe enough to fall asleep. High above the earth, surrounded by the wide green leaves, she could drift into the kinder world of dreams.

When Mildred was in the fourth grade, Porfirio decided that his daughters didn't need any more education. *Girls only go to school to learn dirty things,* he told them, in a way that made the children feel humiliated and guilty. Like many in Guatemala's macho society, he held fast to the belief that women were inferior to men. They belonged in the house, bearing and raising children, cleaning, and cooking. Though his sons and daughters were generally excellent students — Mildred had excelled in almost all of her studies — when one disappointed, every child suffered. Porfirio's thick leather belt waited to catch even the smallest mistake. Only Porfirio Jr., the oldest and their father's namesake, was allowed to continue his studies.

The circumstances of the Alvarado children were far from unique. A 2009 United Nations Development Programme report found that 27 percent of adults over the age of 15 in Guatemala were illiterate, and 65 percent of children didn't study past grade five. Literacy rates for women dragged behind those of men.

The small, poor country struggled with more than literacy. Guatemala was in the midst of civil war when Mildred was born in 1978. She remembers the conflict directly affecting her family twice. One afternoon, the Alvarado children were playing their favorite make-believe game, *vacas* (cows). Some of the kids were pretending to be calves, and the others were *vaqueritos* (cowboys) wielding their father's cold iron brands. The child-*vaquitas* (little cows) were tied to a hitching post in front of the house when a sweeping column of green-uniformed guerrillas appeared.

Mildred, just five or six, was taking her turn as a *vaquita* when the guerrillas approached. *The women are so beautiful,* she thought, gawking as one green-eyed soldier approached and bent down to untie her. The young woman's light skin and clean, pretty fingernails signaled wealth and power. *She must be the daughter of someone important,* Mildred thought. When the young woman met her gaze, she smiled kindly. The small gesture was seared into Mildred's memory. Her own parents rarely smiled.

Pots and pans hung from the young woman's pack, making a low clanging sound as she walked away. Mildred thought that the sound, too, was beautiful. As the troops passed, the green-eyed woman gave the children clear instructions. She told Porfirio Jr., the self-appointed spokesboy for the Alvarado kids, to start a fire in the house so that the Army could see that civilians lived there. It could save their home, she told them.

Soon after, Mildred heard cracking sounds, like fireworks. Helicopters circled overhead, and as a firefight broke out. The plantation was evacuated. For weeks afterward, Mildred's bones felt like they wouldn't stop quivering from terror.

Both Porfirio Alvarado and his wife, Julia Yac, were apolitical. Porfirio was loyal to his boss and to the bottle. Julia, in turn, seemed to be committed only to Porfirio, though even the children knew he was romantically involved with other women. Back when they were in school, the other kids had teased them cruelly, saying that their dad was going to become their own. Julia was quiet and passive. Like her kids, she feared Porfirio's violent temper. She didn't express affection towards her children. Porfirio thought it would spoil them.

When Mildred was twelve, a brother raped her. She approached her mother afterward, crying. Julia shoved a bar of soap towards her, telling her to wash in the river. From then on, Mildred had trouble sleeping and experienced migraines and flashbacks. When she was able to sleep, terrible nightmares brought back every detail of the assault. In the years that followed, she couldn't bear the thought of being physically close to men, much less marrying one. She felt ruined.

At fifteen, friends of her father's boss wanted to hire a live-in maid, and Mildred happily took the job. She moved from the countryside to fancy Zone 14 of Guatemala City, one of the most upscale sections of the capital. Being away from her family was a dizzying relief. During her first two months in Guatemala City, she stayed inside, too timid to venture out even on her day off.

Her new boss, the wife of a cement company magnate, treated her with kindness and respect. Mildred felt loved, almost like a daughter or sister instead of help, even though the *Señora* was only six or seven years older than she was. Mildred looked after the Señora's disabled son, and even accompanied them to the prestigious Nueva Hacienda Country Club. She'd never seen a swimming pool before. The Señora kindly encouraged her to take the boy into the water. For a moment, Mildred felt as if her heart would swell out of her chest from happiness. Her boss encouraged her to eat from the same food court as the country club's wealthy members. "It's no big deal," the young woman told Mildred, smiling. "Take what you want."

Mildred couldn't find words to express her joy and thanks. When she tried to articulate her gratitude to the Señora, she broke down in tears. The appreciation seemed to be mutual. Her boss regularly thanked her for her hard work and even took Mildred shopping and taught her how to dress in the city. Many maids from the countryside wore traditional *traje,* long, colorful wrap skirts, and *huipiles,* embroidered floral blouses. Mildred generally wore fitted skirts, T-shirts, tank tops, and plastic flip-flops, like many others from Guatemala's coastal regions. The kindness shown by her boss bolstered her confidence. After about a year, she felt comfortable enough to divulge the experience of her rape. The headaches and nightmares hadn't ceased. The Señora pulled her into a hug, telling Mildred it was better to let everything out. That way, the woman said, healing could begin.

Photos of Mildred Alvarado as a teenager, from her national I.D. card.

Three years passed. Mildred turned eighteen, and to her dismay, her father suddenly called her home. The Alvarado family now lived in Lago del Pino, working as caretakers at another wealthy family's vacation home. Porfirio said he needed her help, and Mildred never considered saying no. She left the city and began to work alongside her family, her pay cut in half. She thought frequently about her old boss and the little boy she had cared for. The family was trying to immigrate to the United States, and she didn't know if she'd ever see them again. What Mildred had hoped would be a temporary return to her family slid into six years.

It was in Lago del Pino that she met the man who would become the father of her children, a handsome construction worker named Romelio Perez Argueta. Their romance was fast and intense, a kind of love that Mildred had never expected or hoped for. After surviving the childhood sexual assault, she had become resigned to a life alone. Romelio found her funny and engaging. She felt respected and treated like a real person, in a way dissimilar to how she'd seen other Guatemalan men treat their women. After a time, she even confided to Romelio about the rape. He listened compassionately, telling her they could work through it together. Mildred was astonished. She fell deeply in love.

When she found out she was pregnant, Mildred told her sister Patricia, and no one else. Both sisters were thrilled. Patricia ventured into neighbors' orchards at night, harvesting mangoes and oranges to satisfy Mildred's cravings. The pair giggled and dreamed, delighted with the idea of the new baby to come. Mildred thought the pregnancy was the most perfect thing she'd ever had. Together, she dreamed, she, Romelio, and Patricia would start a new life, in a new town. Her baby wouldn't know a day without being held, hugged, and kissed, and she was determined to give her child the affection her own mother hadn't been able to provide. The Alvarado sisters went together to buy baby clothes, and Mildred teased Patricia, saying she would have to be the baby's stand-in father. Romelio was often away because of his job.

It was only a matter of time before their own father found out. At six months, Mildred began to show. To Porfirio, it was bad enough that his unmarried daughter was with child. To him, the fact that she was carrying a light-skinned man's child was even worse. He didn't approve of mixing races. Porfirio was drunk when he discovered the pregnancy, and he beat Mildred so badly her face bled. He made a point to bludgeon her midsection. Mildred was an unfit role model for Patricia, Porfirio said, and pronounced her the shame of the family.

Romelio didn't have the backbone to stand up to Mildred's father, who openly mocked his complexion and ruddy cheeks. Porfirio said he looked as if he wore women's make-up. Romelio kept his distance, and eventually stopped coming around to visit Mildred.

When the baby was born, Mildred named her Susana Pamela. Feeding and caring for the infant made it impossible to save money, and her dream of leaving seemed to be growing more distant. In a moment of courage, she decided to ask her boss — who was also her father's boss — for a one-time loan of 500Q (U.S. $65). With the money, she imagined, she could move back to the capital and work again as a maid. Otherwise, Mildred felt, her future seemed clear: working alongside her family for as long as life decided.

The boss turned her down, then told Porfirio about his daughter's bold request. Another beating followed. Mildred snapped. She'd had enough. She was leaving, and this time she was determined not to return. Seizing Susana and a small bag, she headed to the place she thought she could find work: the busy bus terminal in Zone 4 of Guatemala City. There, scores of homemade food stands fed the city's massive commuter population. She met a woman who hired her to help sell food and rented her a room in a tiny apartment.

About a year passed. One day, while handing a taco to a customer, Mildred looked up to see Romelio staring down at her from a bus window. Her pulse fluttered. She felt as if she'd seen a ghost. Romelio was packed in the rear of the vehicle, one cheek, rosy as ever, pressed against the back window.

She couldn't help it; she took him back. He was her true love. The year apart hadn't changed her feelings for him. Mildred understood that Romelio didn't have the nerve to stand up to her father, in the same way she understood why her mother had never left him. It was simple: They didn't have enough strength.

Soon they were living together, in the little rented duplex apartment in Villa Nueva. Their daughter Susana was joined by a brother, Mario, in 2002 and a younger sister, Fernanda, in 2004. Life reached a comfortable point. When Mildred discovered Romelio's infidelity, it all began to unravel.

Betsy Richards, an Alabama native, was just nineteen when she married, standing alongside Leslie Emanuel in her grandmother's handmade wedding dress at the Cottage Hill Baptist Church in Mobile on June 7, 1980. Betsy's parents looked on skeptically: The groom was a twenty-three-year-old college student, and Betsy herself had just finished high school. The young couple were stubbornly determined to begin their life together.

Having led an insulated, sheltered childhood, marriage felt like instant adulthood to Betsy. Being apart from her family for the first time was exhilarating, as was her liberation from the pressures of a teenage singing career. Her soprano voice had made her a local celebrity, and her family had always stressed that her talent was a gift from God. She had an obligation to use it to uplift and enlighten. Betsy was a natural onstage, content in the limelight. Yet as the singing competitions grew more serious, the pressure to succeed also increased. As the weekends melted into an unending blur of voice lessons, performances, and choir practices, the joy of song faded. Betsy couldn't wait to run her own household and make her own rules.

While they were still dating, Betsy confided her adoption dreams to Leslie. As a Christian, Betsy felt called to adopt. There was no higher gesture of love and charity than to parent an orphaned child. Leslie smiled, appreciating her compassionate heart but underestimating her commitment.

Betsy counted at least 17 different references to adoption in the Bible. The Book of James instructs believers to care for orphans, and Exodus 2:1-10 offers the example of Moses himself, given up by his mother and subsequently adopted by royalty. In the Book of Esther, Mordecai adopts the future Queen Esther after her own parents are killed, raising her as his daughter. "Learn to do good," Isaiah 1:17 commands. "Seek justice. Help the oppressed. Defend the cause of orphans." All Christians themselves are adoptees, Betsy thought, the children of God.

When Leslie proposed, she accepted immediately. The Emanuels began their life together in Mobile, where both had grown up. Betsy worked as a dental hygienist for a local pediatric dentist, Dr. Marion Mac Murphy. She adored the affable Dr. Mac, who sang to his little patients even when they were knocked out. His young clients came from diverse socioeconomic backgrounds, and many were wards of the Alabama state foster care system. To Betsy, the children seemed starved for love. She could scarcely believe, slightly embarrassed at her own naiveté, that she'd never known anyone in foster care before. So many needed help. She couldn't imagine how they grew up without a dedicated family. At night, long after she had gone home, the children's small voices echoed in her heart.

One patient in particular stole her heart. Topaz, a mixed-race two-year-old with a quick smile and gravity-defying pigtails, was a repeat visitor, cheerful despite serious dental issues. When Betsy lifted Topaz into her arms, the child would grin, wrapping a fat baby finger around Betsy's own. When the toddler gazed up at her, Betsy felt twinges of protectiveness. She'd never felt so drawn to a child before. Topaz never failed to be entertained by silly improvised games, like "Bunny on Your Nose." No matter how many times the "bunny," Betsy's finger, landed on her nose, Topaz always erupted in peals of laughter. The simple, open delight tugged at Betsy's heart. Her longing to help Topaz was almost painful. *If only I could adopt her,* she thought.

It was a crazy idea. Nevertheless, after work one evening, Betsy placed a call to an adoption counselor at the local Catholic Charities office to inquire about the possibilities. To her surprise, the nun in charge scoffed at her. "Are you comfortable in a black church?" the Sister asked, condescension coloring her words. "Do you have any black friends?"

Betsy hesitated. "No," she answered quietly. During her childhood and teenage years, the civil rights movement had exploded in Mobile, yet she'd remained oblivious. In her whole life, she'd known only one black person: the family maid, Willie. Of the thousand or so classmates at her private Christian school, everyone was white.

"How would you know what to do with her hair?" the nun snapped. Betsy hung up, feeling defeated yet defiant. Sure, she didn't have any black friends. But did it really matter? She made friends easily. And hair? It could be learned. Still, the nun's disapproval was clear. There was no way she'd allow an adoption to move forward.

That night, thinking about the conversation, Betsy's feelings of defeat transformed into staunch determination. Someday, she vowed, no matter what anyone might think, she was going to adopt. It might be difficult to get her conservative family and some of her friends to understand, as it still wasn't socially acceptable to raise someone else's child as your own. Still, Betsy felt called. After all, as her time at Dr. Mac's office had proven, there was no shortage of needy children in the world. That wasn't likely to change.

Ten years passed. Betsy watched friends adopt, and after having three biological children with Leslie, it felt like the time was right. Leslie was holding down a good, steady job as a corporate controller. Yet when she first brought up the idea of bringing home an orphan from a foreign country, Leslie balked, worried about the family budget. When Betsy showed him a small photograph of a Korean baby with the birth defect ectrodactyly-ectodermal dysplasia-cleft (EEC) syndrome, her husband softened. Like many EEC children, baby Jack was missing fingers and toes. He was just a few months old.

The American adoption agency Holt International could arrange to have the boy delivered to the U.S., Betsy learned. Holt had been founded in 1955 after the Korean War, when two farmers from Oregon, Henry and Bertha Holt, decided to dedicate their lives to finding homes for Korean orphans, as an expression of God's compassion.

Jack came to Tennessee via airplane, escorted and delivered by Holt. Afterward, Holt asked Betsy to write about her experience for their adoption magazine in order to bring attention to special-needs adoptions. She penned a glowing piece. A woman from Iowa read it and contacted her, saying she knew of another Korean baby with EEC syndrome who needed a home. Within days, a picture of the baby arrived in the Emanuels' mailbox. The little girl had misshapen fingers and toes, like Jack, and her dark hair jutted up at a comical angle. Studying the photo, Betsy felt that the baby was supposed to become part of the Emanuel family.

She stuck a picture of the baby, who she called Hannah, on the refrigerator. Jack's photo had been there, too, before he arrived in Tennessee. It was an easy way to keep the boy in their thoughts and prayers while waiting for his adoption to be completed. Betsy figured that seeing Hannah's face would melt her husband's heart, and she was right. A few months later, Leslie agreed that they could adopt again. Hannah became the Emanuels' fifth child.

About a year later, while perusing Precious.org, Betsy found a listing for the child who would become their sixth. She'd developed the emotionally draining habit of clicking through the listings, looking at pictures of child after child, imagining the circumstances of each, alone and unloved. When Betsy saw Bo, a Chinese boy who also had EEC syndrome, she jumped to her feet, yelling out the window for her husband to come inside.

Leslie was cutting their five acres of grass with their cheap 24-inch push mower in the hot Tennessee sun, and he waved her off. When she at last got him inside, she pointed excitedly at Bo's page on Precious.org. "Look at this boy!" she exclaimed. "He has the same birth defect as Jack and Hannah!"

Leslie leaned in. "Yeah?" he said, with a hint of exasperation. "What's your point?"

"I think he needs to be with us, not left in an orphanage," Betsy replied. "The kids could lean on each other growing up. They'd have siblings who understood what it was like."

Leslie's answer was a flat no. Five kids were enough. He went back outside to the sweltering summer heat and the too-small push mower. Two hours later, when he came inside for a drink of water, he found a new face staring out at him from the fridge. It was Bo.

He sighed. "Betsy!" he called, taking care to keep his voice light. In a house with five children, every wall was certain to have a pair of ears behind it. Leslie was crazy about his wife, but the adoption issue was getting ridiculous. "That's not going to work this time!"

She raced downstairs, feigning innocence. "OK, OK," she assured him. "I'm just praying about it."

But when the kids saw Bo's photo on the refrigerator, they knew immediately what it meant. He was potentially their new brother. Finally, one evening during dinner, Leslie turned to his wife. "So when's he coming?" he asked casually. "Who?" Betsy responded, raising an eyebrow. Leslie motioned towards the fridge, a smile tugging at the corner of his mouth.

Despite his conservative nature, Betsy managed to win him over every time. He couldn't resist her generous, upbeat spirit. Nine months later, Bo joined the family.

Dinner at the Emanuel household was Leslie's domain. He always brewed sweet tea according to the tried-and-true Southern recipe, using six teabags and a carefully measured dose of sugar. Most nights, he had dinner on the table by eight. Betsy did children, and he did food. To him, cooking was easier than sorting out who was fussing at whom, or mediating minor squabbles over toy ownership.

Leslie, naturally handy with construction, had knocked down the wall that separated the kitchen from the dining room. The new open floor plan gave everyone more room. Before dinner, the kids would move the schoolbooks that had accumulated on the table to the floor, where they'd remain in haphazard stacks until morning. The living room, painted a warm cocoa brown, was decorated with a huge map of the world that Betsy had found at a teacher's supply store.

When Leslie came home from work each night, around 6:45, he'd start dinner. Betsy and the kids would drift in and out, helping at will or by request. Betsy just couldn't muster the kind of culinary pride that came naturally to her husband. Leslie was a simple cook, a meat and potatoes man, but exacting when it came to following recipes. Betsy chalked it up to his patient, detail-oriented nature and his occupation as a corporate number cruncher. To her, there was nothing wrong with estimating measurements, or even throwing in an extra ingredient or two. When she commanded the stove, things tended to burn.

She took pride in being the unstructured parent, sometimes siding with the kids when trying to convince Leslie of something. He'd recently been cajoled into installing a television over the kitchen fridge. Now it was normal for Steve Irwin and his crocodiles to join the Emanuels for dinner. Though they'd never anticipated adopting more than once, Betsy and Leslie were deeply proud of their lively crew of kids. After Bo had arrived, they'd added one more child, Matthew, to the family in a domestic adoption. The gender balance of four boys and three girls was almost perfect. Almost.

One last daughter would round it out.

Leslie and Betsy Emanuel, recently wed in 1980.
Photograph courtesy Betsy Emanuel.

5. A PRETTY LITTLE GIRL

August 2006–September 2006

Betsy Emanuel called Celebrate Children International the week of August 11, 2006, to share her upcoming travel plans. Sue Hedberg's assistant, Angela Vance, answered, and Betsy began chattering away. Then Angela interrupted. There was bad news. For reasons outside of CCI's control, Jennifer was no longer available for adoption. The referral for the child had been "lost." For a moment, Betsy thought she'd misheard. *Lost? What's that supposed to mean?*

Jennifer's birth mother had allegedly burst into the Guatemala City office of attorney Alfonso Close, Angela explained, accompanied by an armed man. In no uncertain terms, the pair demanded the child's return.

Now, she continued, even Sue didn't know what could be done about the situation. It was the birth mother's right to change her mind about giving her child up for adoption, a possibility clearly outlined in Celebrate Children International's adoption contract.

Betsy struggled to take it all in. Wasn't Jennifer's mother dying? She'd been told the young woman was in the final stages of HIV. Why would she suddenly change her mind, especially now, eight months later? She imagined the situation unfolding in the lawyer's office: a man, probably angry; the cold steel of a pistol; the dying prostitute; and her own sweet Jennifer, who must have been terrified. A flash of anger surged through Betsy's body. The story seemed unbelievable. "Did Alfonso call the police?" she demanded.

Angela told her again that birth mothers had every right to change their minds. Betsy cut the conversation short, asking to speak directly to Sue. To her surprise, Sue repeated the same story, almost verbatim. There had been an armed man. Maybe it was Jennifer's mother's boyfriend, or maybe her pimp. Sue's tone was so coolly indifferent that Betsy began questioning her own initial reaction.

Still, why would Jennifer's mother change her mind if she were dying? It didn't make sense.

Betsy's mind raced through a variety of horrible situations, and she begged Sue to find Jennifer. Like a mantra, Sue told her again that the situation was out of her control. *Jennifer is in God's hands,* Betsy remembers her saying. *Of course He will look after one of His children.* To her, it seemed clear that Jennifer wasn't meant to be with the Emanuels. The agency director's calm manner rankled Betsy. "Don't you trust in God's plan?" Sue asked her.

The question gave Betsy pause, and she swallowed hard against her emotions. Faith was one of the things that had led to the Emanuels' blended family in the first place. There were other orphans who needed homes, and Sue advised Betsy to pray about opening her heart to another child.

Hours later, pictures of other children began filtering into Betsy's inbox. Celebrate Children International had a list of families waiting for available children. If the Emanuels didn't pick soon, Sue implied, they could be left without a referral for an unknown amount of time. Betsy looked through the photos, distracted by thoughts of Jennifer. Where was she sleeping? Was she eating? She imagined the child joining the thousands of children who lived on Guatemala's dangerous streets. *She'll end up a prostitute,* Betsy thought sadly, *like her mother.*

Possibly in an attempt to soothe her worried client, Sue set up a conference call so Betsy could voice her concerns directly to those involved. Lawyer Alfonso Close and Dr. Jose Bran González, a Guatemalan pediatrician somehow involved with Jennifer's case, would be on the line. Since Betsy didn't speak Spanish, Sue acted as translator.

Close spoke quickly, in a high, thin voice. Sue translated swaths of his Spanish into English, repeating the same story about Jennifer's situation. Dr. González kept butting in, but Sue didn't translate his interjections. When the conversation lulled, Betsy piped up and tried to explain the love she felt for Jennifer, though she'd never even met the child. The Guatemalans were condescending in return, especially Dr. González. "You can't have her," he said coldly. "Pick another."

Betsy dissolved into frustrated tears. To her surprise, Sue Hedberg followed suit. It sounded as though CCI's director was pleading with the men, and Betsy thought her weeping squeals sounded like the sounds of a wounded bird. Sometimes Sue reverted back to English, as if by mistake, or maybe for Betsy's benefit. "You don't understand!" she cried out. "Mrs. Emanuel loves her. Mrs. Emanuel really loves her."

Sue's outburst made Betsy feel validated. She announced, more firmly, that her family would wait as long as they had to to make sure Jennifer was safe. "Then you have nothing," Dr. González said curtly, in heavily accented English. "I don't know why you're upset. This one's not available. Just pick another. What don't you understand?"

The call ended uncomfortably. Afterward, Sue told Betsy that she planned to have dinner with Close and "Dr. G" on her next trip to Guatemala, promising to search for the missing child herself. It would be a favor, she stressed, and was not something she usually did.

Betsy felt a warm rush of gratitude. The situation with Jennifer's birth mother was supposed to remain quiet, she understood, because the mother had also asked for Dulce, Jennifer's younger sister, to be returned. Dulce was already in the United States, and her adoptive mother, Mary McGraw, hadn't been informed of the situation. It would just cause problems.

More than once in the days that followed, Betsy reached for the phone to call Mary. Each time, her hand drifted back down to her side. *She didn't seem to want anything to do with me*, Betsy thought, remembering how Mary had quashed the idea of letting Dulce and Jennifer visit. And now, Dulce wasn't even Dulce anymore; the five-year-old had a new American name. Betsy decided to remain silent.

She forced herself to look through pictures of other orphans online. Like before, there weren't many older girls. *Well,* Betsy thought, *they all need homes.* She hesitated for a moment, then began looking through the listings for toddlers. One in particular caught her eye: a beautiful little girl named Maria Fernanda Alvarado.

Sue Hedberg was in Guatemala on business in July 2006. It had been a difficult summer for adoption. Cases entering the Procuraduría General de la Nación (PGN), or Guatemala's Office of the Attorney General, for review were coming out in a trickle. The new chief of the PGN's Children and Adolescents' Unit, a young woman named Josefina Arellano, suspected that many of the adoptions weren't legitimate. That year, she'd instituted a policy of random checks on adoption files. Unlike the previous unit chief, who'd been more diplomatic about compromise, Arellano was strict with adoption lawyers.

Celebrate Children International was used to finishing between fifteen and twenty-five Guatemalan adoptions per month, a sizable number given that the PGN approved an average of 350 adoptions per month throughout the spring. Lately, though, the number of finalized adoptions had plummeted. Only four CCI adoptions wrapped up in June. Some of Sue's clients had waited months for the PGN to approve their adoption paperwork, which was one of the last steps required before a child was granted a visa and could travel to the United States.

At the PGN, adoption cases were supposed to be assigned to one of seven reviewers by a computerized system. Each reviewer would examine the paperwork in their files for signs of fraud and irregularities like misspellings, mismatched information, and doctored photos. Whenever *previos*, or errors, were found, the adoption file would be returned to the lawyer handling the case. In the American adoption community, this was known as being "kicked out" of the PGN. It was common. In fact, Sue told CCI clients that every adoption was kicked out of the PGN at least once. It meant, she said, that their cases were moving farther along in the process. "Don't be sad, be *glad* when you get kicked out!" she told her families.

Some cases were kicked out of the PGN three or four times before getting a stamp of approval. Generally, lawyers had unlimited opportunities to correct errors. One Guatemalan adoption facilitator said she had a case that was kicked out twenty-one times before passing muster. Certain attorneys, like Onelia Estrada Cordon, had so many mistakes accumulate that the PGN banned them from submitting adoptions.

Some adoption cases, like those fraudulently submitted for multiple children under a single child's name, were supposed to be passed to the PGN's in-house investigative unit for review. The PGN investigative team consisted of three or four people working together in a single cramped office. Their workload was massive. Two desks held stacks of adoption files that often towered over a foot high. One longtime PGN investigator said the high amount of previos resulted from the fact that seasoned lawyers weren't actually preparing, or even reviewing, the paperwork submitted under their names.

"Every investigation was full of little boxes of surprises," the investigator said. "There would be similarities of errors for all cases submitted by the same attorney, who'd specialize in one geographic region. You could tell that there were a lot of inexperienced law students and young people preparing the files. It was sad to see such stupid mistakes."

One birth mother said to have voluntarily given her child up for adoption had, in truth, been dead for ten years. Other times, the gender given for a child was erroneous: A photograph of a girl would be stapled inside a boy's adoption file. Falsified ID documents for relinquishing mothers and the children they were giving up were common, and the PGN investigators were forced to trek deep into the countryside in an attempt to verify basic information. Such a trip could take days, but it was the only way to prove whether or not a *cédula* (Guatemala's national ID card) or birth certificate had been recently fabricated.

In the countryside, local civil registrars kept the original copies of ID documents in thick yellowing books, organized in volumes. By leafing through the faded pages, investigators could see if a photo had been carefully cut out and replaced, or if a mother's birth date or address had been changed. If a photo appeared to be doctored, investigators could take a copy of the picture to any listed relatives to see if they recognized their alleged kin. A potentially fraudulent birth certificate for a relinquishing mother could be cross-referenced by a visit to those listed as her parents. When a parent didn't recognize the person in the photo, allegedly their own adult daughter, investigators would know something was amiss. The fact that many rural women didn't have birth certificates was an additional complication.

Guatemalan law required that the records kept by civil registrars be made available to the public. One private investigator who frequently took on private-adoption investigations said that registrars in certain municipalities, such as Escuintla and Puerto San José, provided access to documents only if the person inquiring provided proof of their own identity. "This was because those regions had the highest rates of falsified documents," he said. "After they had your name, they would call people to ask about you." To him, it felt like a veiled threat to stop poking around.

Ultimately, cases with the most serious problems were passed from the PGN to the Ministerio Público (MP), Guatemala's Ministry of Justice, to be sorted out. The MP, a separate government institution, was responsible for investigating and prosecuting crime. "You can identify corruption by watching how fast the files move through the PGN," says Jaime Tecú, who once worked in the MP. "Two similar cases could move at very different paces. Sometimes previos meant fraud. Sometimes a lack of previos meant fraud."

In June 2006, Sue Hedberg arranged a face-to-face meeting with Victor Hugo Barrios, the sub-director of the PGN. He was Josefina Arellano's boss, and both U.S. adoption agencies and Guatemalan lawyers turned to him when advocating for adoption cases to move forward. Barrios had to approve every adoption file, and his signature was required for adoption paperwork to leave the PGN and go on to the U.S. Embassy's visa department. When Sue met with Barrios, she talked about how PGN review was delaying practically all of CCI's adoptions. She had fifty-one cases with the PGN. Barrios approved three of CCI's cases the day of the meeting.

A few weeks later, not much had changed. Just six of CCI's adoptions were finalized in July 2006. One CCI lawyer even suggested that Sue should try to sue the PGN over the review time for one particular case. To clients, Sue said that Barrios blamed the slow processing on a lack of staff at the PGN. There weren't enough people to keep up with the flood of adoptions, and there was no budget to hire additional staff.

Sue also told her clients that PGN's slowness in reviewing adoption cases was the fault of Guatemalan President Óscar Berger and his wife, Wendy. They were "anti-adoption," she said, and Barrios was "under orders" from the president's wife to "slow or stop" them. He was complying by having reviewers "kick out cases for stupid reasons."

Coni Galindo Bran called Mildred hours after taking custody of Fernanda in Guatemala. It was an evening in mid-August, and Mildred was still living in Sabrina's house in Villa Canales. Coni assured her that everything was fine and put Fernanda on the phone, as if to prove it.

"Mama!" Mildred heard her daughter say. "I'm fine." Fernanda's voice sounded small, almost mechanical. She thought it sounded as if the child has been told what to say. "I have my own room," Fernanda continued. "And crib. And baby!" For much of her short life, the child had slept snugly sandwiched between some combination of her mother, aunt, sister, and brother. She'd never had her own bed, much less her own room. "Don't worry," Mildred remembers Coni saying. "The girl is fine here with us. We threw away those old clothes she was wearing."

After the call, Mildred felt her daughter's absence in her bones. She panicked, wondering if she'd done the right thing, and fell into despondency. What kind of mother would leave her child with a stranger? Briefly, the thought of suicide flitted through her mind.

In the days that followed, Mildred tried to focus on keeping house, determined to push the sadness and doubt to the back of her mind. The situation was temporary, she reminded herself. August was almost over, and the baby was due back toward the end of September. A reunion would come in just weeks. She tried to concentrate on her pregnancy, buying healthy food like fresh fruit at the market. Every day, Mildred took time away from her kids to sit alone, in a closet or a corner. There, privately, she'd engage in long one-sided conversations with her rounded belly. It was a tradition she'd created. The talks were calming and felt like an introduction of sorts, from mother to child. That way, Mildred thought, when the baby arrived, it would come into the world already knowing her.

On the afternoon of August 21, 2006, Marvin Josué Bran Galindo, one of Celebrate Children International's adoption facilitators, sent Sue Hedberg an email. "I'm sending you photos of a new girl named Maria Fernanda Alvarado, born May 7, 2004, age 2 years 3 months. She's precious, very well cared for, and in very good health. We received her yesterday, and today we'll bring her to the doctor. . . . I hope you can find a family soon." He didn't say how he had come in contact with the child, or why she'd been given up for adoption. Six tiny headshots of Fernanda accompanied the note.

Sue listed the child on Precious.org that day. "What a pretty little girl!" the advertisement read. Fernanda's description reflected the lack of information, noting that the child's blood work and a medical report would be available "soon" and that only "100 percent paper-ready families," or those ready to adopt immediately, would be considered. In the accompanying photo, Fernanda's wide brown eyes looked uncertain.

Betsy Emanuel thought Fernanda was stunning. Sue told her that CCI had worked with Marvin and his mother, Coni, many times. They were people of faith, active in their church. They even used elderly women from the church to provide foster care for the orphans they handled.

Sue emailed additional photos of the child to Betsy, all grainy and small, as if taken with a cell phone camera. Fernanda wasn't smiling in any of them. Her concerned expression stoked Betsy's compassion. Sue explained that Fernanda probably missed her mother and grandmother, whom she had lived with. She had been relinquished because her family was too poor to care for her.

On Friday, August 25, about a week after being told Jennifer was unavailable, Betsy confirmed her interest in adopting Fernanda. Sue had already sent documents on the child, including a copy of a birth certificate that stated that Fernanda had been born to Mildred Alvarado in Guatemala City in May 2004. Two medical receipts were also enclosed, dated August 22, 2006. The first was from the office of Guatemala City pediatrician Dr. Napoleón Castillo Mollinedo, stating that he'd examined Fernanda and found her healthy. On the second, the word "PERSONAL" had been typed in the field meant for a doctor's name. That receipt, printed on stationary from a clinic forty minutes outside the capital, stated that Fernanda had tested negative for HIV and hepatitis. No doctor had signed it.

Later that day, Sue sent the Emanuels a new power-of-attorney document appointing a man named César Augusto Trujillo López to act as their new legal representative in Guatemala. The Emanuels signed and notarized it and sent it back to Sue. Betsy couldn't get the worried little girl out of her mind.

The Emanuels received a DVD from Celebrate Children International about two weeks after signing up to adopt Fernanda. In the video clip, a striking, dark-eyed Fernanda stood before a burgundy couch on which two women were sitting. One cradled a baby in her arms. Fernanda stood still, and then her face blossomed into a bright smile and she began jabbering happily, speaking in sounds instead of words. Her hair was pulled back in a neat ponytail, and Minnie Mouse danced across the front of her light pink dress. Several adult voices could be heard in the room, and a camera flashed repeatedly as someone photographed the girl.

The adults in the room spoke a combination of Spanish and English. Sue, standing just outside the video camera's frame, questio-ned and chatted with others in the room in Spanish. "And we can go forward with this case, right?" she asked.

Marvin Bran, a stocky twenty-something in a striped button-down shirt, responded. "Right," he replied. "But they haven't sent me the papers..."

"No?" Sue said. "Who, Alfonso? You haven't spoken with Alfonso?" The adults continued speaking, oblilquely discussing the child's situation as the video camera remained trained on the toddler. The conversation moved from time frames and finances to personal matters. Fernanda's grin started to fade. Sue inquired about why she was being offered for adoption.

"The first day that we had her, she was very shy and only cried," Marvin answered. "And when someone hugged her, she cried. But now she's fine. The mother lived with the father, but they weren't married. At first, she lived with him, but he left her. These are people who aren't educated; they don't have options for good jobs." He didn't mention how he'd become involved with the child.

Fernanda stood in the center of the frame, now silent and unsmi-ling. "And is she healthy?" Sue asked. "And her teeth, how are . . .?"

One of the women in the room cut her off. "They're good," she said, reaching out to grab Fernanda by the jaw. She pulled the little girl's face towards her. "Show her your teeth, my love," she said. "She wants to see your teeth."

Fernanda stared back blankly. The woman tried again. "Your teeth, my love," she repeated, baring her own at the child in an exag-gerated smile. Fernanda remained uncooperative, turning back to face Sue and the video camera. Her mouth was clamped into a small, hard line.

Then Sue tried. "Fernanda, can you give me a smile?" she asked. "Can you give me a smile?" The child stared at her.

"Please? No?" Sue continued. "Nothing? You don't have teeth? I think you have teeth."

They gave up. The next time Sue spoke, she was addressing someone on the phone, asking questions about a file. "Alfonso, please, talk with Marvin…" she directed, the rest of her words drowned out by the cries of other children in the background. The camera panned past Marvin Bran, who sat in an armchair and was now speaking into a hot-pink cell phone. "Alfonso, a pleasure," Marvin said eloquently. "Good afternoon. I have a little something to bother you with…"

Sue reached forward and scooped Fernanda into her arms. The camera followed her, refocusing. Sue looked pudgy in a blue shirt and white pants. Her blond hair hung in a shoulder-length bob.

From behind the camera, a female voice called out in perfectly accented Spanish, "*Hola, muñeca!*" Hello, doll! "Fernanda!" the unknown woman exclaimed, trying to get the child to look towards the camera. Instead, Fernanda stared intently at Marvin Bran, her gaze locked on his face. Oblivious, he continued chatting on the phone. "*¿Cómo estás?*" the woman asked pointedly. *How are you?*

Fernanda trained a serious gaze on the camera. Then, seconds later, her attention reverted back to Marvin.

Sue looked away from the child and into the camera, pausing for effect. "She is to die for, Elizabeth," she announced dramatically in English, calling Betsy by her full name. "She is to die for." Leaning in, Sue planted a kiss on the little girl's cheek. Fernanda stared back with wide eyes. She seemed uncertain.

One of the women in the room tried asking the toddler a few last questions, in rapid succession. "What is your favorite food? French fries? Yes or no? Yes? Do you like French fries? Do you like tacos? Cheese?"

Fernanda remained silent. Sue loosened her hold and let the little girl slide to the floor. Fernanda toddled toward the couch, where three other children waited. Two were babies, and one looked to be a year or two old. She placed one hand on Marvin Bran's knee to steady herself. The clip ended abruptly.

Sue Hedberg holds Maria Fernanda Alvarado in a video clip sent by her to the Emanuel family, fall 2006. Video courtesy the Ministerio Público, Guatemala.

6. DAVID AND GOLIATH
1990–2000

For the U.S. Embassy in Guatemala City, facilitating international adoptions was politically delicate. An internal cable from the
Embassy, dated August 1990, defined its objectives bluntly: "providing expeditious service to U.S. citizens adoptive parents, enforcing
the "orphan" provisions of our immigration law, and insulating the
Embassy from charges of complicity in child trafficking. . . ."

It was a difficult task, and a learning process. Over two decades,
as the adoption caseload continually increased, the U.S. Embassy
struggled with pressure from adopting Americans, a lack of resources, and the challenge of verifying the authenticity of "orphans"
brought forward by adoption attorneys.

"Because Guatemalan attorneys can earn thousands of dollars
for each international adoption case they handle, many employ
shoddy or illegal practices, including the preparation or purchase
of false documents," the Embassy told the Secretary of State in the
August 1990 cable. "Given our limited investigative resources and
our commitment to providing American citizens with expedited
service, we cannot thoroughly investigate the truth of every adoption
document presented to us." The Embassy found it "impractical" to
comply with Immigration and Naturalization Services (INS) guidelines that asked them to deem all orphan cases "clearly approvable"
before they were passed to the INS for visa processing.

In the same memo, the Embassy described a litany of abuses and
fraud they'd observed. "The current system provides fertile ground
for abuse," the cable stated. "Numerous interviews with natural
mothers of adopted children have revealed that many attorneys in
"private" (relinquishment) adoption cases exploit the absence of
effective oversight, engaging in questionable legal practices: notari-
zing documents although not present; obtaining the signatures or

thumbprints of natural mothers on blank pieces of paper, which are filled in at a later date; drafting social workers' reports for the court-appointed social workers, who in turn pass those documents off as independent studies; and postdating or backdating documents whenever convenient." The Embassy found such "indifference to documentary proof" to be "disconcerting."

"One of the Guatemalan adoption attorneys whom we trust recently told Embassy officials that he believed that fewer kidnappings had occurred in the past year, but that they were 'still a problem,'" the cable continued, noting that the Embassy believed that kidnappings were uncommon. They did, however, suspect that many birth parents sold children to adoption attorneys.

The memo outlined the U.S. government's plan for handling the minority of adoption cases that showed obvious signs of fraud. As the Embassy didn't have the resources to scrutinize each document in an adoption file, they decided to focus on one particular element: the consent, or relinquishment, form. That way they could avoid "overloading ourselves and causing long delays for adoptive parents anxious to return to the United States with their children."

"The pitfalls of this approach are obvious," the Embassy explained to Washington. "We undoubtedly approve petitions that do not merit classification as 'clearly approvable.'" The Embassy had "given up active efforts" to determine whether a child's grandparents or extended family were in the picture, and because child-selling wasn't technically illegal in Guatemala, it had been "making no effort to determine whether or not adoptive parents or their legal representatives are making payoffs to natural parents. . . ." The cable noted that the key to improving the adoption process was the promotion of legal reform in Guatemala.

Over the next seven years, the U.S. Embassy in Guatemala City continued sending regular updates about adoption fraud back to Washington. In 1991, they requested guidance in dealing with "unscrupulous" adoption attorneys, saying that they believed that fifteen to twenty lawyers were involved in "what we consider shady legal practices." They believed that the attorneys' exorbitant fees lent credibility to the idea that "legal services are not the only commodity changing hands." Ongoing efforts to verify consent led to a new practice of interviewing all relinquishing birth mothers at the

Embassy. They estimated that 7 percent of adoptions included fraud such as baby-selling, impostor mothers, false birth certificates, or the deception of birth mothers by attorneys.

By 1994, the Embassy was referring to adoption as a "service industry," noting that the Guatemalan public was sensitive to the issue. "More significant than gross numbers or a nationalistic reaction against adoptions is the fact that child stealing and baby trafficking do occur in Guatemala," one cable read. During one weekend in March 1994, the Embassy noted, "graffiti reading *Gringo Roba Niños* (*Americans Steal Children*) and *Yankis Roban Niños Fuera* (*Child-Stealing Americans Out*) had been painted "all over Guatemala City." That same month, Guatemalan authorities issued arrest warrants for various adoption attorneys and foster mothers. One foster mother from Mixco had been arrested with two undocumented children, one of who turned out to have been kidnapped. Local newspapers reported on groups of undocumented children discovered in unlicensed nurseries, and the Embassy told Washington that even American adoptive parents had been affected, "both personally by police detention and derivatively by the detention of escorts and adoptive children at the airport." The situation, the Embassy said, was a "virtually uncontrolled adoption environment."

The Embassy came up with a new way to prove whether or not impostor birth mothers were relinquishing children: by testing their DNA. In February 1995, after 18 months of scientifically testing suspicious cases, the Embassy sent an update to the Secretary of State. "Even positive tests can mask fraud," the cable noted. The first sample ever drawn from an alleged birth mother and a child had been negative. Since then, a "significant minority" of women had failed to show up after being called in for testing. When negative results came back, the Embassy noted, the children involved entered a kind of "adoption purgatory" by disappearing "back into the same foggy background from which they came."

In one case, a birth mother returned to the Embassy, distraught, a week after testing. "She told us that the attorney had threatened to kill her if she told us the truth," the cable stated. Two months previously, the woman's son had been kidnapped. "The mother heard nothing about her three-year-old until the day she was brought to the Embassy by the attorneys and told not to talk to us. . . . The mother decided to file a criminal complaint against the attorneys, at great personal risk to herself."

Filing criminal complaints could be dangerous. In a June 1995 cable, the Embassy mentioned a case involving an "alleged Mafioso" attorney who had founded a "private orphanage for homeless and displaced children" in Guatemala. Three criminally fraudulent adoption cases were tied to the attorney, and the Ministerio Público had lost the complaints "either to error or corruption." Furthermore, the Embassy said, "both alleged birth mothers met untimely and violent deaths soon after our investigation of [redacted] began."

This 1995 cable stresses the importance of combating international child trafficking. The Embassy was worried about becoming "tacit accomplices by ignoring what is often right in front of us. . . Supply and demand are two sides of the same coin. We toe a fine line in balancing customer service with battling the unscrupulous and greedy. . . . The issue is the following: Are we not morally (if not legally) obligated to prevent what is otherwise clearly reprehensible as well as criminal under any penal code — kidnapping, the illegal separation of biological parents from their children?"

In its own words, the U.S. Embassy had realized, unequivocally but sadly, that child stealing and other serious fraud were ongoing in Guatemalan adoptions. ". . . It would certainly be expedient of us to ignore such facts and issue orphan visas without hesitation," the Embassy wrote to the State Department. "It would also be dead wrong."

The cable was an appeal for help, outlining the continuing efforts that had been made over the years to inform both the Department of State and the INS about adoption corruption in Guatemala. "Virtually nothing has changed over the years, except some of the players," the Embassy noted. It partially blamed the INS, for "regularly approving" all cases without ever asking questions. ". . . We urge that efforts be made at the Washington level to improve interagency communication on this specific issue."

A year later, in November 1996, the issue of fraud was raised yet again in another cable from the Embassy to the Secretary of State, citing the cases of two women who had recently tried to change their minds about giving children up for adoption and were subsequently threatened by adoption attorneys. "Because of the lack of control in the Guatemalan adoption process, a birth mother cannot rely on the legal support or intervention of the Guatemalan authorities in an effort to regain custody of her child," the cable said. "Poor, uneducated, and unsophisticated, she is David to the savvy, unscrupulous Goliath of an adoption attorney. Unfortunately, the birth mother's ultimate fate probably will not mirror that of David, who was the final victor. Without an understanding of the legal system or the as-of-now unavailable resources of a family advocate, she will likely never regain custody of her child."

Two distinct processes could lead to a child becoming a legal orphan under Guatemalan law. The first was "abandonment," also known as a judicial adoption process. Just 1 to 2 percent of children in adoption processes were declared orphans through abandonment proceedings, which could take up to seven years to complete. A potential custodian, usually an adoption lawyer or facilitator, could initiate abandonment proceedings by presenting a child to a family court judge and saying that the child's parents or relatives couldn't be found. Next, an advertisement featuring a picture of the child would be placed in the newspaper for ten days to broadcast the fact that the child had been found. That way, in theory, if anyone was looking for the boy or girl, they'd see the ad and come forward. Yet half the Guatemalan population could not read, and fewer still could afford throwaway luxuries like newspapers. It was also relatively easy to run an overexposed picture, or a photograph of a different child.

If no one came forward to claim the "abandoned" child, the judge would then decide who the child's new legal guardian would be. In many cases, custody would be assigned to whoever had brought the child forward, usually an adoption lawyer or facilitator or the director of an orphanage or *hogar* (private nursery) seeking legal custody. According to investigators and Guatemalan government officials, certain judges had arrangements with specific nurseries, and some were suspected of accepting bribes for quick declarations of orphanhoood. "They usually took one to two years," says Maria Soto,[4] a law student who worked in adoption and handled hundreds

---

[4.] The name has been changed.

of cases for five different lawyers. "But when you paid, they moved fast."

Some nursery directors who didn't work in adoptions heard about the judicial bribery through word of mouth. Judge Roxana Maribel Mena Guzmán at the First Court of Children and Families in Guatemala City was said to charge around 10,000 quetzales (U.S. $1500) per abandonment, says Shyrel Osborn, director of the Amor del Niño hogar in Guatemala City. Osborn says she was approached by an intermediary at a Christmas party, who detailed the crooked expedited abandonment process and made her an offer. She declined.

The remaining 98 to 99 percent of Guatemalan children in adoption processes went through a private process called relinquishment, or notarial adoptions. Relinquished children typically had living mothers, fathers, and relatives. During a relinquishment process, a child's parent or custodian would sign custody directly over to another person, commonly an adoption attorney or facilitator, who would then offer the relinquished orphan to an adoption agency. Through the mid-2000s, a relinquishment adoption process in Guatemala usually took between four and six months, making it one of the fastest ways in the world to adopt. ". . . An international adoption attorney knows that one of the most important criteria on which his clients will judge his performance is the speed with which he can push the adoption through the Guatemalan legal system," stated a 1990 internal cable from the U.S. Embassy in Guatemala. "He also knows that representing U.S. citizen parents is very lucrative; if he can finalize a handful of such adoptions, he can get rich quick."

Payments to birth parents were often arranged quietly. Typically, they were broken up into three lump sums, to make sure that the relinquishing mother showed up each of the three times her presence was required: for the first DNA test, for an interview with a social worker, and for a second DNA test.

In a relinquishment procedure that ran into complications, such as a failed DNA test or a birth mother who changed her mind, a child could still be declared a legally adoptable orphan through abandonment. Ultimately, any child could be declared an orphan if strategic bribes reached the correct hands, according to Guatemalan government authorities, adoption lawyers, and private investigators.

Once orphan status was obtained via relinquishment or abandonment, the child's adoption case file would be presented to the Guatemalan Attorney General's Office (the PGN) for review. A 2010 report by the UN Commission Against Impunity in Guatemala (known by its Spanish acronym, CICIG) confirmed that the PGN review of adoption files was vulnerable to corruption, finding that state actors in fact played a crucial role in the facilitation of illegal adoptions. PGN reviewers were noted even to have signed off on adoptions for children whose cases were being investigated by Guatemala's Ministry of Justice.

After PGN reviewed an adoption file and all documents were found to be in order, the child in question still had to meet the U.S. government's own definition of an orphan in order to for a U.S. visa to be issued. The Immigration and Nationality Act of 1952 defined an orphan as a child with only one or no parents and stated that if a birth parent existed, he or she had to irrevocably relinquish all parental rights in writing. If an orphan had a living parent, he or she had to be single.

The marriage stipulation caused problems. Sometimes, when a married Guatemalan woman relinquished a child, an adoption could be salvaged with a quick fix, such as altering the woman's ID card to read "single." If that didn't work, or if the forgery was caught by American or Guatemalan authorities, another option would be to initiate an abandonment proceeding for the child and have him or her declared to be an orphan under Guatemalan law. Then the fact of a living parent, married or not, would be eliminated from the child's records. Finally, if all else failed, a child with a mother and a stepfather (or a father and a stepmother) could always be offered to a family in Israel instead of the United States. Israel didn't have the same kind of restrictions on the marital status of birth parents.

The year after the Guatemalan Civil War officially ended, the U.S. Embassy in Guatemala City sent a memorandum to the Secretary of State in Washington. The Embassy was concerned. The cable, dated June 1997, disclosed that Post (The U.S. government uses "Post" as a synonym for "Embassy") saw a staggering "80 percent increase in international adoptions destined for the United

States." According to numbers from the PGN, 542 children were adopted into the U.S. in 1996, and in 1997, the number ballooned to 1,388. The Embassy memo went on to say that American contacts at adoption agencies had told Embassy personnel that the surge was "caused by the shutting down of international adoptions in other countries such as Paraguay and Ecuador. . . ."

The memo continued: "Post has been contacted by a number of agencies that are interested in starting programs in Guatemala. They are feeling pressure from their clients to use Guatemala due to its availability of children, the relative ease of the process, and the severe restrictions of adoptions in other countries. . . . To date, the GOG [government of Guatemala] has not been able to keep up with the increase in international adoptions."

Five months later, in November, the Embassy sent a formal request to the Secretary of State for all Guatemalan children in adoption processes, not just those with suspicious cases, to undergo mandatory DNA testing. The November memo noted that the Guatemalan newspapers had continued to publish "reports of baby stealing and other anomalies in international adoption," as well as accusations of baby theft and child trafficking. "So far, the U.S. Embassy has not been accused of involvement," the memo said. It noted that Canada already required DNA testing for all cases. The Department of State mandated DNA testing in October 1998, a year after the Embassy made its recommendation.

Adoption files would now be accepted only from attorneys, not agents or adoption facilitators. Every child also would now undergo DNA testing to evaluate whether the woman giving him or her up was really the child's biological mother. "Once the DNA results have been received," an October 1998 memo from the U.S. Embassy stated, "INS will evaluate the case to determine whether further action is necessary. If no fraud is suspected, the case will proceed to the Guatemalan courts. . . . INS will conduct further investigation if it is deemed necessary." One official at the Ministerio Público says that when testing began, about 180 women were shown to be unrelated to the children they were trying to relinquish. That same year, the "International Adoption Safeguards" page on the U.S. State Department's website noted that the U.S. "abhors" adoption corruption and "consistently takes a strong stand against fraudulent adoption procedures."

By July 1999, international concern about child trafficking in Guatemala had grown so intense that the United Nations sent special rapporteur Ofelia Calcetas-Santos there on a fact-finding mission. The number of Guatemalan children adopted internationally had quadrupled in fewer than ten years. Calcetas-Santos's mission was undertaken on the working assumption that children were already being bought and sold for the dual purposes of prostitution and adoption. She was supposed to figure out just how serious the problem really was.

In Guatemala, Calcetas-Santos met with a variety of organizations, private citizens, and government officials, including staff from the U.S. Embassy. During one interview, American immigration officials "confirmed various aspects relative to the payment received by biological mothers," the existence of intermediaries, the "frequently unethical" practices of social workers and attorneys, and various industry-related fees and expenses. Most of the people Calcetas-Santos met with affirmed that baby buying and selling were common.

Still, when blatant wrongdoing surfaced, little was done to rectify the situation. After a meeting with the visa unit of the U.S. Embassy, for example, Calcetas-Santos learned that a single Guatemalan woman had successfully given up thirty-three children for adoption over the course of three years. They were all supposed to have been her own biological children. No one caught the error because the woman had relinquished two children per month, the legal limit. Since Guatemalan authorities usually didn't save documentation on children who left the country in adoption, the impostor birth mother's repeated relinquishments had gone undetected. All thirty-three "orphans" had been successfully adopted into the United States. No one had figured out where the children had actually come from. It was also unclear who, if anyone, should be responsible for investigating.

The special rapporteur presented her findings to the UN Human Rights Commission on January 27, 2000. "What started out as genuine efforts to place children in dire need of homes turned into lucrative business deals, " she stated. "The information provided . . . suggests that Guatemala has the weakest adoption laws in Central America. Trafficking of children is not even typified as a crime under the law. It is reported that a stiffer penalty is imposed for the theft of a car than for the theft of a child."

Following Calcetas-Santos's report, UNICEF commissioned the Latin American Institute for Education and Communication (known by its Spanish acronym, ILPEC) to investigate Guatemala's adoption process and how it affected the rights of children. The 61-page ILPEC report was released in early 2000. It began with a clear indictment: Guatemala had indeed failed to uphold elements of the UN Convention on the Rights of the Child, the most widely and rapidly accepted human rights treaty in history. A decade earlier, in 1990, Guatemala had been the sixth country in the world to ratify the treaty, despite the ongoing civil war. The agreement had gone on to gain ratification from all but two UN member-states, Somalia and the United States.

The ILPEC investigators reached their conclusions after months of fieldwork, including a review of documents related to a random sampling of ninety finalized adoptions. Out of the ninety cases, eighty-two birth mothers[5] gave the same reason for relinquishing children: Each cited a "precarious economic situation." The wording concerned the ILPEC team. "It seems that the mothers are generally quite clear on what they need to say when appearing before the family courts and embassies to make their statements," the ILPEC report stated. ". . . According to social workers from the family courts, they express themselves with the same clichés."

There was one obvious way to uncover the truth. ILPEC's team decided to meet with a small selection of birth mothers in person, and randomly selected sixteen case files from the ninety. In those sixteen files, only two birth mothers had given legitimate addresses. The fourteen others, the ILPEC report noted, had been fabricated or "very intentionally" misrepresented. "In some cases," the report noted, "a gully or ravine was located at the address indicated, while other addresses corresponded to a park or to places of extremely difficult access." Based on interviews with judges, social workers, and nursery directors, ILPEC concluded that a "sector of middlemen, or *jaladoras,* who act as intermediaries in the trafficking of children existed, "actively seeking out" pregnant women in public places

---

[5.] Not all provided answers.

like markets, parks, buses, or streets and offering them up to 5,000 quetzales (U.S. $640) for their unborn child.

The report concluded that the interests that most often prevailed in adoption in Guatemala weren't those of the children. Instead, the adoption process was "overwhelmingly preoccupied with satisfying the demands of the parents," in addition to lawyers, notary officials, and adoption agencies. American agencies were chastised for advertising children on the Internet "as if they were manufactured according to the public demand." Furthermore, ILPEC stated, the high demand for children and "the poverty experienced by most Guatemalan families" had created a situation "where the processing of adoptions occurs according to the 'laws of supply and demand,' effectively resulting in the trafficking of children." Owing to the "fragility of the existing laws in Guatemala" and the fact that children were being treated as commodities, ILPEC suggested suspending "all direct and private adoptions." The report ignited instant controversy.

A coalition of eight American adoptive parents and adoption advocates calling themselves "Families Without Borders" formed and published a 63-page refutation. They said the positions of UNICEF, and by extension the ILPEC team they had funded, were "overly idealistic. . . misguided and dangerous." They called the ILPEC report "sensationalistic" and "steeped in error."

"...We strongly object to UNICEF's linking of intercountry adoption and 'child trafficking'.... Their inflammatory rhetoric regarding children as "exports" due to intercountry adoption is intolerable and is neither accurate NOR in the best interest of the children," the Families Without Borders rebuttal stated. "The lobbying of UNICEF has successfully disrupted adoptions in India, Romania, El Salvador, Honduras, and many other countries." The coalition was concerned that Guatemala might be next.

Cribs are lined up inside one Guatemala City nursery in January 2009.

7. "ARE WE READY FOR A FALL?"

2001–2006

Deconstructing the Guatemalan adoption industry was confusing even to expert investigators. Because the business was comprised of various networks, many investigators tried to map the money that trickled down along chains of associates. Human rights organizations, private investigators, Guatemalan authorities like the Ministerio Público, and even the International Commission Against Impunity in Guatemala all created simple flowcharts in an attempt to clarify the different chains of command. No two charts were the same.

It was clear that $20,000 to $30,000 per case originated in the United States, in the bank accounts of American families who wanted to parent Guatemalan children. Money would be given to an American adoption agency to begin the process. The agency would send between $15,000 and $23,000 to a Guatemalan attorney, facilitator, or "contact" for a single child, or case. The Guatemalan lawyer representing an American adoptive family was often the person who held custody of the child being offered.

Then things got complicated. Each American adoption agency worked with anywhere from one to a dozen different in-country contacts. Because the relationship between an agency and its in-country contacts generally wasn't exclusive, it was common for the same Guatemalan child to be offered to families simultaneously by more than one agency as the contact or facilitator linked to the child could offer him or her to more than one adoption agency. Free-market capitalism then decided the child's fate: Whoever found a paying client first landed the case.

The pervasive simplicity of falsifying documents and flimsy oversight by the Guatemalan government of orphan classifications led to the emergence of different adoption networks, many of which operated in their own unique fashions. Determining who was in charge of a certain network was difficult, and proving it legally was even harder. The adoption files that lawyers presented to the PGN never mentioned the names of the jaladoras or any supporting lawyers, facilitators, contacts, or even the American agencies they were working with.

According to estimates from U.S. and Guatemalan authorities, between 500 and 600 Guatemalan attorneys worked in adoption. Each adoption case had a mandatory and a notary, who authenticated papers in the case file. Yet the inclusion of a certain lawyer's name on an adoption file didn't necessarily mean that he or she had much to do with the handling of the case. A countless number of recent law school graduates, students, and others would collect the various pieces of documentation that comprised a complete adoption file. In those situations, a file would be passed to a registered attorney or notary for a signature before it was submitted to the PGN for review. Sometimes, the signing lawyers paid off those preparing adoption files. Sometimes, those preparing adoption files paid off the signing lawyers. Sometimes, lawyers or notaries did everything themselves.

Then there was the dizzying issue of the jaladoras, the people who "pulled" or found babies and children for adoption. They were sometimes referred to as "facilitators" to American agencies or adopting families. Other times, jaladoras worked for intermediaries who might also be called facilitators. Various middlemen might connect the baby finders to the adoption lawyers. They included pediatricians, obstetricians, midwives, civil registrars, "lookouts" or recruiters, *casas cunas* ("crib houses," or nurseries), and cuidadoras. The links in the chain sometimes grew so numerous that the lawyers and notaries themselves might not know where a child they were placing had come from.

"Sometimes, jaladoras would take the same baby from notary to notary," says one Guatemalan private investigator frequently hired by adoption facilitators confused about their own cases. "Lots of times, the intermediaries knew where birth mothers were, but they would hide them. When an intermediary or jaladora had almost everything paid for, she would tell the notary that she'd lost the mother and that she needed more money. That was how she kept extracting money... The intermediaries were the ones who really profited."

Most lawyers and notaries were white-collar Guatemalans who never went to the "bad neighborhoods" where jaladoras often operated, explains the investigator. Furthermore, some rural regions were just too far away to travel to in order to ascertain a certain child's origins. "If they had [visited], they would have saved themselves a lot of grief," the investigator says. "But they wouldn't, because it was a money issue. . . . Intermediaries and jaladoras placed the births in faraway places in order to discourage the notaries from looking into them and checking out the paperwork."

Intermediaries, *buscadoras* ("finders"), and jaladoras operated in different ways. Some would offer a mother a few hundred dollars outright for a child. For a mother lacking birth control and/or food, selling a child could stave off hunger, possibly helping the rest of the family, or provide a means to buy material possessions like clothes or a television. In a country as poor as Guatemala, such cash offers could be hard to resist. The nation's infant mortality and chronic child malnutrition rate remained among the worst in the Western hemisphere even in 2010, according to the U.S. Department of State. UNICEF's 2006 child hunger report card maintains that 80 percent of Guatemalan children in rural areas were chronically malnourished and that half the total Guatemalan population under the age of five suffered from moderate to severe stunting and/or abnormally slow growth and development owing to a lack of food. A report from the mid-1990s found that urban Guatemalan women gave birth to an average of five children each, whereas their rural counterparts commonly had six or more. Abortion was, and remains, illegal except to save a mother's life.

Some jaladoras used deceit to obtain children. One ploy, according to studies done by the Myrna Mack Foundation in conjunction with the Guatemalan government and human rights organizations, was to work in rural communities far from the capital, offering educational grants for the children of largely illiterate and highly isolated indigenous women. The birth mothers were told to bring their children to Guatemala City to claim the grant. There, after being led to believe that it was for the grant, they would be asked to affix a signature or thumbprint of consent to documents. Later, the papers could be turned into adoption relinquishments.

Casas de engorde, or "fattening houses," were sometimes advertised as places for pregnant women to carry their babies to term while living and eating for free. But before the babies arrived, the women were told they owed money for food and rent. Their infants could be used to pay off the debts.

Honduras, the country along Guatemala's southeast border, also had casas de engorde. "Newspaper headlines here have blared reports related to baby trafficking since 1985, when the first 'fattening house' was reported," Lisa Swenarski wrote in the *Christian Science Monitor* in May 1993, a year after Honduras suspended international adoption because of corruption. "These casas de engorde are private homes where children are kept until adoptive parents are found. . . ." Swenarski's article went on to cite sources claiming that hundreds of Honduran children were "stolen or obtained in other illegal ways in order to 'sell' them for adoption to couples from the United States." A 1991 cable from the U.S. Embassy in Guatemala to the Secretary of State in Washington noted that articles from the Guatemalan press alleged that adoption attorneys were involved in "purchasing children for international adoption, complicity in child kidnapping, and running illegal foster homes known locally as 'fattening houses.'"

Other "maternity houses" were also advertised in Guatemalan newspapers, and the ads were typically paid for by adoption lawyers or facilitators who would subsequently offer infants to American adoption agencies. Adoptive parents were often told by their agencies that unwed teenage mothers used the homes to hide pregnancies that would bring negative stigma to their families in the countryside.

It was a partial truth. Young women did, in fact, travel to the capital from rural towns to work as housekeepers and sometimes became pregnant. In some cases, their babies weren't voluntarily relinquished. Various rackets were used to separate young, unsuspecting rural woman from their babies. For example, sometimes after hospital deliveries, women were presented with inflated bills for medical services. Doctors, nurses, and midwives often worked in conjunction with the people who'd employed the young women as a maids, or within other adoption networks. A baby could serve as compensation for a debt.

Sometimes a mother was told that her son or daughter had died at birth. The concept of going to a hospital to give birth was unique to some rural women who'd migrated to the city for work, many of whom spoke Mayan dialects as their first language. Most didn't know to ask for a death certificate, and if they were presented with a document, there was a good chance they wouldn't be literate enough to understand what it said. "In a separate, gruesome news item," the U.S. Embassy noted in an internal memo dated December 2003, "the AG [attorney general] and the PGN are also investigating claims by at least eight Guatemalan couples that newborns were taken from them and transferred to Roosevelt Hospital in Guatemala City, where the staff claimed the babies needed emergency medical treatment and later died." One section of a five-part investigative series published by the Guatemalan newspaper *Al Día* that same month detailed the kidnapping of a baby from Roosevelt Hospital in Guatemala City.

Some adoption industry contacts played a role in more than one part of the business. Guillermo Bosque, an adoption facilitator, is said to have owned a private medical clinic where women could come to give birth adjacent to a private nursery, both of which were named Un Mundo Nuevo (A New World). Susana Luarca, the outspoken adoption lawyer, ran a hogar Asociación Primavera in Guatemala City and had an additional child care facility with the same name in rural Palín. Luarca's name never appeared on the paperwork for the adoption cases she handled; instead, she typically enlisted other lawyers, like Enriqueta Noriega Cano, to sign her files. Other attorneys had standing agreements with certain hogares and orphanages, like Alfonso Close's exclusive deal placing children from the hogares run by the Spanish evangelical organization REMAR, which had begun working in Guatemala in 1992. REMAR's mission was to rehabilitate ex-convicts, drug addicts, and "other marginalized members of society" from Spain by sending them abroad to Latin American countries to work with troubled and abandoned youth. In 1997, a report by Human Rights Watch detailed the severe physical and psychological abuse of Guatemalan boys at the hands of REMAR staff, including beatings with baseball bats and firewood. The organization came under greater oversight and has since regained a largely positive reputation.

Cuidadoras, known as foster mothers to most Americans, were paid by intermediaries or attorneys to care for children in adoption processes. Though they were supposed to care for no more than two children at a time in their homes, some cuidadoras would care for four or five. They typically made anywhere from 500Q ($65) to 2,000Q ($250) per child per month. U.S. adoption agencies often inflated "foster care fees" for their clients, charging monthly expenses that reflected the cost of living in the United States instead of in Guatemala. Celebrate Children International's standard rate for foster care was $400 per month, about the same price other agencies charged. In interviews, many cuidadoras said that their employers often provided the cheapest supplies possible to save money. Many also complained of skipped or late payments.

Hogares were also commonly used to care for children in the process of adoption. The Guatemalan government lacked hard statistics on how many hogares were in operation. Although the Secretaría de Bienestar Social (Guatemala's Social Welfare Secretariat, or SBS), distributed licenses to hogares, many weren't inspected or reviewed. In 2007, the Office of the Human Rights Defender in Guatemala estimated that 10,000 "orphans" were living in more than 500 nurseries, half of which were hidden across the countryside.

To an impoverished woman with a family ravaged by hunger, selling a child was an obvious, if heartbreaking, option. In Guatemala, 44 percent of women between twenty and twenty-four had had a child before the age of twenty, according to a 2006 study by the Allen Guttmacher Institute, and the rate among uneducated women rose to 68 percent. Another 2006 survey found that 8 percent of Guatemalan women reported their first sexual experience as rape. Birth control was not readily available.

Karla Ordoñez, an adoption facilitator who worked with various U.S. adoption agencies, including Celebrate Children International, says she frequently got calls from pregnant women asking for help: "Most of the time they needed a house or food. Cases fell through when the birth mothers changed their mind. Part of the money would have already gone to the woman, so you couldn't get it back." American agencies wouldn't want to hear the truth about what was happening, Ordoñez explained. She estimated that for every two hundred adoptions, fifty to sixty cases had problems.

Birth mothers typically made a fraction of the money that the intermediaries, jaladoras, and lawyers made, researchers agree. The sale of a baby netted Q3,00 to Q15,000, or $40 to $1900. Female children were more valuable than males as there was greater demand from American families for adoptable girls. One Guatemalan adoption facilitator said that the network she worked with offered American agencies boys for $19,000 each and girls for $22,000. Prices were also adjusted according to age: Younger children and babies were more expensive than older children, who also were less desirable to Americans.

Many women, including Mildred Alvarado, remained ignorant of the fact that Americans were paying tens of thousands of dollars to adopt Guatemalan children. One adoptive mother ended up paying more than $75,000 for one child's adoption. Many Guatemalans found the amount of money Westerners would pay for a child stunning. In Guatemala, it was uncommon for the wealthy upper class to take in poor children, let alone pay hundreds of thousands of quetzales for them. The concept was foreign.

Around the world, adoption industries struggled with corruption. In 2001, U.S. Immigration and Naturalization Services halted all Cambodian adoptions because of trafficking concerns. U.S. citizen Lauryn Galindo, a woman who had arranged about 800 Cambodian adoptions, was later arrested and convicted on federal charges of money laundering and conspiracy to commit visa fraud. In Romania, a formal moratorium was issued on international adoption, and implemented in June 2001. Months later, an article by journalist Kate Connolly in the British newspaper *The Guardian* said that a Romanian government commission had discovered a "catalogue of horrors," involving global child trafficking rings, drugged babies, and stolen identities.

Officials from the Marshall Islands also imposed an adoption moratorium after a 500 babies reportedly were adopted in Hawaii after being born to Marshallese women who had been flown to the island over the course of three years just to relinquish. Trouble also surfaced in China. In the *Cumberland Law Journal*, Patricia J. Meier and Xiaole Zhang wrote that a Chinese organization called the Hengyang Social Welfare Institute had been "buying babies from traffickers since 2002" while collecting "$3,000 per child in mandatory contributions" from adoptive parents. In May 2001, Moldova issued a ban on international adoptions, citing an ongoing investigation into falsified documents and illegal actions by government officials.

The U.S. State Department announced an estimated 50 percent increase in the number of Guatemalan children who would be applying for orphan visas in 2002, stating it was "due in part to the suspension or delays of adoptions in Romania and Cambodia." In the same bulletin, it was noted that "problematic cases" such as "children . . . obtained by illegal means, perhaps even stolen" had surfaced in Guatemala, along with a "high incidence of corruption and civil document fraud." Still, the U.S. government made no attempt to discourage citizens from adopting from Guatemala.

In February 2002, Ambassador Prudence Bushnell at the U.S. Embassy in Guatemala City sent a cable to the Secretary of State in Washington. It was copied to the commissioner of the INS, the Department of Justice, and three other American Embassies: those in Tegucigalpa, Honduras; San Salvador, El Salvador; and Mexico City, Mexico. Ambassador Bushnell was a veteran diplomat who had not only survived the 1998 Al-Qaeda bombing of the Nairobi Embassy, but had also warned the State Department of security concerns beforehand. She was known for her directness and candor. The subject heading of the memo was "U.S. Adoptions in Guatemala; Are We Ready for a Fall?"

The cable started with a call for help. "Recent huge increases in adoptions destined for the United States have brought into question the ability of the Embassy to manage the risks adequately," the ambassador wrote bluntly. "If we do not take action now, we run the real possibility of a scandal that could result in the USG [U.S. government] being accused of abetting child trafficking."

She continued, "The Embassy is between a rock and a hard place. On one side, we are absolutely committed to serve the thousands of insistent U.S. adoptive families, who are always eager to enlist the help of their congressional representatives. On the other, we have a moral imperative to do everything in our power to ensure that each child has been given up legitimately and honestly."

In order to avert "potential disaster," Ambassador Bushnell said, the Embassy's INS office urgently needed an infusion of resources. The number of orphan applications had "skyrocketed." The most "recent twist" in adoption fraud observed by the Embassy was an influx of migrant women coming to Guatemala from Honduras and El Salvador in order to give birth and relinquish infants. According to the ambassador, the women were probably traveling to Guatemala because of "strict adoption laws in their home countries," or a perhaps because of a "shortage of babies here." Whatever the case, she wrote, the "complete lack of accountability" in the issuance of Guatemalan cédulas, or national identity cards, meant that "foreigners and Guatemalans looking for a new identity can be documented easily with a new, authentic cédula."

When the Embassy's INS office had delays in adoption case processing during the summer of 2001, the Embassy was "flooded" with inquiries, from both the public as well as members of Congress. "The number of inquiries soon outstripped the INS's ability to respond quickly," Bushnell explained in her cable. "And then people used other means (multiple Congressional contacts, White House, etc.) to send duplicative inquiries, further clogging the system." In January 2002, when Guatemala's newly appointed director general of migration decided to uphold a long-standing legal requirement related to passport issuance, the outcry from U.S. families was so great that the Embassy started "almost immediately looking at ways of waiving the passport requirement for the children's immigrant visas."

The U.S. government needed to face the issues head-on, Ambassador Bushnell stated, and needed to communicate effectively to the American public and the U.S. Congress what was being done and why. Passing the Hague Convention on Intercountry Adoptions, an international agreement intended to protect children's rights in adoption, seemed like a good start. The Hague Convention tried to prevent fraud by outlining clear guidelines for safeguards and "good practices," such as mandates for government recordkeeping on adoptable children, the prohibition of excessive fees, and discouraging the practice of choosing children on the Internet.

The close of the ambassador's February 2002 memo foreshadowed a grand reckoning. "If we cannot come up with the resources to investigate the suspicious cases in a timely manner," Bushnell wrote, "we need to consider the consequences of being accused of abetting baby trafficking someday." A "fall," she suggested, could be imminent.

Some Guatemalan politicians had their own aspirations surrounding the Hague Convention. On August 13, 2002, congressional deputy Dr. Carlos Mauricio Vallardes de Leon proposed a bill entitled the Law of Adoptions. "In effect for Guatemalan society, international adoption has become synonymous with the illegal trafficking of children," the proposal read. "Until now, there has not been a legislative answer which duly regulates this institution in such a way that it impedes the frequent and uncontrolled abuses which have converted the child into an object of traffic. . . ." The draft bill was meant to lay the groundwork for Guatemala to ratify the Hague Convention on Intercountry Adoption.

To adoption attorneys in Guatemala, Hague compliance meant that millions of dollars of profit might be lost as the industry ground to a halt. Reform measures would have to be drafted, proposed, voted on, passed, and implemented. Getting a new adoption system up and running could take years. A group of outspoken lawyers, calling themselves La Asociación de Defensores de Adopción (the Association in Defense of Adoption, or ADA) and led by attorneys Susana Luarca, Roberto Echeverría, and Enrique Urizar Maldonado, organized a fierce political campaign. They were supported by another organization of lawyers, the Guatemalan Family Law Institute, that also opposed the proposed reforms. "The Institute's argument is that 'Lawyers have the right to put on pressure, and the mother has the right to say no,'" the U.S. Embassy in Guatemala stated in an August 2005 memo.

In a blog entry published on the American website GuatAdopt. com, adoption attorney Susana Luarca stated: "I, and many others, am fully convinced that the Hague Convention is detrimental to adoptions and that it should be defeated around the world. . . . We've just begun our first phase in raising funds to initiate an aggressive, effective, and widespread pro-adoption educational campaign. . . . The ADA is poised to file an amparo[6] supported by over two hundred lawyers in case any law that restricts adoptions is passed by Congress overnight."

Luarca herself was the founder of two nurseries where children lived during adoption proceedings. Through the summer of 2003, the ADA stepped up its battle plan, receiving help from American allies equally concerned that adoptions would stop or become restricted if new child-protection legislation was put in place. American websites like GuatAdopt.com solicited donations, targeting adoptive parents. Advocacy organizations like the Joint Council on International Children's Services (JCICS) also worked to drum up sentiment among their memberships, which consisted largely of American adoption agencies with a clear financial stake in maintaining a flow of adoptable children for their clients.

JCICS was the primary interest and lobbying group for American adoption agencies. With the help of politicians like Senator Mary Landrieu (Louisiana) and Senator Norm Coleman (Minnesota), lobbying groups including the Congressional Coalition on Adoption Institute helped steer the United States towards adoption-friendly legislation. JCICS met regularly with officials from the Department of State and participated in high-level meetings related to adoption policy with foreign officials. They repeatedly provided testimony as child welfare experts at congressional hearings. According to minutes from a December 13, 2005, JCICS board of directors meeting, two of Senator Landrieu's staffers approached JCICS for recommendations on the use of $300 million of USAID money earmarked for "projects in foreign countries related to adoption."

JCICS encouraged adopting Americans to fight for the children of Guatemala and to lobby against Guatemala's attempts towards ratifying the Hague Convention in 2003. At the same time, in the U.S. Congress, Senator Landrieu co-introduced the Intercountry Adoption Reform Act, a new bill meant to "modernize, streamline, and strengthen the international adoption system." The proposed bill, according to Landrieu's website, would result in "eliminating much of the red tape and paperwork" in foreign adoption by creating

---

[6.] An *amparo* is a feature of the Guatemalan legal system that is essentially an appeal of something that might happen in the future.

a new adoption-specific office within the U.S. government and enabling the State Department to "provide greater diplomatic representation and proactive advocacy in the area of international adoption." Acting Deputy Director of U.S. Citizenship and Immigration Services Robert Devine called parts of the proposal "troubling," since they would eliminate an "important check" in the process: the U.S. government's being able to "review foreign adoptions and refuse to recognize them for immigration purposes when fraud, public welfare, or other particular issues are present."

On August 13, 2003, Guatemala's Constitutional Court issued a 51-page ruling signed by seven judges stating that Guatemala's ratification of the Hague Convention on Intercountry Adoption violated the country's own constitution. Therefore, they concluded, it was illegal. Guatemalan Vice President Juan Francisco Reyes López (acting on behalf of the President), the Ministry of Foreign Relations, the Ministerio Público, and the Guatemalan Congress all had deemed the Hague ratification constitutional. The Constitutional Court and the PGN had not.

"The darkness is over," Susana Luarca announced in a blog entry posted on Guatadopt.com. At the time, she was married to the one of the Constitutional Court judges, Ricardo Umaña.

Just a month later, in September 2003, another international adoption scandal broke, this time involving nine Guatemalan children that had turned up in Costa Rica in what the *Miami Herald* described as a "makeshift nursery allegedly being used as a transit point for infants en route to foreign couples who wanted to adopt." The Florida-based American adoption agency International Adoption Resource, Inc., was implicated in the network and, according to the *Florida Sun Sentinel*, had paid the rent on the home where pregnant Guatemalan women were brought. A report from the Florida Office of the Attorney General noted that one woman had given up her thirty-month-old son for about $630. International Adoption Resource denied any wrongdoing, and the agency's lawyer told the *Sun Sentinel* that "one man's trafficking is another's humanitarian effort."

Raids continued in Guatemala. On May 31, 2004, the newspaper *El Periódico* published an article called "Alarm Growing from the Theft of Children of Adoption," describing the raid of nine illegal nurseries and the recovery of twenty-six children. On May 14, four women in Chimaltenango, Guatemala were reportedly arrested for running illegal nurseries, and authorities confiscated thirty ID cards for local women, birth certificates for two hundred children, and three hundred photos of Guatemalan children posing with foreigners. On May 19, a nursery in Guatemala City was raided, and the press reported that seven to nineteen children had been found. "A mother whose three-year-old was stolen in the same neighborhood filed the complaint that led to the raid," the U.S. Embassy in Guatemala noted in a July 2004 memo detailing the operations. "Police found the child, who had been falsely documented after the abduction. A number of other children were also found to be awaiting new documentation."

In the same cable, the Embassy acknowledged that they'd broken a "previous annual high for adoption visas" and that "the time it takes to complete an average adoption here appears to be getting shorter." The memo said it was because the Guatemalan adoption process had a "reputation for being relatively quick," and because adopting Americans had "no shortage of Guatemalan children to choose from." Adoption referrals for week-old babies, the memo said, were "likely being arranged prior to the birth of the [children]."

When yet another investigative series about adoption ran in the Guatemalan newspaper *Siglo XXI*, the U.S. Embassy sent a summary to the Department of State in Washington, saying that they generally agreed with the journalists' findings. ". . . The authors conclude that the interests of Guatemalan children are not preeminent under this system," the August 2005 memo stated. "While some columnists argue that the series exaggerated the methods that lawyers and their handlers use to convince or otherwise deceive mothers to give up their children, Post believes that the series presented a realistic and non-sensational view of the adoption process in Guatemala."

The cable went on to detail various offenses mentioned in the press, including the purchase of babies, birth mothers being tricked into signing blank documents, the kidnappings of children from Guatemala City hospitals, and deceiving birth mothers by telling them they were "needed for blood tests when really DNA testing is the motive." The Embassy wrote that seasoned lawyers were suspected of "compelling new hires in their law firms to sign fraudulent adoption papers on their behalf to avoid possible prosecution themselves,"

Other Western nations began distancing themselves. Canada, France, Germany, the Netherlands, Spain, and the United Kingdom all banned citizens from adopting Guatemalan children because of corruption. By 2005, the United States was one of only a handful of Western nations that still participated in adoptions from Guatemala. Like many other adoptive American families, Betsy and Leslie Emanuel were oblivious to much of the fraud.

8. RISK VERSUS REWARD

September 2006–November 2006

On the afternoon of September 6, 2006, Mildred began hemorrhaging while mopping the floor at Sabrina's house. The new baby wasn't supposed to arrive for several more weeks. When the bleeding started, Sabrina and Rony helped her into their car and drove to the Sanatorio San Antonio de San Miguel, a private medical clinic less than thirty minutes away.

The clinic's drab brown storefront was no wider than a garage door. The reinforced doorway opened directly onto the crumbling sidewalk. A small blue badge from an alarm company, Grupo Golden, sat on the building's face. It wasn't a particularly nice part of town. An old sign showing a mother and child dangled precariously from the clinic's roof. It looked as if it had hung there for decades. Another sign, this one pale blue, stretched across the front of the building above the doorway, advertising X-rays, pediatric care, and ultrasounds. The sign had a realistic graphic of three masked surgeons in blue scrubs operating on a body. Between them, a tall Jesus stood, an arm draped around one doctor's shoulders, motioning with his free hand towards the patient's open midsection.

A security guard eyed Mildred and Sabrina as they entered. A black shotgun hung lazily at his side. The reception area was an institutional pale green, including the ceiling. A single naked bulb illuminated the reception window, which looked thick enough to be made of bulletproof glass. A few folding chairs to one side stood empty. There were no other patients at the clinic.

A physician emerged from the back of the clinic, introducing himself as Dr. Miguel Paniagua. He was a stout man with a friendly, casual manner. They walked into a small examining room, and Dr. Paniagua asked a few questions and looked at Mildred's belly. "I can't feel the baby," she said, worried. She felt fortunate that Sabrina and Rony had been around to help her.

"Everything's fine," Dr. Paniagua reassured her. The clinic smelled sour, like vomit. "I can hear a heartbeat," he said. "I'll give you something for the pain."

He left the room, and Sabrina followed. They spoke for a moment outside in the corridor. To Mildred's surprise, she thought she saw Rony's father and stepmother, Toño and Lily, outside. *It's so kind they came to check on me,* she thought, watching the group talk. After a few minutes, a nurse came in and gave her injections. She blacked out within seconds.

A day later, when Mildred cracked open her eyes, she struggled to recognize her surroundings. The walls were pale blue, and morning light filtered in through a set of blinds. Her head pounded as she tried to lift her chin. It was the Sanatorio San Antonio medical clinic; she was in a hospital room. A sharp pain spidered across her waistline. Glancing down, she realized she was no longer pregnant. Surgical tape bound her hands and feet to the bed frame.

"What's going on?" she called out weakly as a nurse in blue limped past. "Where's my baby?"

No one answered. Then Sabrina came to her bedside, offering three tiny pills and a cup of water for the pain. Mildred took them and became comfortably numb and dizzy. She asked after her baby. "The doctor ordered for her to be kept apart," Sabrina said casually. She left the room.

A different nurse walked by the doorway, and Mildred called out again, trying to suppress a feeling of panic. "Where's my baby?"

"You've had an operation," the nurse replied. She motioned towards Mildred's bound ankles. "It's for your own good, so you don't hurt yourself. Don't worry, you had a girl. She's fine."

But after Mildred asked, yet again, for the child, the nurse told her that the baby was sick. One of her lungs was bad.

"Why did they take her out?" Mildred pressed. "It wasn't her time." The pills she'd swallowed made her feel as if she were floating away. The nurse ignored her and left the room.

In the hallway, Mildred glimpsed a woman who looked like Coni walking by, carrying a pink bundle in her arms. *Maybe that's her,* she thought. *My girl.* She didn't trust her eyes. She closed them and drifted back into sleep.

The small discharge receipt from Sanatorio San Antonio, dated September 9, 2006, lists Lilien de Bautista as having paid 4,200Q, or $538 dollars, for "medical services" rendered to the patient Mildred Alvarado. The woman, known by Mildred as Lily, had the same name as Rony's stepmother. The field on the receipt meant for the doctor's name had been left blank.

Sue Hedberg was in Guatemala at the time of Mildred Alvarado's C-section. Three days later, on the morning of September 10, 2006, Sue emailed pictures of the newborn baby to the Emanuels. She had arrived in Guatemala on the first of the month and had hit the ground running. Before leaving the U.S., she had told her clients that she planned to see at least 95 CCI children during her eleven-day trip. She instructed them not to email her unless absolutely necessary, as she'd be too busy working to respond. She also asked for prayers, saying that she had "some difficult problems to solve" during her trip.

Betsy opened Sue's email excitedly, eager to see more snapshots of Fernanda. The last batch of photos Sue had sent, taken exactly a week before, showed the child playing in what appeared to be someone's home. Betsy wasn't sure if Fernanda lived in an orphanage, a hogar, or a foster home. In the pictures, the little girl appeared to be well cared for. She wore a smart jean jacket with frilly pink trim and an embroidered Strawberry Shortcake emblem and plump red strawberry. Fernanda was gazing into the camera, clutching a stuffed animal and grinning in delight. *She's just darling,* Betsy thought, smiling to herself.

But the new images weren't of Fernanda. Instead, the 32 pictures were of a newborn. The infant was wrapped in a pink fleece blanket, her pink and white onesie dotted with tiny flowers. She was too young to crack her eyes open. Sue's email was just three sentences. A new baby had been born, and Fernanda now had a little sister. She, too, was in need of a home.

Betsy's heart lurched. The thought of separating Fernanda from her baby sister made her cringe. Sue's brief email offered little in the way of detail. But when CCI's director quoted her a price for baby Ana Cristina — an additional $25,000 — Betsy realized the situation's futility. The cost of adopting one child had already strained the family's budget. Taking the infant on would be all but impossible.

She begged to talk to Marvin Bran, thinking she could convince him to come down on his fees. Since Sue said he was such a good Christian, she was sure he'd recognize her own similar motivations.

Ridden with guilt, Betsy declined Sue's offer. CCI went on to refer newborn Ana Cristina to another Christian family, Bethany and John Thompson[7] of Alabama. Neither the Emanuels nor the Thompsons had any idea that three days before, the tiny newborn wearing pink daisies had been cut from her mother Mildred's womb as she lay unconscious in a private medical clinic on the dusty outskirts of Guatemala City.

In early October, Sue added Betsy Emanuel to Celebrate Children International's private Yahoo listserve. List membership was by invitation only, and not all CCI clients enjoyed the privilege. Betsy was thrilled.

In a typically sunny manner, she introduced herself to the group on the morning of October 6, 2006. "Good morning, Ladies," she wrote. "We were thrilled to accept the referral of a sweet and brave girl last spring, but her birthmother (HIV-positive) changed her mind. . . . We are just sick over this and have now lost all touch with this child. Sue has not given up hope of finding her. . . . We are worried for her, and have cried a river over this, but know that Sue and CCI have done all they can for her at this point. Her future is in God's hands."

"We know and trust that His plan is perfect," Betsy continued, "and are very thankful He has now allowed us to move towards the adoption of beautiful little Maria [Fernanda]!! We can't wait to hear her giggles in person. . . . We have no idea where things stand right now. Like all of you, we are just hungry for info or an update. . . . We

---

[7.] The names have been changed upon request.

are very thankful for Sue's gift of love for kids in need and her work, day and night, for all of us who want to adopt them."

Within hours, Betsy felt the warm embrace of her new online family, 150 members strong. Many were Christian stay-at-home moms, whose faith had led them to choose CCI. Some had adopted many times before, and some were first-timers. Almost all were women. Over half maintained personal blogs detailing their family lives, faith, and spirituality. Others used their blogs exclusively to track their adoptions, under titles like "Andrew's Journey Home," "Princesa Gabriela," and "My GuatAngels." By heavily linking to each other, the blogs created an informal directory of CCI clients.

The waiting mothers-to-be read carefully about each other's lives, and often, relationships forged online blossomed into real-world friendships. The women took pains to stay up-to-date on each other's adoptions, posting upbeat comments and empathetic notes on each other's blogs. Most shared conservative Christian values.

On the listserve, discussions ranged from general child care tips and home-schooling advice to specific adoption issues. A "prayer chain" let list members collectively pray for God and Sue to "bring CCI babies home" in uncomplicated, fast adoptions. Whenever problems arose, encouraging messages of compassion and solidarity filled the listserve.

"Referrals," or children, could be lost for a variety of reasons. At times, children died partway through the adoption process. According to posts made on the CCI Guatemala listserve, at least five adoptive mothers were told their sons- or daughters-to-be had passed away. The boy that Jane G.[8] was adopting died six months into the process, as did Fara W.'s girl. Jill N. was told that her first referral, a seven-month-old baby named Pablo, had choked to death in a freak accident. Another client experienced the deaths of two referrals in a row. Members of the listserve showered each with condolences and prayers.

Declarations of faith occurred daily. "God is in this [adoption], and nothing can stop Him," one adoptive mother wrote, "No matter how hard the governments may try." Because many seemed to feel that the adoption process was shrouded in mystery, blaming nebulous entities like "the government" for hang-ups and delays was

[8.] The names have been changed.

simple and convenient. Sue reinforced this belief by regularly telling clients the Guatemalan government was "anti-adoption."

Sue often used the list to reassure clients. In one email, she told them that she thought of "each and every one of you by name every day." In another, she wrote about how thankful she was that those "on our group" consisted of devout believers. "I often wonder how people with no faith get through the adoption experience," she mused, saying she'd seen many people become "resentful, bitter, and angry," whereas others successfully "let God work in their lives."

List members traded stories about how they'd come to adopt. "It's funny, but when the Lord was softening my heart toward adoption in the summer of 2002, I was afraid and couldn't quite take the first step to do it," Jennette Johnson wrote. "It seemed overwhelming. . . . One morning at church on Sunday, a woman came up to me and said, 'Jennette, you need to go down to Guatemala and get yourself a baby. I have a friend who can make it happen.' That friend was Sue. I was blown away that the Lord used her to speak to me in such a clear way. . . ."

The list regularly heaped praise on Sue, who was referred to in divine terms as a "saint" or "angel." "Sue will do whatever it takes to get our children to us in the fastest and most efficient way possible," posted Cindy P. "She knows exactly where all our cases are at any given time and will do whatever it takes to make the bumps a little easier to go over. That really goes for her whole staff and the attorneys that she works with in Guatemala. Too bad PGN hasn't figured out who they are dealing with yet!!"

Sue's own notes to the list could be abbreviated or lengthy. At times, she passed along advocacy opportunities or provided general updates. Many of her posts read as if they'd been written quickly, with little attention to grammar, punctuation, and spelling. The CCI Guatemala listserve served as a kind of virtual pulpit, where the agency director could inform and inspire her clients. For example, with regard to various press clips about adoption, Sue explained that the media chose to portray Guatemalan adoptions in a "negative light," which gave them a "bad rap." She wrote about how police in Guatemala City tended to "hang out" around the hotels where adoptive parents stayed to "create problems" and extort families.

Sometimes, Sue's tone was curt. On October 28, 2006, she sent a warning to the list after nervous chatter erupted about the possibility of Guatemala's reconsidering the ratification of the Hague Convention. "Please enjoy each other's friendship," Sue instructed sternly. "However, I ask yet again, DO NOT post things from other sites . . . this is our CCI group, and I will make statements that I feel are true, necessary, and important. Everything else is considered rumor."

After the C-section, Sabrina brought Mildred back to the house in Villa Canales. Her stitches were infected, and oozing pus. When Sabrina examined the incision, she pronounced it strange. She said she'd had C-sections before, and they'd always been easy. Mario and Susana were subdued and quiet. They understood the loss of their two sisters. Mildred was told that the baby was safe with Coni, who was generously paying for medical care out-of-pocket.

Sabrina soon stopped coming home. When she did, she acted brusque and distant. Whenever possible, Mildred asked about her daughters. Sometimes she found the backbone to be forceful and got in loud arguments with Sabrina, who'd tell her to stop worrying. Mildred believed that Coni had both Fernanda and Ana Cristina. After one particularly heated discussion, Sabrina's daughter, Kaylee, approached her mother, arms stretched upward. The child wanted a hug. In a strong motion, Sabrina struck her across the face. The girl turned to Mildred in pain, blood running from her mouth. Mildred felt terrible.

The air was heavy with tension. Rony also came home less frequently. When he did, he brought his friends, twenty-somethings with baggy jeans and black *Santa Muerte* (Grim Reaper) tattoos snaking up their arms and necks. He remained kind to Mildred, frequently reassuring her that her children would return. When Sabrina was around, he tended to ignore the Alvarados all together.

One night, a small band of Rony's friends were downstairs, excitedly discussing a carjacking that had occurred in Atitlán, a town not far away. Rony bragged about installing the seats from the stolen vehicle in his own Mazda.

As Mildred listened to the rowdy bunch crow over the theft, she realized why people in the market always gave her such a wide berth when she mentioned that she lived with Rony and Sabrina. Rony's friends seemed like gangsters, common criminals. The words of Mildred's old landlady and confidante Marjorie rang in the back of her mind. *How can you trust people you don't even know?* Selling *chiles rellenos* by the highway in Villalobos seemed like a lifetime ago, though just two months had passed. Now it seemed that Sabrina neither liked her nor trusted her anymore and was keeping her around just to make sure she didn't go to the authorities to ask for help getting her kids back.

Mildred and Patricia began planning their departure from Sabrina's house. Patricia had ferreted away a small amount of money from her old job at El Pulpo. Both sisters had also saved money from doing laundry for neighbors in Villa Canales. Before they had a chance to solidify their plan, Mildred began receiving threatening calls on her pay-per-use cell phone. She thought that the caller's voice was disguised by a machine, though it sounded distinctly male. "Don't look for Fernanda or the baby," the voice told her. "If you try anything, the children will be killed. Stay quiet." Sometimes he just heaved long rasping breaths without saying anything.

Terrified, Mildred told Sabrina and Rony about the calls. She passed her phone over to them so they could inspect the number. "I know who that is," she remembers Sabrina saying. "It's just someone who's jealous of me. Pay no mind to those idiots; just ignore them."

Mildred tried her best, but the calls kept coming. One time, the same male voice, instead of threatening, passed on a warning: "Don't trust Sabrina," he said. "How dumb are you? She isn't who you think she is. You are so stupid for believing she is helping you. What kind of mother are you? Demand your children back!"

Mildred told Rony and Sabrina immediately. They acted concerned. "Did you see what number they were calling from?" Rony asked. Some calls were from a blocked number, and others appeared to be from a local cell. Rony agreed with Sabrina, saying the calls must be from someone they knew. It was probably some kind of prank. "Don't worry about it," he told Mildred. "Your children will be back very soon."

But Sabrina still refused to give her a date when the children would return, and Mildred grew more agitated with the passing of each day. To kill time, she sat in front of Sabrina's television set with her two remaining children. Neither Susana nor Mario attended school. Mildred couldn't afford uniforms for them. She fell into the lives of the soap opera characters on TV. She didn't know whether she should keep waiting for Fernanda and Ana Cristina to be returned or whether she should move her family out of Sabrina's house as soon as possible. Escaping into fictional drama was better than wallowing in reality.

Roughly three weeks after Ana Cristina's birth, Mildred received word from Coni Galindo Bran. *Finally!* she thought, feeling a thrill of excitement. She pressed the phone firmly against her ear, expecting Coni to nail down the details of the children's return.

Instead, the older woman explained that baby Ana Cristina had medical problems. She might be suffering from a rare blood-borne illness, according to the pediatrician Coni said she'd taken her to see. Mildred was sure a person like Coni would take the baby to a good doctor. A blood test from Mildred, Coni continued, could determine whether the disease was hereditary. The test might save the baby's life.

"When will the girls come back?" Mildred asked.

"It depends on the test," Coni replied, and hung up.

Mildred held the phone in her palm. What if she went in for the test and Coni still kept the girls? If she couldn't make Sabrina and Coni return them, maybe the authorities could. She called the police to try to explain the situation. An officer answered in an abrupt, unfriendly manner. His hurried tone made Mildred stammer, and her childhood speech impediment of swallowing her *r* sounds became more prominent than usual. She recounted what had happened: moving into Sabrina's house, giving Fernanda to Coni for care, Ana Cristina's birth. The story was hard to follow.

The officer explained that the police department wouldn't be able to do anything to help her. They didn't have any available vehicles. He advised Mildred to play it cool, not to let on that she'd spoken to the police. She wasn't sure if he was being serious or trying to humiliate her.

Sabrina didn't drive, so Rony's father and stepmother met Mildred and Sabrina in Villa Canales on the morning of October 25, 2006. All four piled into the Toyota Tercel. Sabrina had told Mildred the night before that she believed Coni would return the girls that very day, and since then, Mildred had lost herself in daydreams of holding her daughters. She felt happy that she'd chosen to wait things out at Sabrina's house.

In Guatemala City, they arrived in Zone 15, where the gleaming Edificio Multimedico building stood. The towering high-rise was home to various high-class doctor's offices and boasted medical facilities that rivaled those in developed countries. They pulled into the parking garage below the building and parked next to Coni Galindo Bran and her husband, Oscar Bran Herrera. It was the third time Mildred had seen Coni, and she was as unsmiling as she remembered.

The men, Oscar and Toño, remained in the parking garage while the women got into a shining elevator. Coni told Mildred that Fernanda was waiting upstairs. Mildred broke down in relief and began to weep from joy. She'd been right. She was finally getting her girl back, after two long, surreal months. "Thank you, Doña Coni," she gasped, trying to smile.

Instead of showing any warmth, Coni reprimanded her. "Stop crying," she said forcefully. "If you don't, it will look suspicious. We'll all end up in jail." The young man operating the elevator, dressed in a neat uniform, looked on with undisguised curiosity. Coni's words instantly changed the mood. Mildred realized she'd been dead wrong; Coni had no intention of returning her daughters. The attendant shot Mildred a sympathetic look as she stepped out of the elevator.

The lab sat behind an unmarked wooden door. Inside, a young Guatemalan woman with blond hair greeted them. She was chubby. Coni embraced her, kissing her cheeks and calling her Kimberly. Kimberly referred to Coni as "Mother." *Coni has a daughter?* Milded's thoughts felt slow, bogged down in anguished confusion. *But Sabrina said she didn't have family. . . .*

Fernanda was with Kimberly. Mildred gazed into her daughter's lovely face, her heart racing. Her girl didn't seem to recognize her, though only two months had passed. The toddler's clothes were stiff and new, and she seemed subdued. Tears pooled in Mildred's eyes. Fernanda's hair had been cut into bangs and dyed black. Before, her fine hair had been lighter, with a reddish cast. Mildred tried to act as if everything was normal, not wanting to scare the toddler. She was too afraid to say anything out loud to her girl. Fernanda didn't speak either.

The staff in the office seemed to know Coni and greeted her warmly, kissing her cheeks and asking after her family. Mildred was ushered into a small room and told to sit in a chair in the corner. A nurse tied a rubber band around her arm and drew a vial of blood, then asked her to open her mouth. She raked a cotton swab across the inside of Mildred's cheek.

Kimberly carried Fernanda into the room. "Don't touch the child," Mildred remembers her saying softly. "Keep your arms at your sides." It felt like a threat of sorts. When her daughter was placed on her lap, Mildred couldn't conceal her emotion. Tears rolled down her cheeks. She held her arms clamped at her sides, afraid to speak. Kimberly hovered a few feet away.

The slight weight of her daughter felt warm against Mildred's thigh. She felt dazed and confused. Fernanda seemed like someone else's child, failing to recognize her. The nurse stepped back and snapped a Polaroid picture. Mildred didn't know she was inside one of the three labs approved by the U.S. Embassy to administer DNA tests for children in adoption processes. The photo that had just been snapped would help establish, to authorities in both the United States and Guatemala, that Maria Fernanda Alvarado was a legitimate orphan.

"Good morning, friends," Betsy Emanuel greeted the CCI Guatemala list in late October. "Sue's email says that Fernanda's DNA will be done today! BM (birth mother) interview may also be done at the same time (not sure yet). Pray for an easy time for mom and child to see one another again. If she's a typical 2 yr old, I'm sure she'll want to fling her arms around her mom's neck. I can't even imagine the torture of this myself. It has got to be so hard to see your beautiful toddler after several weeks and then say goodbye again. My prayers are with her, whoever she is! Please pray for a quick match. . .

Thanks so much to all of you for your prayers, this group is remarkable! Betsy Emanuel, mom of 7 in TN, waiting on Fernanda.[9]"

She scanned the text to make sure there weren't any silly typos or spelling errors. Most of the emails she wrote were dashed off between wrangling children, and this one wasn't any different. Betsy hit the send button and paused for a moment, lost in daydreams.

A week later, the results of the DNA test came back. It stated that Fernanda was indeed the biological daughter of Mildred Alvarado. Betsy found the photograph of the pair deeply disturbing. Both Fernanda and her mother Mildred stared dead into the camera. Mildred wore a red tank top, and her black hair was pulled back in a ponytail. A few loose strands had escaped and framed her face. Her right arm was held stiffly at her side, and Fernanda looked as if she was perched, somewhat precariously, on one of her mother's thighs.

At first glance, Betsy wondered why Mildred wasn't holding Fernanda. As soon as the thought crossed her mind, she chastised herself for being callous. Giving a child up for adoption was a sophisticated, difficult decision. She silently commended Mildred for choosing a bright American future for her girl instead of a life of poverty.

Fernanda's small hands were raised in clenched fists, and her mouth was pulled into a tight, serious line. Mildred's eyes looked red, and her face was visibly puffy. It wasn't a happy image. The longer Betsy studied it, the more unsettled she felt. As noble as she imagined Mildred to be, there was no denying she looked downright miserable.

She decided to ask Sue about the picture. Sue explained that the young woman was probably a drug addict, as were many Guatemalan women giving children up for adoption. She urged Betsy to remember that the child would have a life filled with opportunity and possibility in the U.S. If Fernanda remained in Guatemala, there was no telling what could happen to her. A child as pretty as her could easily end up in a brothel.

Betsy almost shuddered when thinking about little Fernanda, possibly alone and unloved. Sue was right; it was a good thing she'd

---

[9] Betsy's email actually said "Maria," which is how she referenced the child. She didn't know that the double first names common to Guatemala were shortened to the second name rather than the first.

agreed to adopt the toddler, even though she'd hoped to provide a home to an older child. Besides, who was she to question another mother's choice based on a single image?

Five days after the meeting at Edificio Multimedico, Coni still hadn't called with the results of the blood test. Mildred snapped. She'd ignored the threatening phone calls as Rony and Sabrina had instructed. But they still hadn't ceased. She had no idea if Ana Cristina was dying or not, and Sabrina hadn't mentioned a word about either Fernanda's or the baby's return.

The breaking point came when a woman who said she was Sabrina's landlady stopped by to collect the rent. Mildred held the door open, staring at her. *Rent? Landlady?* She was at a loss for words. Sabrina had always said she owned her house.

The betrayal caused an unraveling of confidence, and a painful clarity seared Mildred as she considered the amount of naïve trust she'd placed in Sabrina. Over the past two and a half months, she'd been manipulated. She still had no idea why Sabrina and Coni wanted her daughters, but they did, and she realized she had to do something about it. The women weren't going to return them.

At first, Sabrina had acted as if she was growing to trust Mildred, slowly revealing slices of a colorful history that included prostitution, disposable income, and dance halls. She was a foreign creature to Mildred and Patricia. They'd never attended a party, and neither sister knew the most basic dance steps. They'd never even worn high heels before.

These casual glimpses into Sabrina's troubled, glamorous past broke up the tedium of Mildred and Patricia's daily lives. She was like a *telenovela* (soap opera) heroine come to life, someone who'd expertly used men and relied on her wits. Patricia had never had a boyfriend, and Mildred had been only with Romelio. The Alvarado sisters played a captive, willing audience to Sabrina's stories. How different Sabrina's parents had been from their own, they marveled. How different Sabrina's hard, short life had been from their own hard, short lives.

Sabrina didn't seem like a bad girl turned good anymore. The landlady's surprise visit, compounded by the strange phone calls and lack of information about the girls, ruined the last of Mildred's faith in Sabrina. The faint tendrils of pride she'd felt as Sabrina's confidante withered. *I have never been a charitable cause to her,* she reflected. *I have never been a real confidante.* Instead, she'd been a fool.

She quietly told Patricia to go to the market and find a *flatero* to move them. They left without telling anyone. Everything now seemed sinister, and a host of malicious motives flooded Mildred's mind as she considered why Coni and Sabrina would want her children. The Alvarados moved back to the part of Villa Nueva Mildred knew best, a few blocks from where they had previously lived. Their new one-room apartment room was small and lacked windows.

The first night in the new apartment, Mildred looked down at her ringing cell phone's screen. It was Sabrina. She hesitated, then slowly lifted the phone to her ear.

"Do you really think I don't know where you are right now?" Sabrina snarled. Mildred remained silent. "It's on you, Mildred, whether the girls stay alive," she continued. "Don't think that I don't know where you are."

The line was abruptly disconnected.

Mildred began receiving death threats the next day. Sometimes they came multiple times in a single day. Some days, there were none. At times, Mildred thought she recognized the voices of Lily and Toño, Rony's parents. The message was always a variation on the same theme: Her daughters would die unless she kept quiet and minded her own business. Their bodies would be chopped up into pieces, which would be strewn around Zone 9 of Guatemala City. Mildred would be informed of where to pick up her children's heads, legs, and arms. Sometimes the killings of her two remaining kids, Mario and Susana, were detailed. Sometimes the calls foretold Mildred's own death, or worse, Patricia's. Patricia found a job in a Chinese restaurant, and the threats started reaching her there too, on the restaurant's phone line. The Alvarados felt like they were being watched.

One afternoon, a call came in. It was the same male voice that had previously warned Mildred about Sabrina. Again, the anonymous voice offered unsolicited advice.

"The children are in Villa Canales," he said. "They are in San José las Rosas. Behind the gates. Take the 21 bus. Doña Coni goes to the park with her grandchildren on Sundays before church. Go early." The bus he mentioned was named the *Milagro*, or Miracle.[10]

He hung up, and Mildred wasn't sure if she should be elated or terrified. She couldn't imagine who might want to warn her or help her. *Could it be Rony?* Her head swam. Surely Rony would tell her outright if he wanted to help. For the hundredth time, Mildred felt trapped in an unending dream. Was it simply another trick, a scheme to kill or disappear her? It certainly could be. Yet the voice *had* been right about not trusting Sabrina. *It's worth it,* Mildred decided.

Mildred and Patricia set out for San José las Rosas early on Sunday morning, traveling together as a safety precaution. When they arrived, they found a yellow metal gate and a few guards at the private community's entrance. They told the guard they were there to work as maids, and he let them in. To their crushing dismay, Coni wasn't in the park. After a few hours of wandering, Mildred sent Patricia home. They'd left the children, Mario and Susana, alone in the tiny apartment, curled up together atop the single mattress. They wondered if the kids would be gone or dead upon their return.

When Patricia got home, she called Mildred to say she'd arrived safely. Everyone was fine. Mildred walked on alone, imagining Fernanda's bright smile and the possibilities of Ana Cristina's face. Would the baby look like her? How would she recognize a face she'd never seen?

Time passed, and suddenly Mildred, fantastically, caught sight of a woman that looked like Coni, alone, climbing into a black SUV. The vehicle was parked along the side of the street. Mildred's feet became rooted to the ground in fear. Before she could find her voice to call out, the black truck disappeared up the road.

It was encouraging, still. Mildred approached the house closest to where the SUV had parked, knocking on the white iron gates protecting the doorway. A blond woman swung open the small trap door and peered out.

"Does Doña Coni live here?" Mildred asked.

"Maybe," the blond answered mildly. "Who wants to know?"

"I wash clothes," Mildred answered, biting her cheek. "I heard she might have work."

[10.] Most buses have nicknames, generally female, painted on their exteriors, such as "*Esperanza*" (Hope) or "Wendy."

The blond studied her eyes for a beat. "Come by later," she replied, closing the door.

Mildred gazed at the white bars for a moment. Coni's house was solidly upper-middle class, with roses and vines climbing the decorative latticework. To Mildred, it looked like the home of a wealthy woman. She retreated across the street and considered whether or not to call the police.

Throughout the country, Guatemala's *Policia Nacional Civil* (the National Civil Police, or PNC) lacked both logistical supplies and respect. A continual shortage of fuel and vehicles hampered police work. As of July 2003, 2,300 officers, or about 12 percent of the total police force, had been implicated in such crimes as corruption, robbery, extortion, and extrajudicial killings. It was common knowledge that some police worked as hired assassins to supplement their meager incomes. The corruption's long, sordid history stemmed from wartime, when certain precincts had engaged in activities like *operaciones de limpieza,* "social cleansings" that included the torture and killings of demonstrators, prostitutes, and students. One special unit of police detectives, later known as the DINC, directed the infamous 1980 siege of the Spanish Embassy in Guatemala City, in which thirty-six demonstrators were burned alive.

The salaries of the police were significantly smaller than those of the armed private security guards stationed in the doorways of Guatemala's cafés, delis, and shops. In March 2010, Guatemala's Interior Minister announced that 70 percent of police lived in poverty. A 2004 had report previously found that only half of the force had elementary school educations. The untrained, underpaid officers investigated fewer than 3 percent of all reported crimes — let alone solved them. Police officers were known for extorting victims, sometimes blaming them for the very crimes they were reporting. Fifty-eight percent of victims didn't report crimes at all. One 2006 report on corruption sponsored by USAID found that 40 percent of households in Guatemala reported having paid bribes to traffic cops in order to avoid having their cars seized.

When Mildred called the police, an operator answered and asked if she'd already filed a *denuncia,* or complaint, against Coni and Sabrina. Because she hadn't, the operator said, the police would-n't be able to do anything.

When the black SUV returned to Coni's house, Mildred advan-ced. Coni immediately caught sight of her. The iciness of the older woman's earlier demeanor was gone. Instead, she seemed emotional and charged. "How did you find this address?" she said with anger. "What the fuck are you doing here?"

She didn't seem to care if anyone heard her. The crass language surprised Mildred. Wealthy people weren't supposed to be so impo-lite. Mildred herself almost never used such foul words. "I've come to get my daughters back," Mildred said. Her voice came out flat and steady, and its strength amazed her.

"What daughters?" Coni tartly replied. "As if you don't know!" Mildred answered. Four men spilled from the house, surrounding them. They'd heard the yelling. One young man held a gun that looked, Mildred thought, like the rifles used by the police. Another, in blue jeans and a white polo shirt, brandished a small pistol. He grabbed Mildred by the ear and dragged her inside.

A small veranda gave way to the interior of Coni's home. They sat down around a table. The men addressed Coni formally, as Mother. Mildred's mind whirled. She was still struggling to come to terms with the fact that Sabrina hadn't really been helping her, and was at a loss to understand Coni's own motivation in kidnapping her children. *Is this about a personal grudge?* Mildred wondered briefly. *But I don't even know her! What could I have done to deserve this?*

Sounds of young children echoed through the house. Coni addressed the man who had dragged Mildred in as Marvin. Down a corridor, Mildred glimpsed a girl she thought might be Fernanda. The child was quickly enveloped by the darkness of the hallway.

Mildred broke down in tears, begging to hold her daughter. Coni refused, frantically repeating that the child wasn't Fernanda and that Mildred was crazy. The older woman demanded, over and over, that Mildred reveal who'd given out her address. Coni said she felt ill, and one of her sons brought her a blood pressure pill. "If something happens to my mother," Marvin snarled at Mildred, "I'll leave you dead on the side of the road. Who the fuck gave you this address? Answer me, you idiot whore!"

Mildred tried to explain about the anonymous voice, and brandished her cell phone to show them the number. No one believed her strange account. Finally, Marvin lunged forward and slapped her roughly across the face.

"I don't know," Mildred replied, flustered and afraid. "I don't know." She dropped the cell phone in her lap, raising her hands to shield her face. "I just want my girl," she stammered, her speech impediment mangling her words. "Give me my girl. I'll leave, and I won't say anything about any of this. You'll never hear from us again."

One of the men started to make phone calls to Sabrina, Rony, Rony's father, Toño, and his stepmother, Lili, urgently telling them to come over. Coni seemed angry. Mildred was placed in the back of the black SUV. The others got into another car and pulled away.

So this is it, Mildred thought. *This is my end.*

They'd drive to a ravine or overpass, she figured, where she could be killed quietly and cleanly. The rate of murder of women had more than tripled in Guatemala since 2000. Many corpses showed signs of sexual abuse or mutilation and sometimes turned up unidentified in a garbage bag of body parts. Guatemala's *Procuraduría de Derechos Humanos* (Office of the Human Rights Ombudsman) reported that between 2002 and 2005, the murder rate for women had risen 65 percent.

Theories abounded about what had caused the gruesome trend. Some people blamed the thousands of gang members in the country, hypothesizing that the unidentified female corpses were casualties of violent initiation rites. Some had even tried to tie the killing of women to the adoption industry. No one knew.

If Mildred was killed, there was a high probability that no one would ever investigate. She understood that she didn't matter.

The black SUV and the other vehicle drove to a parking lot in San Miguel Petapa. Sabrina, Rony, and Rony's parents met them there, along with others. Two men wearing what looked like bulletproof vests climbed out of a pale-blue car and hovered around the edge of the group. Mildred was pulled out of the van. She stood silently.

A raucous argument broke out over who had snitched. It seemed that everyone there had a stake in the matter, and each person,

Mildred realized, was in disagreement with the next. They were in business together, and the business revolved around children. Coni was clearly the boss. The quarrel escalated to the point where the men drew their guns. It became clear that these weren't the first children Sabrina had sold to Coni. The older woman grilled Sabrina about what happened with Mildred. "This always happens with her," one person complained, motioning towards Sabrina. "Things get out of control. She can't handle it."

"But she *was* under control," Sabrina whined, "until one of you called her. That's not my fault. I never even got the money."

"Don't lie," Toño told her. "Don't lie about the money. I gave it to you myself."

Everyone was yelling at once. Emboldened by the chaos, Mildred piped up. "I will call the authorities," she said, "and I will tell them everything. I want my children back."

Some of the group laughed.

"You?" One of the men spat towards her. "You have nothing, you are nothing. If you call the cops, you'll never see your sister or your daughters again. Just go ahead, try. If you do, we'll kill them."

"I won't," Mildred said, terrified. "I won't do anything. I promise. Please, just let me see them, one last time."

Her promise seemed to calm the mood, and the guns were put away. After a few more words, the other people got back into their cars. Mildred was put back in the black SUV and driven to a neighborhood she didn't recognize. "Get out," the man said. She swung the car door open quickly, heart racing.

Moments after the black SUV pulled away, the two strange men in the light-blue car pulled up.

One of them called out to her. "Are you going to file a complaint?" There was a pause, and no one spoke. The same man called out again. "We have family in the Ministerio Público, inside the PGN, and inside the police. We will find out if you do anything. And if you cause any trouble, you will die."

"I won't," Mildred said. She couldn't stop trembling and was having trouble thinking clearly. "I won't do anything."

She was left standing on the corner, alone but alive.

Maria Fernanda

Add to My Child Page

(May not work for AOL users)

What a pretty little girl! This child will be going to the MD this week and bloodwork and a medical report will be available soon. This child can only be considered by 100% paper ready families. This means that you have an I 171 H in hand and a dossier in hand completely authenticated. We cannot hold a child such as Maria Fernanda while a family becomes paper ready.

See all the children from **Celebrate Children, International** who are on the photolisting.

Child Name:	Maria Fernanda
Birthdate:	07-May-04
Sex:	F
Developmentally Handicapped?:	NO
Physically Handicapped?:	NO
Child/Sibling Group ID:	191716
Date Added or Last Updated:	21-Aug-06
Country:	Guatemala
Number of Children:	1
Singles accepted?:	YES
Can either parent be over 45?:	YES
Must both parents be over 35?:	NO
Can the family already have children?:	YES
Is travel required?:	NO

*Mildred Alvarado only had one photograph of her daughter, Maria
Fernanda, when she filed a missing child complaint in 2006. Her son Mario
stands in the background. Photograph courtesy Mildred Alvarado.*

9. GONE

Days later, back in Villa Nueva, Mildred considered the futility of her new circumstances. Going public with the abductions meant there was a chance that the girls might be found. Yet it also meant they might be killed in retaliation. If she remained silent, were they more likely to remain alive? Mildred wasn't sure. Fernanda had been gone for almost three months, and the pain hadn't lessened. The risk of speaking out was worth it, she finally decided. There was nothing left to do but gamble.

On November 21, she stood outside the Villa Nueva branch of the Ministerio Público. It was her second attempt to file a complaint. The week before, she'd shown up but had been too afraid to walk through the front doors. After the first attempt, she'd returned home to answer a call from a low, angry voice that said he knew she'd gone to the MP building. "The girls will be killed immediately if you keep this up," he told her.

Mildred wasn't sure if someone at the MP had tipped off the caller or if she'd been followed. It was hard to think. She felt overwhelmed. Living without her children was as bad as she imagined death would be. As she waited in line at the Ministerio Público for the second time, she nervously struck up a conversation with a security guard outside. He casually inquired about her reason for visiting and listened patiently as she related her tale. "It's good you came here," he said. "What happened to you is serious. It's a crime."

His words gave her confidence. Inside, Mildred filed a formal denouncement against both Sabrina Hernández Donis and Coni for the kidnapping of her two daughters for the purpose of adoption. From what she had seen at Coni's house and afterward, in the parking lot, Mildred believed that the Galindo Brans were making money buying and selling children. She wasn't sure what Coni's full name was or how to spell it, but she was able to provide a description of her address and Sabrina's, too. Mildred's old job at the car parts store left her with the quirky talent of noticing and remembering details about cars, and she was able to supply the make, model, and license plate number of Coni's white Nissan. Officer Isaac Payes Reyes typed up the report.

Mildred thought he had a mean, tough face. *That's good,* she thought. Tough faces usually covered for soft hearts.

Yet Reyes clearly thought her story was crazy. "OK, woman," he said. "It's best to just say that you sold them. Just tell me the truth. It will make everything easier."

"I didn't sell them," she told him. Her voice wavered with emotion. "Come to my house if you don't believe me. I sleep on the floor. My clothes are in a cardboard box. If I sold them, wouldn't I have money?"

After giving a sworn statement, Mildred was told to contact the Departamento de Investigaciones Criminológicas (Department of Criminal Investigations, or DINC) in Villa Nueva, where she lived. On the morning of November 23, she went to the office armed with her new criminal complaint file from the Ministerio Público. The DINC building was swarming with people waiting to obtain criminal background checks, a necessary step for many job applicants in Guatemala. She took her place in the dusty line. Vendors had set up carts, hawking chips and soda to the crowd.

Inside, Carlos Cujá, a stout investigator with a boyish face and glimmering gold teeth, received her kindly. He squirmed in his seat as she cried. He wasn't sure what to make of Mildred's story, but he was sympathetic. Another officer, Nelson Adán Orellana, transcribed her complaint. Despite the fact she'd willingly given Fernanda to Coni, the most appropriate charges were *sustracción agravada,* or aggravated abduction or kidnapping. Before 2007, the Guatemalan criminal code lacked provisions regarding the disappearance or theft of a minor.

The fact that the Ministerio Público had sent Mildred might have encouraged the police detectives to pay attention to her case. That same day, Detective Cujá and Third Officer Crispín Véliz chauffered Mildred to Coni's gated neighborhood in an attempt to ascertain her address. That way, the detectives could read the number of her electricity meter and check electric company records to see who owned the home. A black SUV was parked outside the house.

As it turned out, Coni owned not one but two homes in San José las Rosas. The detectives began filing paperwork for permission to raid both houses. The next day, detectives brought Patricia to the precinct so she could give a statement in support of her sister's testimony.

Eight days later, the police detectives wrangled the necessary search warrants and brought together a multidisciplinary squad to raid Coni's houses. The team included PGN representative Julia Victoria Zacarías Rodríguez, police detective Orellana, and two officials from the Ministerio Público. In the early morning hours of November 29, 2006, before 7:00 am, the team set out.

Third Officer Véliz took notes about the raid by hand. He recorded certain details, describing the first home as a pale-pink house with a black gate. It was, in fact, orange. Vivian Bran Galindo answered the door, he wrote, and let the detectives in to search. The report noted she was the 35-year-old daughter of Coni Galindo and Oscar Bran. No young children were found in the home. At the second house, Marvin Bran's wife, Mariela Solís Ramírez, answered the door. The police noted that she was 22 years old and married, though they didn't record who she was married to or make any mention of Marvin's name. Again, they found no children.

It seemed as if Lilia Consuelo Galindo Ovalle de Bran, known as Coni, had anticipated the raids. Among the neighbors, it was common knowledge that Coni's daughter Kimberly worked as a cuidadora in her mother's own home. Some claimed that up to eight pregnant women also lived inside Coni's house, waiting to give birth and then sell the babies in adoption. Others claimed there were even more. It was rumored that Coni's son, Marvin, had contacts inside the local branch of the Ministerio Público. Upon arriving, the police detectives found a few random children's things that were easily explained away by the fact that Coni had grandchildren of her own.

As the detectives discussed the failed raids, Mildred felt the outlook was bleak. She realized, darkly, that a ticking clock loomed overhead, and the new awareness filled her with heaviness. Fernanda and Ana Cristina had to be found before they were given to new families, far away under a foreign sky.

When Betsy Emanuel woke up on the morning of November 30, 2006, she found an exciting email in her inbox: official pre-approval from the U.S. Embassy in Guatemala for the Emanuel family's adoption of Fernanda. It was carbon-copied to Sue Hedberg at Celebrate Children International and to Marvin Bran. The pre-approval letter meant that the Department of Homeland Security, the government arm responsible for reviewing American citizens' applications to adopt foreign children, had reviewed the Emanuels' case. They'd looked over the family's home studies, tax documents, and related materials, as well as paperwork like DNA results related to Fernanda. Everything seemed to be in order, and the U.S. government found no reason to object to the proposed adoption.

Betsy was beside herself with joy. Receiving the pre-approval was deeply reassuring. Betsy knew that adoptive parents trying to adopt from Guatemala weren't always so lucky. Sometimes, the United States refused to grant pre-approval or ordered an investigation into the potential adoptee's situation, for instance if they received an adoption application for a child whose exact name or identity had recently been used in another application.

After losing the referral to adopt Jennifer, Betsy had tried her best to refrain from indulging in homecoming fantasies about Fernanda. She wanted to avoid further emotional pain in case something else unexpected happened. Now, with U.S. Embassy pre-approval for the adoption to progress, she felt safer. For a moment, Betsy imagined Fernanda's arriving in December, just in time for Christmas.

Later that morning, Betsy called Angela Vance at the Celebrate Children International office in Florida. She was eager to chat, excited to discuss the next steps of the process. After a few minutes of small talk, though, Angela stopped her, saying she had bad news. Betsy's heart raced. For reasons outside of CCI's control, Fernanda could no longer be adopted. Like Jennifer, the child's referral had been "lost."

Betsy dropped the phone into the receiver in disbelief. *How could this happen again?* she wondered, feeling a sudden hot streak of anger and helplessness. The fantasy of Fernanda's Christmas homecoming abruptly evaporated. Drawing a few deep breaths, Betsy collected her poise and called back, apologizing to Angela for hanging up so rudely.

Angela's explanation of what had happened with Fernanda was familiar. Betsy felt instantly uneasy. Apparently, the child's mother had changed her mind about the adoption, deciding that she wanted to keep her daughter. She'd gone directly to Marvin Bran and demanded Fernanda's return. Things got violent. A man with a weapon had accompanied the young woman, and Angela said that Marvin had been scared.

Betsy had heard enough. Despite her best efforts at control, her voice trembled with a mix of anger and pain. She could understand losing one referral, but now a second? She demanded to speak with Sue.

The agency director confirmed the account that her assistant had relayed and then offered a possible explanation, noting Mildred's haggard expression in the DNA picture. Perhaps she was trying to settle a drug debt by relinquishing the child, or by getting her back. Sue reminded Betsy that she'd even inquired about the young woman's troubled expression. Maybe Mildred was a drug addict.

Betsy's heart raced. Like many other in-process adoptive parents, she felt like the child was already her own daughter despite the fact the adoption was far from finished. She felt a fierce sense of maternal protectiveness for the girl's well-being, believing the child to be unwanted and unloved. She took a moment to reconsider the troubling photograph of Fernanda and her birth mother, recalling the plaintive desperation that seemed to radiate from Mildred.

Sue explained that she wasn't sure where Fernanda had been taken. The details of the reclamation were too traumatic for Marvin Bran to get into, she said, and she hadn't wanted to push him. Betsy remembers Sue saying that they couldn't risk searching for Fernanda because the threat of violence was too great.

Betsy couldn't understand why Sue was so nonchalant about the situation. *What if Fernanda's life was at stake?* "Well, Sue," she began, trying to keep her voice even. "Maybe I can go to Guatemala and try to find her myself?"

The words came out more sharply than she'd intended. Sue immediately rebuffed her, saying that such actions held the potential to endanger CCI's other in-process adoptions from Guatemala. She implied that if Betsy stirred things up and caused a scene, she might be responsible for the loss of many other referrals to CCI clients. Marvin had already threatened to stop working in adoption all together, she continued, because of what had happened with Fernanda. He was scared. Sue said she'd had to beg him to keep working on CCI's cases.

Then she brought up faith, reciting a few Bible verses that alluded to the virtues of unquestioned faith. God was in control, and He had a plan. She reminded Betsy that plenty of Guatemalan children were available for adoption. "Pray about it," she told Betsy. Perhaps God would soften her heart to accept another child in need.

There seemed to be plenty of children, Betsy thought, since Sue was so busy. Though she didn't know it, weeks earlier, Sue had sent an email to one of her business partners, Olga Sullivan at Adopt International in Texas, mentioning that she was simultaneously handling 172 Guatemalan adoptions.

Days later, Betsy remained confused about what to do. She didn't understand how visiting Guatemala could jeopardize the adoptions of other children through CCI. She didn't understand how Sue could be so cold about losing Fernanda, on top of losing Jennifer. It was almost as if they were merchandise, Betsy thought. Her confidence faltered. Sue had made a valid point about trusting God, yet she still wanted a hard explanation of what, exactly, had transpired with Fernanda. The man-with-gun story wasn't enough. Everything was happening too fast.

In search of solace, Betsy penned an email to CCI's Guatemala listserve about the missing children. "As devastated as we are," she wrote, "I know that His eyes are on them and He will provide all that they need. That is a hard thing to trust, but what choice do we have but to dig deep and pull out our strongest feelings of faith? Adoption is a privilege for any of us no matter what our reasons are for doing it. . . ."

In prayer, Betsy tried to reconcile the concept of adoption as a manifestation of love and charity with the disturbing, vague details of what had transpired with Jennifer and Fernanda. Days later, she remained worried. Fernanda's disappearance troubled her more than Jennifer's. As hard as she tried, Betsy couldn't purge the little girl's bright smile from her mind. Her gut said something was wrong.

The Emanuels weren't the first family to be perplexed by adoption circumstances with Celebrate Children International. On January 21, 2006, Indiana teacher Tiffany Cargill[11] turned to the Florida Department of Children and Families (DCF) for help with her problems with CCI. In an email to the state agency, which granted operating licenses to adoption agencies in Florida, Tiffany explained that she'd paid CCI $15,200 to adopt from Guatemala, with a balance due of $9,500. "Then Wednesday, Sue Hedberg called me and demanded that we pay $300 a month for foster care," Tiffany wrote. "I told her that wasn't in our contract. . . . She said that either we pay it or we don't get our baby." Furthermore, Sue told her, if Tiffany didn't pay and the baby ended up in an orphanage, "no one would ever be able to adopt her."

Shortly after contacting DCF, Tiffany Cargill retracted her complaint. "We would like to avoid any retribution if at all possible," she told DCF. "At this point, CCI suspects we have filed a complaint, but I don't think they are certain." She was afraid of losing the child she was trying to bring home.

Janey and Robert Brooks[12] began the adoption process with CCI in the spring of 2006. *They're Christian and they're in with God,* Janey had thought when choosing an adoption agency. *That's good enough for me.* Sue's emails were kind and compassionate. When she offered the Brooks family two female infants to choose from, they chose the younger baby. In the fall of 2006, the couple traveled to Guatemala to meet their future daughter. When they arrived, they say, the baby was malnourished and lethargic, with an angry rash. Janey discovered that the child's caretaker had been putting sweetened coffee in her bottle instead of milk. The child was clearly neglected. Also, when Janey had asked the bellboys at the Radisson for the green suitcase of baby supplies that CCI supposedly kept in storage there, they'd hadn't seemed to know what she was talking about. Panicked, Janey called CCI, unsure of how to handle the situation. One of CCI's adoption facilitators, Clariss Bracamonte, had come to the hotel to retrieve the baby, saying she was going to take her to a doctor.

[11.] The name has been changed to protect confidentiality.
[12.] The names have been changed to protect confidentiality.

After the Brooks got back home to the U.S., they received a certified letter from CCI telling them to enroll in parenting classes, complete three additional home studies, and undergo a psychiatric evaluation in order to continue adopting. When they asked Sue why such additional measures were needed, she replied that it was because Janey had "acted inappropriately" and, at times, "irrationally" to CCI staff and in-country contacts. Janey felt like the fact that she'd expressed outrage over the condition of the neglected, sick orphan had led to the requests. Like Tiffany Cargill, she wrote to DCF to complain. When questioned, Sue told DCF that she'd made the requests because Janey's behavior had prompted "concern" about her ability to "handle stressful situations" once her potential daughter arrived in the U.S.

Janey Brooks wasn't the only one asked to undergo a psychological evaluation. Carrie McFarland,[13] a Celebrate Children International client who was a professional psychologist, was also asked to do so after she expressed concerns about how her adoption was unfolding. CCI had given Carrie an adoption referral for a nameless female infant who was a few days old and lacked a birth certificate. CCI staffer Tammy Grega had told Carrie via email that the baby's mother was "actually born in El Salvador but is not a Guatemalan citizen," but that CCI's Guatemalan lawyer Alfonso Close "assures us that the cédula is in good order." Worried, Carrie asked for copies of the birth mother's ID, medical reports for the baby, and other documentation.

Sue responded to her request in an email typed in all capital letters. "CARRIE, I CANNOT PRODUCE DOCUMENTS THAT ARE NOT READY NOW," the message said. In a few sentences, she explained that "a lot" of information is "not available" in international adoption and would not be provided. She told Carrie that a complete referral would consist of photos of a child, a copy of the child's birth certificate, and a medical report with blood work, nothing more. "IS THAT SOMETHING YOU CAN LIVE WITH?" she asked.

Carrie was taken aback; to her, the tone of the email was unnecessarily aggressive. A few days later, she says, Sue informed her the adoption wasn't going to work out. She provided two reasons: The baby's mother had changed her mind, and it might not be possible to get the

[13.] The name has been changed to protect confidentiality.

paperwork for the case in order. She sent Carrie digital snapshots of five other babies to choose from. Carrie chose another but remained concerned. She typed the name of lawyer Alfonso Close into an internet search engine and found an article from the November 11, 2006 edition of *Siglo XXI*, a Guatemalan newspaper, that claimed Close was being investigated for "anomalies" in some of his adoption files. The article had been published almost a year before Carrie started trying to adopt with CCI and Close. The automatic English translation was confusing, and Carrie asked CCI about the piece. CCI staffer Tammy Grega wrote back, telling Carrie that the article was very old and calling it "baloney." Later on in the adoption, the last name of the new child Carrie was referred to inexplicably changed on the birth certificate and other documentation. The last name of the birth mother of the baby also changed. It was when Carrie demanded an explanation that Sue told her she needed a psychiatric examination in order to continue adopting. Carrie refused and filed a complaint with the Florida Department of Children and Families.

Jillian Richman,[14] a CCI client whose husband spoke fluent Spanish, called Alfonso Close directly to check on their adoption. Jillian was worried because the U.S. Embassy had refused to grant pre-approval, and no one seemed able to explain why. Sue had told her that Alfonso Close was "the only one" capable of handling "difficult cases" and that he could "work miracles." Yet when Jillian's husband spoke to the lawyer, his version of events didn't match Sue's. Jillian bluntly told the agency director that she thought CCI wasn't being honest with them about errors in their case. Sue responded by email, telling Jillian that God was in control, not her, the U.S. Embassy, or the PGN. "God in his eternal foreknowledge will build your family in His time," she said. The religious references failed to stop Jillian's persistent questions about the discrepancies. Days later, Sue told her she must undergo psychiatric evaluation if she was to continue adopting with CCI.

Rachel Robinson[15] was also told to have a psychological evaluation in order to continue her adoption with CCI. She refused to comply and instead hired a lawyer. Rachel was a devout Catholic, and

---

14. The name has been changed to protect confidentiality.
15. The name has been changed to protect confidentiality.

lately she'd begun wondering about Sue Hedberg's own motivation and faith. She certainly didn't seem very compassionate.

In Guatemala, Josefina Arellano, the young woman who served as head of the adoption unit at the PGN, was getting frustrated. Adoptions with signs of criminal fraud were sent from the PGN to the Ministerio Público, the institution responsible for criminal investigations and prosecutions, for review. Yet the MP didn't seem to be doing much with the files. Sixty-nine different adoption cases had been passed to their office since January 2006, and nothing had happened. It was now November.

The prosecutors and investigators at the Ministerio Público were political appointees, subject to frequent turnover. They faced the daily fear of losing their jobs, or possibly their lives, if the wrong person happened to be investigated. Death threats were common, and some staffers had bodyguards. Three to four prosecutors were assassinated annually. Instead of using filing cabinets, some MP investigators kept small, padlocked metal safes to house important documents. These safes, it was hoped, wouldn't be stolen or tampered with. Josefina Arellano understood how the Ministerio Público functioned because she'd worked there before the PGN. One problem with investigating adoption cases was that you never knew what kind of "interest" might be "touched" by a seemingly benign inquiry.

"People are scared of talking about adoption because of these kinds of connections," says one adoption facilitator whose network included a lawyer who'd defended alleged narco-traffickers. One of the more prolific adoption attorneys in Guatemala, Francisco García Gudiel, had rumored ties to drug cartels because of his earlier defense of alleged members of the Mexican crime syndicate Los Zetas, and others connected to drug kingpin Otto Herrera. García Gudiel had also led the 1993 defense of three men, including the grandson of former dictator Efraín Rios Montt, who were accused of attacking Guatemalan human rights activist and Nobel Peace Prize winner Rigoberta Menchú.

Guatemalan attorney Julio Roberto Echeverría Vallejo (known in adoption circles as Roberto Echeverría) had defended retired Army Colonel Byron Lima Estrada; his son, Army Captain Byron Lima

Oliva; and former presidential military staff sergeant José Obdulio Villanueva when they were tried in what is considered to be the most high-profile criminal case in Guatemalan history. Echeverría's clients were convicted of masterminding the 1998 assassination of Bishop Juan Gerardi, the Catholic bishop who had published *Guatemala: Nunca Más,* a detailed report containing thousands of statements from witnesses to and victims of violence and repression during the wartime. Almost all of the abuses were attributed to the Guatemalan Army.

In his role as an adoption lawyer, Echeverría worked for various American agencies, including Adoptions International, Inc., Carolina Hope Christian Adoptions, Karing Angels International, and Families Through International Adoption (FTIA). Echeverría also worked closely with the American adoption advocacy group Joint Council for International Children's Services, as well as the Guatemalan lobbying group La Asociación de Defensores de Adopción. Echeverría was a powerful man, with many ties to the Guatemalan government. JCICS later appointed him to act as the organization's official "Guatemala representative," saying he would "significantly increase the effectiveness of Joint Council's advocacy efforts in Guatemala." Echeverría offered pro bono legal services to the American group and spoke in the United States, addressing members of Congress in adoption-related briefings alongside JCICS director and friend Tom DiFilipo.

Echeverría's sudden death in July 2010 at age 38 sparked an outpouring of grief in the American adoption community, where the story that he'd died in a car crash circulated. "It wasn't an innocent car accident," one Guatemalan prosecutor from the Ministerio Público speculated. "Echeverría was killed because his car was blown up." About a month after the "crash," Guatemalan newspaper *El Periódico* published an article by Luis Ángel Sas under the headline "Muerte de Echeverría: ¿accidente o homicidio?" (Echeverría's death: Accident or Homicide?). The lawyer's burnt body had been found inside his car, the article reported, after the vehicle had apparently run over cement steps and inexplicably caught fire.

The lack of action from the Ministerio Público was just one of Josefina Arellano's frustrations. A former law school valedictorian, she was an ambitious young woman who liked to get things done.

She believed in the possibilities offered by accountability, justice, and reform. At the PGN, she'd instituted a new system of random checks on adoption files, designed to expose fraud. Forged documents consistently made it past PGN reviewers, including fake medical records and birth certificates and, occasionally, falsified DNA results. To Arellano, it was unclear if the reviewers were simply overworked and drowning beneath the massive amount of paperwork or if they were taking bribes to approve the fudged files.

For PGN staffers, it could be difficult to verify the facts of an adoption case thoroughly and expeditiously. As soon as someone began to look into the details of a certain case, the child in question might be shuttled to another location. Between the networks of casas cunas and the hundreds of cuidadoras sprinkled throughout the nation, it could be impossible to locate a baby. Confirming a child's true identity also presented challenges. At one point, an investigator from the PGN's in-house investigative unit showed up at a DNA lab to observe a child and her mother undergoing their DNA test. The investigator says she stood directly next to the pair, in the frame, as the Polaroid picture was taken. Later, when the child's file was resubmitted, the investigator was surprised to see that she'd been erased from the picture.

Furthermore, when certain adoptions were called into question, the names of those handling the case would often change. When the adoption file was resubmitted for review, the original lawyer's name would be replaced with another lawyer's name. It was maddening. Some attorneys would pay recent law school graduates 2,000Q per signature. It was a common practice for established lawyers to protect their reputations by having a "newbie" sign for them.

The PGN was also being pressured by American families. Potential parents would call in anger, fuming about the slow pace of the adoption process and demanding that "their" children be "released" by the PGN. Some were downright rude. After some explaining, though, they'd usually come to understand that it wasn't that the PGN didn't want them to get the babies. The delays were a typically the result of paperwork or case problems, not an issue with the idea of adoption in general.

Many adopting parents were terribly misinformed about their cases. Often, they would call to check on a case that hadn't been submitted yet. One adopting mother arrived in Guatemala to pick up a child who'd died months before. Some Americans reported being asked to pay additional fees to get their adoption files through PGN review, though PGN didn't charge fees. Josefina Arellano wasn't sure who was pocketing the money, the notaries or the American agencies.

Sue Hedberg told the Emanuels that they might be able to adopt another child from Guatemala in just four months. The time frame was startling. Though Betsy's faith in CCI was wavering, she believed that the events that had occurred were outside of Sue's control, as the agency director had said. Betsy thought that the losses of Jennifer and Fernanda had happened because of the people in Guatemala associated with their case files: Alfonso Close and Marvin Bran.

Betsy told Sue that she wouldn't accept a third referral from either man. Sue seemed annoyed. Turning down children reflected poorly on CCI, she said. Things would be more difficult.

John and Bethany Thompson, the young couple who'd been adopting Fernanda's baby sister, Ana Cristina, had been informed of their lost referral via email. Sue urged them to pick another child quickly. "I know from experience that the sooner you can move on, the better it is for everyone," she wrote to them on November 29, 2006. The Thompsons signed up to adopt another baby who'd been offered to Sue by Marvin Bran.

Betsy understood that it was going to be hard for Sue to tell Marvin that her family was refusing to accept another referral from him. She felt pangs of guilt. The man had been beaten, after all, trying to help her family adopt. Nevertheless, there was no way she was working with him again.

Both Betsy and her husband had concerns about their attempts to adopt from Guatemala. Yet when it came to the question of what to do next, their perspectives differed. Leslie remained committed to Jennifer, the first child they'd tried to adopt, feeling they should follow up and, if at all possible, wait for an abandonment decree to be issued. Betsy felt ready to move on, thinking of other children who needed families.

Sue sent the Emanuels more photos of Guatemalan children. The options were almost all infants or young babies. Betsy felt defeated. *I don't know if I have any feelings left,* she thought to herself. In exasperation, she made a premeditated appeal to Sue's ego.

"What do you think, Sue?" Betsy asked. "Why don't you pick a child for us? Whichever one you think would be the best." She figured that they'd be matched with an older girl as soon as one came along. Instead, Sue paired them with Lady Diana, a baby who was just months old. She had been born on October 1, 2006, and apparently named by her birth mother.

Betsy couldn't believe it. She'd told Sue more than once that their family didn't want to adopt an infant. Neither she nor Leslie had the energy to wrangle a baby. It almost seemed as if Sue's referral of a baby was retaliation for Betsy's refusal to work with Alfonso or Marvin.

Sue informed the Emanuels that the adoption fees would, again, go up. Since the new baby was even younger, her adoption would be more expensive, just as Fernanda's was more than Jennifer's. Lady Diana's process would cost somewhere around $24,000 total. A lawyer named Elmer Belteton would handle the case. Elmer babies, Sue said, came home the fastest.

Before formally assigning Lady Diana to the Emanuels, Sue asked them to send a letter to the U.S. Embassy stating that they were no longer interested in adopting either Jennifer or Fernanda. Betsy worried that the letter might enable another family to adopt the girls, if they ever turned up. Sue reassured her that a new power-of-attorney form would be required anyway. She refused to start Lady Diana's adoption until Betsy sent the letter, and the Emanuels had only twenty-four hours until the baby would be referred to another family.

On December 1, 2006, the Emanuels officially accepted the referral of Lady Diana. They decided to call her Emily Belle. Their new power-of-attorney document said that their lawyer was now Carmen Esmeralda Pantaleón, not Elmer Belteton, the man Sue had said would handle the adoption. Again, the Emanuels paid no attention to the change in names. Betsy remembers Sue saying that the person listed on her power-of-attorney form had little to do with the "contact" that actually handled the child. Instead of replacing

Fernanda's picture on the fridge with Emily Belle's, Betsy moved both photos to her dresser.

What the Emanuels didn't know was that two weeks before, on November 28, 2006, the name of their new lawyer had appeared in *Siglo XXI* on a list of twenty-one adoption lawyers whose files were being investigated by the Ministerio Público. Josefina Arellano, the head of the PGN, said that some of the cases even contained forgeries of her own signature. Aside from Pantaleón, other CCI contacts on the list included Alfonso Close, Francisco García Gudiel, Alfonso Cacacho Ralda, and Luis Roberto Aragón Hernández. The Emanuels' new lawyer was under investigation for alleged kidnapping and falsifying documents. All of the lawyers were free to continue working despite the investigations.

Less than a week after accepting the referral to adopt Emily Belle, Sue called Betsy with heart-wrenching news. She'd found Jennifer.

The little girl, now nine, had turned up in a private girls' home called Fundaniñas in Guatemala City. Miraculously, the child had reappeared by pure chance. Sue told Betsy that she happened to have overheard a conversation in attorney Close's office that included Jennifer's name. She'd never heard of the orphanage Fundaniñas before, but she took it upon herself to go and visit to check up on Jennifer. The girl was doing fine. Sue told Betsy that Jennifer's mother had turned up dead in Mexico.

Sue reoffered Jennifer to the Emanuels for just $3,000, promising that all other fees would be forfeited. Sue said she planned to use an elderly lawyer named Felix who was retired and wouldn't charge as much as other lawyers for the adoption.

Hogar Nuestro Señora de la Asuncion, or Fundaniñas, was founded in 1989 by Isabella de Bosch, one of the wealthiest women in Guatemala, and was subsidized by donations from Rotary International. De Bosch's husband was the man behind the Pollo Campero fried chicken empire, the largest fast-food chain in Latin America. Fundaniñas housed and schooled girls aged three to eighteen. They were expected to go out into the world and become upstanding citizens, adding value to society despite their humble and often brutal beginnings.

In a 2010 meeting at the Fundaniñas office, in the most upscale section of Guatemala City, the organization's board of directors told me that each girl residing at the orphanage had been referred there directly from the Guatemalan court system. The Fundaniñas board, which consisted mainly of manicured women with heavy jewelry, insisted that Fundaniñas wasn't involved in adoption, though they did have a partnership with Buckner International, a Dallas, Texas–based evangelical ministry and international adoption agency dedicated to "helping orphans, at-risk children, and families."

To Betsy, the fact that Jennifer had been found was extraordinary. Sue had made good on her promise. Betsy's faith was buoyed. The orphanage where Jennifer now lived, Sue explained, would need some "convincing" to allow Jennifer's adoption to begin anew. They didn't do many adoptions.

Betsy cautiously asked for more details, and for a copy of the death certificate of Jennifer's mother. For the third time, the Emanuels reconsidered their adoption plan. First, it had been Jennifer. Then Fernanda. Then Emily Belle. And now both Jennifer and Emily Belle?

The thought of adding two more children to their large household was daunting, especially to Leslie. The Emanuels agreed they felt a responsibility to Jennifer and would help her however they could. Now nine years old, she was probably cognizant of her thwarted future with their family in the United States.

Following Sue's advice, Betsy began sending presents to Fundaniñas. Her mother helped her put together about $700 worth of toys and children's clothes — all new with tags, as Sue had ordered — as a "goodwill gesture". The presents were practical, including toothbrushes, bras, underwear, and pajamas in a range of sizes appropriate for thirty-three girls of various ages. Sue said she couldn't return to Fundaniñas empty-handed and that such tokens were expected. She instructed the Emanuels to send the boxes to CCI's Florida office, saying her husband, Dave, would hand-deliver them to Guatemala.

Thelma de Saravia, Fundaniñas's spokeswoman and treasurer, says they never received the gifts. She explains that Sue Hedberg approached Fundaniñas "as if she owned it. She just walked in through the gates without permission, without talking to anyone. She started taking pictures, asking the girls, 'Who wants to be adopted?'"

She goes on to say that Sue showed up unexpectedly one day with an unnamed American couple in tow, asking how much Fundaniñas charged for adoptions. "We said no, we don't use adoption lawyers, and we wouldn't charge if we did," says de Saravia. "We only use our lawyer. She asked our lawyer, 'Well, how much do *you* charge?'"

A few days after the Emanuels started trying to figure out if they could manage the adoptions of both Jennifer and Emily Belle, Sue told them that Jennifer's adoption would actually cost $17,000. She explained that she'd try to "play hard ball" with Fundaniñas in hopes of bringing the fees down to $12,000.

It was too much for the Emanuels. Betsy reminded Sue that she'd been quoted a different price for Jennifer. There was no way her family could afford Jennifer and the baby too. Sue told her that she wasn't being fair to Jennifer.

The words echoed in Betsy's conscience. She imagined Jennifer, alone and grieving over her mother's death, confused about the Americans who had said they loved her and then vanished. She thought of Fernanda's charming smile, wondering if she had a bed to sleep in and why her birth mother had suddenly wanted her back. Finally, her thoughts strayed to tiny Emily Belle, given up at birth and living with a foster family somewhere in Guatemala.

The more Betsy thought about the situation, the less things made sense. How could Sue have offered Jennifer at one price, then raised it? Could she believe anything Sue told her about the third referral, Emily Belle? And why was no one except her concerned about finding Fernanda? *The whole country of Guatemala isn't much bigger than Texas,* Betsy thought to herself. In reality, the small country was the size of Tennessee. *How hard can it be?*

During her next conversation with Sue, Betsy announced that she might as well go to Guatemala herself to search for Fernanda. Sue became agitated, insisting that it was too dangerous. Maybe in six months or so, Betsy remembers her saying, when things were calmer, it would be possible.

Furthermore, the agency director implied, she was starting to doubt the Emanuel family's will to adopt Emily Belle. If she did in fact decide that the Emanuels were no longer fit to adopt, then the baby would be placed with another family. Betsy understood that there would be no hope for another referral.

10. DEALING WITH THE DEVIL

December 2006–October 2007

Mildred returned to the police station often to check in with Officer Cujá, the round-faced, gold-toothed detective who'd helped orchestrate the November raids on Coni's houses. She believed that her daughters would be found, despite an apparent lack of progress with the investigation. She also visited the local branch of the Ministerio Público regularly, sometimes two or three times a week. That way, the investigators would understand how serious she was. Ariel Guevara, the investigator assigned to her case, seemed calm and focused.

Guevara crafted an order for the police to find Coni and Sabrina after Christmas, with the intent of obtaining depositions from both suspects. A judge had to approve the request before action could be taken to apprehend the two women. Because Mildred didn't know Coni's full name, one order was for the detention of "Cony and her children," and one was for Sabrina Donis. If the warrants were acted on, then copies of the suspects' cédulas would be obtained and their current addresses would be recorded.

Months passed after the orders were in place. Nothing seemed to happen. In February, Mildred got a job cleaning offices for a Nicaraguan man and used the earnings to finance her travel to and from the various government offices. By March, she was thoroughly frustrated. It had been six months since the girls were taken.

In a moment of desperation, Mildred even called her estranged parents. Her mother told her to give up, saying she was a fool for thinking she could get the children back. Her father was accusatory, saying she must have done something to deserve what happened.

She also went to the press, approaching Latitud, a television channel that aired national news broadcasts in the afternoon between soap operas. A reporter there interviewed her and three

147

other women, all of whom were trying to locate missing children. The resulting piece aired during a break from the popular soap opera *Prueba de Amor* (Test of Love). Mildred held up the only photograph she had of Fernanda. It showed the little girl standing in a bucket of water during a bath. A few days later, Mildred called Latitud and learned that a woman had phoned the station. The woman said her neighbor Coni Galindo was a good Christian incapable of stealing children. That week, the reporter who'd worked on the piece received a threatening phone call.

Mildred herself was still being threatened regularly. When the threats came, she panicked, powerless to stop her body from shaking. She would curl into a ball and remain beneath her bed sheets until the feelings of terror passed. She felt as if her bones were trembling uncontrollably, in the same way they had as a child, when the army and the guerrillas had opened fire on each other in her family's backyard.

One afternoon, an anonymous caller told Mildred that the Ministerio Público knew where her children were. It was a terrifying but plausible concept. Mildred went to Ariel Guevara's office to confront him. She glared into his surprised face. He, too, was short and dark-skinned. They stood almost eye-to-eye.

"What is going on?" she demanded. The words poured out. "Either you help me, or I'll go somewhere else! Are you getting money to stay quiet?"

He looked at her oddly. "No," he answered. He seemed scared. Slowly, Mildred realized he was offended. "I'm a father myself. I'm trying to help you."

"Sorry," she continued. Tears began streaming down her face. "You should know how I'm suffering. I'm going through a lot." Before Guevara could speak, she backed out of the room. She didn't want to hear any excuses.

At home later that day, Mildred reflected on the conversation and felt foolish. Her outburst seemed absurd. She didn't have enough money to return to Guevara's office to apologize until three days later. "I'm so sorry," she told him, her eyes trained on the ground. "I've never done anything like that before. I still want you to help me." He was gracious and told her he understood. From then on, he called Mildred every so often to check in.

She continued pressing forward, visiting every person she could think of. On March 20, 2007, she went to the PGN in Guatemala City and filed a formal denouncement of the kidnappings of Fernanda and Ana Cristina. If the children were in adoption processes, the PGN would probably have records.

Victor Hugo Mejicanos, chief of the PGN's *denuncia* (complaint) unit, typed up the complaint. "Stop it, stop crying," he told Mildred. She'd sat in his beige office and sobbed all the way through her testimony. "I'll help you," he said. "Just tell me the full story."

Mejicanos, a small man with restless eyes, worked as a private lawyer in addition to his government job. His bookshelves were adorned with hundreds of tiny elephant figurines, presents from appreciative clients. They represented loyalty, the quality he admired most. His favorite elephant, a small animal with a brown cat hair pelt, had come from Mexico. Mejicanos habitually did pro bono legal work in exchange for future favors. When he needed a quick raid, say, on a brothel, he boasted that he was able to call on loyal police officers that wouldn't extort or tip off the brothel owners beforehand.

He told Mildred that he believed she'd been genuinely fooled, and instructed her to keep coming back for help. Mejicanos promised he'd do anything he could to help find the children, and he gave Mildred his special cell phone number. He kept one line exclusively for favors and charity. Mildred didn't know that he'd made the same promise before to other poor mothers who'd come into his office begging for help in finding lost children.

Mildred asked how she could repay him for his kindness. He mentioned that he could use someone to clean his office, and she began scrubbing his floors at night.

Still, nothing happened. Mildred fell into a normal routine three times a week: traveling to the PGN in Guatemala City, stopping to visit the Ministerio Público in Villa Canales on the way home to Villa Nueva. She didn't like calling to check in, preferring to look people in the eye. Sometimes she leafed through photos of children being adopted at the PGN, but she did so half-heartedly. Something in her gut told her that the girls weren't going to turn up at the PGN.

All of the officials said they were continuing to look into the case. In January, the police detectives unsuccessfully searched a house in Guatemala City for the girls. Because of the complaint Mildred had filed at the PGN with Mejicanos, a Guatemala City minors court judge, Judge Ricardo Gómez Damman, was now involved. He'd reordered the police detectives and the national police to find the children. None of them had. In late March, Judge Gómez issued orders to immigration that banned Fernanda and Ana Cristina from leaving the country. In April, the Ministerio Público obtained a copy of Sabrina's national ID card. The Ministerio Público issued orders for Coni and Sabrina to be arrested and formally charged with kidnapping. Neither suspect was captured. As summer crept closer and the one-year anniversary of Fernanda's abduction approached, little progress seemed to have been made.

Betsy found Rachel Robinson's blog by accident. She'd been perusing fellow CCI clients' blogs, trying to learn what others were experiencing. After reading it, she instantly knew something was wrong. At first, Rachel detailed adoption proceedings for two Guatemalan children, an infant boy, Luis, and a four-year-old girl, Valentina. Then Valentina stopped being mentioned.

That day, Betsy sent a vague note to Rachel, asking how her adoption was going. Rachel responded that night, asking Betsy if she was using CCI and signing her email "Hugs!" The warm gesture was enough for Betsy to pour her heart out in a long reply, summarizing the last fifteen months of adoption difficulties. "I just wondered if you might share with me what happened, *if* anything did happen with Valentina," she asked Rachel. "I just need to keep up with what is going on so I can know how to deal with Sue and CCI. . . . If I am intruding, please forgive me. "

Rachel answered quickly. The adoption facilitator handling the adoption of both Luis and Valentina was none other than Marvin Bran. A few hours later, the women were on the phone comparing notes. After successfully adopting from China, Rachel and her husband, Steve, had begun trying to adopt Valentina in August 2006. They started adopting infant Luis a month later. She'd been told that both children were under the care of Marvin Bran's sister, Kimberly, in their mother Coni's home.

The Robinsons traveled to Guatemala with their toddler daughter to meet their future children in November 2006. They rented an apartment in Antigua, a picturesque city just outside the capital that was a popular tourist destination, planning to stay until the adoptions were finished. The couple paid CCI about $45,000 up front.

When Valentina was dropped off at the Robinsons' apartment in Antigua, they noticed that the four-year-old's stomach was pocked with what looked like scars from cigarette burns. Her body was bruised. She was prone to fits of rage, and her violent episodes were so bad that the Robinsons worried for the safety of their own young daughter.

The day baby Luis was supposed to be dropped off, he never arrived. Rachel said she called Sue in Florida, worried, and that the agency said she didn't know what had happened. A little while later, an unknown person with a Spanish accent phoned Rachel, explaining that Luis was sick. The person said the child had been taken to the doctor. The next day, Rachel says she learned that the baby was in intensive care. She didn't know where, or what his prognosis was. Sue told her that he might die.

A week later, Luis arrived. He'd apparently suffered dehydration from a case of rotavirus. His cuidadora told Rachel that she'd return to pick the child up for a family court hearing in a week. Sue told Rachel not to believe anything the foster mother said. During a phone conference with both Rachel and Sue on the line, Marvin Bran said he agreed that the foster mother was lying. Rachel didn't know what to believe about anything in the adoption.

During her time in Antigua, Rachel befriended other CCI families who were also temporarily living with children they hoped to adopt. Many had endured adoption complications and no longer trusted what they were being told by Sue. Each hired the same private firm, Adoption Supervisors Guatemala (ASG), which would "check" on adoptions and provide updates. Because many adoptive families signed contracts forbidding them to contact anyone in Guatemala without their agency's permission, ASG usually rendered its services secretly. Marco Tulio Mérida Cifuentes, a well-connected Guatemalan lawyer who spoke perfect English, was known to be the man behind ASG. Typically, his company charged $3,500 to report on a single case. The Robinsons hired him immediately.

Mérida told them that Valentina's documents appeared to have been forged and that baby Luis didn't have any paperwork at all in any of the courts. Rachel called Sue to ask if there might have been a mistake, explaining she'd learned that the child hadn't been through court yet.

Sue seemed agitated. "Why do you need to know the family court case number?" Rachel remembers her asking. "You aren't entitled to it. You need to stop nosing into things. This is why we don't like families to foster — it always causes problems. You need to stop and desist!" When Rachel asked why the baby's social work report hadn't been written yet, Sue said it was probably because Marvin Bran hadn't paid off the social worker.

Valentina's violent rages continued. The housekeeper tending to the Robinsons' apartment explained, in broken English, that the girl said she'd been stolen from her mother. Frightened, the Robinsons thought about calling Sue yet again. They decided against it. Instead, they hired a local child psychologist in Antigua to evaluate the four-year-old. After a few hours, the psychologist determined that the child had been sexually abused and was emotionally disturbed and cognitively impaired. Worse, the doctor believed the little girl's account of having been forcibly taken from her mother.

The Robinsons were still afraid to call Sue, who'd told them that Valentina was a healthy orphan. Rachel worried that Sue would tell Marvin Bran about the abuse and that he might punish Valentina. ASG's Mérida told Rachel that the little girl's adoption file had been rejected by the PGN because of seven different *previos,* and that Luis's adoption still hadn't gotten pre-approval from the U.S. Embassy.

Ultimately, Rachel told Sue about the doctor she'd hired to examine Valentina. Sue didn't believe the abuse allegations. "Kids lie all the time," she told Rachel. "One girl told me that the President of Guatemala had raped her. *That* wasn't true."

Another family who was said to have adopted Valentina's biological brother contacted Rachel after getting her contact information from Sue. The other woman mentioned that Valentina's biological mother was alive. The social work report that had been shown to Rachel claimed she was dead.

Convinced they were involved in a fraudulent process, the Robinsons halted Valentina's adoption. Sue allegedly refused to refund any money to them, saying she'd already paid her contacts in Guatemala. The Robinsons continued with Luis's adoption.

A month later, in February 2006, Rachel called the PGN to see if Luis's case had been submitted for review. It hadn't, although Sue said it had been submitted months before. When Rachel confronted her about the misinformation, Sue insisted that the PGN "lies all the time" and accused Rachel of not trusting God with her adoption. As a Christian, Sue said, she was troubled. Two weeks later, the Robinsons were told they needed to undergo psychiatric evaluations in order to proceed with Luis's adoption.

Betsy felt sick listening to Rachel's bizarre story. It sounded like something out of a movie. If Valentina had been abused while under Marvin Bran's care, what might have happened to Fernanda? She wondered if she'd been lied to about Jennifer and Fundaniñas. With what Rachel had gone through, anything seemed possible.

"My head has just been spinning all day," she wrote to her new friend the day after their conversation. "It's like you know something bad, but you just ignore it and try not to believe it . . . and then . . . you just finally know that you have to face it and deal with it."

The Emanuels became two of the hundreds of Americans who hired attorney Marco Tulio Mérida Cifuentes and Adoption Supervisors Guatemala. He knew the adoption business inside and out.

Mérida's expertise came from experience. Before he "supervised" cases, he worked on the other side of the industry, facilitating adoptions for American adoption agencies. "I think Marco is one of the smartest lawyers," said Shyrel Osborn, co-director of the Amor del Niño nursery in Guatemala. "It was like he could see into the future and switched sides from adoption provider to the adoption-mess-cleanup attorney."

To information-starved adoptive parents, Mérida's reputation was stellar. He returned emails and phone calls promptly, unlike some American adoption agencies. ASG's business was bolstered by regular mentions and English-language advertisements on the popular website GuatAdopt.com. Mérida offered his services pro bono to the site. ASG's services ranged from simple document translation to "help" with DNA tests. The company also offered "counseling" to other lawyers involved in complicated cases, with the goal of achieving case "completion."

Online, ASG didn't specify how it obtained information. Clients say that Mérida, who was commonly known as "Marco Tulio," and his partner, Luis Roberto Aragón Solé, visited courts, government offices, and adoption contacts to collect data. Many prospective adoptive parents were told that simple negligence on the part of a lawyer or agency, such as a file being left on a desk for weeks, delayed their adoptions. Mérida didn't like to use email to discuss business; instead, he encouraged clients to communicate by phone. He didn't like leaving trails.

Mérida and Aragón ran another company called Bio Family Trace, which shared ASG's office and phone numbers. Bio Family Trace engaged in similar work for the same American clientele, locating birth parents for a fee after the completion of an adoption. The two men also worked at a larger law firm in Guatemala City called Desprosa, whose mission statement said that God was at "the center of our business activities."

When Betsy called Mérida, he listened attentively, saying he was familiar with CCI. For $3,500, he checked the status of Emily Belle's adoption. Her file had been "misplaced" at the PGN, he said. Matters were further complicated by the fact that the baby's mother was from El Salvador. Mérida promised to straighten out any confusion over the baby's nationality with the proper authorities. He confirmed that Jennifer was indeed living at Fundaniñas, the private girls' home in Guatemala City. But when it came to Fernanda, he balked, telling Betsy that the case was too risky to handle. He refused to accept additional payment to investigate the child's situation. It might damage his reputation, he said. Dangerous people were involved, and if he investigated, his own family might be at risk for retaliation. He was afraid of the "bad" people who worked in adoption, he said.

Nevertheless, Mérida told Betsy, he'd pulled a few strings at family court. He told her that three different adoption cases existed in relation to the child, all stamped with the name Maria Fernanda Alvarado. Each contained a photograph of a different child, with different birth dates. It appeared that Fernanda's identity was being used for the adoptions of three unique children.

Mérida offered nothing more. He seemed to be a careful, intelligent man. If anyone could have found Fernanda, Betsy thought, it would have been him.

A secret email listserve of dissatisfied CCI clients sprang to life. Rachel invited Betsy to join in May 2007. The list was private, with an initial membership of just five women. It was titled with the acronym "DWTD," for "Dealing with the Devil."

On the list, Sue was openly referred to as "a weenie" or "the Turd." The women vented to each other about their situations, sharing and then poring over each other's case details. They felt powerless to protect the children they were adopting, or even to understand what was happening in the process. The resulting anger and disempowerment leaked out in the form of sharp sarcasm and dedicated detective work. The women collected and shared information about CCI "contacts," gleaned from blogs, adoption forums, and conversations with other CCI clients. The solidarity was emboldening, to an extent. Each list member still had the ultimate goal of successfully adopting through CCI, and each was afraid to voice concerns or questions to Sue. No one wanted to anger her or risk the chance of losing a referral. Each of the five women had retained the services of Adoption Supervisors Guatemala.

There didn't seem to be any good reason that one family could adopt a child in four months and another took more than eighteen, when both were using the same Guatemalan contacts. The women were infuriated. Once in a while, exasperation led to otherwise unthinkable ideas. Janey Brooks mentioned she'd heard about a certain attorney who offered expedited case processing through the PGN for $1,500.

"Hey, it's worth more than $1,500 to find out *who* to write the $1,500 check to," Rachel Robinson replied. "I don't know, though; I tried to wire Marco (Mérida) thousands to use as a bribe, and he swore it didn't work that way. I hated to think of myself doing such a thing — but desperate times call for desperate measures. . . ."

In May, the Robinson's adoption of baby Luis wrapped up. They flew to Guatemala to pick him up. Rachel promised Betsy she'd ask Marvin Bran about Fernanda. On May 15, 2007, Marvin and his mother Coni met the Robinsons in the lobby of the Guatemala City Crown Plaza hotel to talk about the adoption. Marvin Bran was clean-cut, with immaculately pressed clothes. He wore heavy cologne, and his dark hair was cut short, military-style.

Rachel mentioned Betsy's concern about his alleged beating. Marvin raised an eyebrow. He'd never been tied up, the young man said, or pistol-whipped. Neither had his mother. Coni said nothing, looking grim.

Rachel searched his dark eyes and believed him. Marvin explained that Sue Hedberg had told him the Emanuel family had changed their minds about adopting Fernanda, that they didn't want her. Fernanda's mother tried to take her children back, Marvin said, and then tried to extort money from him. He told Rachel he'd left the small sisters at Luz y Esperanza, a nursery in Zone 4 of Guatemala City.

He went on to angrily call Sue a liar, saying that she stole from people "all the time" and that she owed him money, including $10,000 for baby Luis. "We can't give him to you until the debt is collected," Coni explained to Rachel, as a tear rolled down the older woman's cheek. The Robinsons phoned Sue immediately. "I'm having a financial dispute with Marvin," Sue said. Apparently, Marvin owed her money from another adoption case, and that by not paying for Luis, things evened out. She told Rachel again to stop being nosy and that she'd settle things with Marvin.

Before they parted ways, Marvin asked Rachel to deliver a message to the Emanuel family. If they were still interested, he said, he could help them adopt Fernanda in an independent process. It would be directly through him, and Sue would be effectively cut out of the picture.

Rachel raced to phone the Emanuels. Betsy listened attentively, struggling to make sense of the new version of events. The last remnants of her faith in Sue Hedberg and Celebrate Children International were shattered.

When Mildred approached the Office of the Human Rights Ombudsman in Guatemala City for help, the man she spoke to eyed her skeptically. "It would be a lot easier to find your kids if you just admitted you sold them for adoption," he told her coolly.

She grimly shook her head. She'd almost come to expect such accusations when talking to authorities for the first time. "If I sold them, why would I be sitting here?" she asked him, a note of sadness in her voice. Nine months had passed. "If I sold them, I'd know who I sold them to! I'd go get them!"

He suggested that she turn to Fundación Sobrevivientes (Survivors' Foundation), a women's rights organization that helped women who'd lost children to adoption. Mildred had never heard of them.

The day after her visit to the ombudsman, Rony's stepmother, Lily, showed up at the Chinese restaurant where Mildred's sister Patricia worked. She told Patricia to have her sister call immediately. It was urgent. Mildred called the police to let them know, and an officer was sent to sit beside her and listen while she called Lily back.

"Why are you being so stubborn?" Lily demanded. She knew that Mildred had visited the office of the Human Rights Ombudsman. "We will take the girls to Tecún Umán[16] if you won't cooperate. Take 5000 quetzales. If you don't, we will kill you."

"I don't care," Mildred answered. The police officer had affixed a recording device to her phone and was supposed to be taping the conversation. "I would give my life for my daughters. I want them back."

"Then it's settled," Lily replied. "You've signed your babies' death sentence."

It was the last time Mildred was threatened by phone. The repeated warnings had started to lose their power, and she no longer trembled when they came. The frequency of the threats had also lessened. Mildred didn't know what happened to the police recording of the conversation, or if it had really been taped at all. She assumed the police filed it away.

[16.] Tecún Umán is a town on the northern Guatemalan border, next to Mexico.

In the meantime, her criminal complaint was being passed from court to court. On May 11, a judge from the Twelfth Penal Court of Guatemala City looked over the complaint and decided it fell under the jurisdiction of the court system of Mixco, where Mildred, Coni, and Sabrina all resided, not that of Guatemala City. The case was sent to Mixco's Second Penal Court. But once it arrived, the Mixco court refused to accept the case. Their branch was closing and wasn't taking on any new cases. As with most jurisdictional conflicts, a decision would be made by the Camera Penal Court, part of Guatemala's Supreme Court. On July 22, 2007, the higher court ruled that Guatemala City would handle the criminal proceedings against Coni and Sabrina.

Now two judges, four courts, the Villa Canales police detectives, the national police, the PGN, the Villa Canales branch of the Ministerio Público, the Human Rights Ombudsman, and the press all knew about Mildred's situation.

During one of her many routine visits to check in about the investigation, Mildred asked police detective Carlos Cujá about Fundacíon Sobrevivientes, the nonprofit mentioned by the Guatemala City Human Rights Ombudsman. Cujá hadn't heard of them, but Mildred decided to visit the organization anyway.

August 2007 was a turbulent month for Guatemalan adoptions. First, the U.S. State Department instituted a new rule for all Guatemalan children in adoption processes: Now, instead of a single DNA test, two would be required. In an August 6 press release, the U.S. Embassy stated vaguely that "due to concerns . . . the United States government must apply an extraordinary level of scrutiny to adoption cases." It was thought that two DNA tests, one at the start of the process and one at the end, would prevent baby-switching and relinquishments of children by women posing as their mothers.

Months before, on March 13, 2007, the U.S. Department of State had noted, "Although we understand many U.S. families have adopted children from Guatemala in the past, we cannot recommend adoption from Guatemala at this time." Guatemala finally seemed posed to ratify the Hague Convention. Nevertheless, many

U.S. adoption agencies, including Celebrate Children International, continued providing new adoption referrals.

Then, on August 11, 2007, Casa Quivira was raided. Guatemalan authorities combed through the private nursery run by Florida native Clifford Phillips and his Guatemalan wife, adoption lawyer Sandra González. The hogar was being investigated by the Ministerio Público for various signs of fraud, such as forged documents. González and another attorney, Vilma Desire Zamoya, were arrested. The police removed 46 babies and children, placing them in other nurseries for care while their IDs and adoption paperwork were reviewed. All were under the age of three. The story garnered international media attention.

Sue Hedberg sent an email to clients on August 13 saying she wasn't familiar with Casa Quivira, but she knew enough to be opposed to what she said they stood for: adoptions to gay couples. Sue told clients that what they might be reading in the newspapers wasn't accurate and that the raid was a "political move, an anti-adoption move." She said the Casa Quivira children hadn't been stolen; instead, they had been voluntarily relinquished, "just like all your children have been!"

A crush of posts from worried adoptive parents appeared on GuatAdopt.com. "It is really shocking to see this responsible, well-run institution represented so wrongly," posted Elissa Kent, who said she'd recently adopted from Casa Quivira. Others questioned why the nursery had been raided at all, choosing to believe that the investigation was politically motivated. Hannah Wallace, an agency director who served on the JCICS Guatemala caucus, called the raid "an outrageous abuse of power" that was "part of the ongoing attempt to discredit adoptions" in general.

Within a few weeks, an American lobbying effort took off. GuatAdopt.com site moderator Kevin Kreutner posted on behalf of Casa Quivira's in-process families, encouraging phone calls, letters, and emails to elected officials with the goal of pressuring the U.S. government to in turn pressure the Guatemalan government to allow adoptions of Casa Quivira children to move forward. The babies should come to the U.S., the lobbying position implied, despite pending questions about their histories.

Kreutner posted a sample message for people to download, personalize, and send. "On the night of August 23, in the pouring rain, all remaining babies were loaded into two vans and driven to undisclosed locations by armed authorities. . . ." it said. "The basic human rights of these babies are being violated. . . . We are writing you because we know that Guatemala is a strategic partner to the U.S. and we give millions of taxpayers' dollars in aid to Guatemala. Therefore our government should be able to make requests on the behalf of its citizens and on behalf of the welfare of the 42 remaining children caught in this political mess."

The message was met with appreciation and energy from the adoption community. "Let's go, people, fire up those faxes," Melissa T. posted. "There are over 4,000 of us in process. . . . Don't wait until it's your child or mine that is missing or stuck in the system. . . ."

Lobbying targets included the Department of State Office of Children's Issues; John Lowell, consul general at the U.S. Embassy in Guatemala; eight senators and fourteen members of Congress who sat on the subcommittee funding Guatemala-related programs; and senators including Sam Brownback of Kansas and Tim Johnson of South Dakota, both of whom were adoptive parents themselves. The Congressional Coalition on Adoption Institute, a pro-adoption organization, also took up the Casa Quivira battle. With the help of JCICS, they drafted a letter and obtained signatures from 28 members of Congress, then overnighted it to Óscar Berger, the President of Guatemala.

The mounting pressure from the Americans couldn't, however, change the sad truth of the situation. After a month of investigation, the Ministerio Público and the PGN found that half of the women who'd given babies to Casa Quivira couldn't be found. It was nearly impossible to ascertain where the children really came from, and nine babies appeared to have forged names and details. One had been given the identity of a stillborn baby who'd been born 22 years previously.

On August 1, 2007, adoption facilitator Carla Gabriela Girón Rosales, known as Carla Girón, presented a formal request to Judge Mario Fernando Peralta. Her request was made in defense of the rights of two children, the sisters Maria Fernanda and Ana Cristina Alvarado. Judge Peralta's courtroom was in the heart of Escuintla, a bustling urban area about two hours outside of Guatemala City. He presided over the Juzgado de la Niñez y de Adolescencia y Adolescentes en Conflicto con la Ley Penal, a court that handled issues pertaining to children and teens. He was well known to Ministerio Público investigators in the capital, who referred to him, jokingly, as "Danny DeVito." The pudgy, talkative judge bore a striking resemblance to the American actor. He was long-winded, animated, and suspected of accepting bribes to declare "abandoned" children to be orphans.

Judge Peralta was known for giving rapid declarations of abandonment for children brought before him. The Ministerio Público was building a case to try to strip the judge of his impunity so that they could prosecute him for more than forty cases of authorizing adoptions based on fraudulent documentation. In abandonment proceedings, Judge Peralta would decide where the child in question would live and receive temporary care. He allegedly favored a few particular nurseries: attorney Feliciano Carillo Gudiel's Hogar Nuevo Amanecer, attorney Barbara Cofiño Vides's Hogar Luz de Fátima, facilitator Guillermo Bosque's Hogar Nuevo Mundo, and attorney Susana Luarca's Asociación Primavera. The Ministerio Público had since 1996 investigated each of these nurseries at least once for allegations related to adoption fraud. Judge Peralta also regularly sent abandoned children to Hogar Luz de María, run by two sisters, Claudia Briola Palacios and Dinora González Palacios.

Carla Girón was an adoption facilitator. She'd gotten her start in the business by working with her stepmother, Miriam Elena Monterroso Bonilla, a well-known lawyer who'd placed hundreds of children over ten years. The two had a tumultuous relationship but had worked together until Carla branched out on her own, allegedly taking some of her stepmother's business contacts and clients with her. She became successful, building connections with multiple American adoption agencies, including A Field of Dreams, Adopt International, Adoption Blessings Worldwide, Adopt an Angel. Carla still used her stepmother's contacts, she said in an email to one American adoptive parent, including one person who worked inside the *Registro Nacional de las Personas* (Guatemala's central registry of persons, also known as RENAP) and accepted bribes of 2,500 quetzales ($320) for issuing a birth certificate in ten days.

The Alvarado sisters had been relinquished for adoption, Girón stated, but now their mother, Mildred, had disappeared. Carla needed to have the girls declared abandoned so that their adoptions could move forward. The documents she presented stated that Mildred had willingly given her children up about seven months previously, on December 12, 2006. Attached to the petition for abandonment were six notarized documents — three concerning Fernanda and three concerning Ana Cristina.

Each set of docouments said the same thing: Mildred had given permission for the girls to live with Girón in Retalhuleu, a rural region near the southwestern coast of Guatemala. Additionally, the request explained, it had already been proven that Mildred was the mother of Fernanda and Ana Cristina; a DNA test had been administered at one of the three U.S. Embassy–approved DNA labs. The results showed a 99 percent match.

An attorney who often did favors for Girón had notarized the documents. His name was Amadeo de Jesús Guerra Chacón, and he lived a few blocks away from Marvin and Coni Bran in San José las Rosas. "I make the irrevocable decision," the testimony read, "for my daughter to be adopted and emigrated to the U.S. by Timothy Dale Stark and Dawn Marie Stark."

Timothy and Dawn Stark, two pastors from Illinois, had no idea their names were on the Alvarado sisters' paperwork. Two months before, they'd begun trying to adopt a little boy with the adoption agency Adoption Blessings Worldwide. The adoption facilitator on the case was Carla Girón. The Starks had never heard of Fernanda or Ana Cristina Alvarado.

Judge Peralta didn't feel responsible for determining things like whether or not the information in adoption paperwork was authentic. The judge was a longtime proponent of international adoption. He took pride in seeing Guatemalan children leave the country for the United States, where eager families awaited them. The documents Girón presented to him were politely worded, a standard request for judicial assistance on behalf of the children. They also noted that Girón wanted to remain involved in the case. Judge Peralta saw no reason to deny her request. There was no explanation of how or why she had become involved with the children.

Following protocol, he arranged for an abandonment hearing to be held so that anyone interested in the girls could come forward and declare their intent. A court date was set for a little more than a month later, on September 6, 2007.

After the Camera Penal court decided that Mildred's criminal complaint should be handled in Guatemala City, the next steps happened quickly. Arrest warrants for both Sabrina, whose full name was Mirla Sabrina Donis Hernández, and Coni, identified as Lilia Consuelo Galindo Ovalle de Bran, were approved on September 4, 2007. The charge was aggravated kidnapping. Although Ministerio Público officials had first requested the warrants five months earlier, the process had stalled while the courts bickered over jurisdiction. Judge Gómez in Guatemala City, who was presiding over the case, ordered the police to hand over all of their casework to Ariel Guevara, the Ministerio Público investigator Mildred had scolded.

Both Sabrina and Coni were arrested on October 10 and brou-ght to the precinct to give statements. The two women said they didn't know each other, though they hired the same defense attor-ney, Elfego Orozco. Orozco, an acquaintance of Coni's son, Marvin Bran, had a bleached mustache and wore heavy gold jewelry. He regularly used Marvin's office to make photocopies. Both women denied having any role in the kidnapping of the Alvarado sisters. Each said she had no idea who Mildred Alvarado was or why they were being accused. Orozco arranged bail for both women, and they were set free.

On October 12, 2007, the criminal charges against Coni were updated. The organized crime unit of the Ministerio Público decided to tack on two additional charges: Instead of being charged with aggravated kidnapping alone, Coni now was also facing human traf-ficking and conspiracy charges. The older woman and her lawyer voluntarily appeared at the Ministerio Público on October 25 to give a revised statement. "What's being done to me is a crime," Coni said. "I demand that Ministerio Público investigate. . . . Let her [Mildred] go to jail and pay for the damage she's done to me physically, morally, and psychologically."

She also mentioned, vaguely, that her son had paid "some people" to look around, and they'd found out that the children were being handled by "an Escuintla court." Her lawyer, Orozco, elaborated on her statement, saying in an official deposition that the children his client was accused of kidnapping were actually involved in two ongoing cases that were being handled by two separate Guatemalan courts: the Third Court of Youth and Children in Guatemala City and the Escuintla Court of Youth and Children. According to Orozco, two separate adoption processes had been opened for each of the Alvarado sisters: two using Fernanda's identity and two using Ana Cristina's. He even offered two case numbers: "182 or 184" in Escuintla, and 600-64-2007 in Mixco.

11. FUNDACIÓN SOBREVIVIENTES

November 2007

Norma Cruz sits behind her desk at the offices of Fundación Sobrevivientes in Guatemala City, January 2009.

A female security guard eyed Mildred through the iron bars protecting the doorway of Fundación Sobrevivientes, a shotgun slung loosely over one of her shoulders. The building's exterior had no discernable signage and looked like any other residence on the block, with heavy bars covering all of the windows. The Fundación was in Zone 1 of Guatemala City, the oldest section of the capital, known for housing the National Palace and the Mercado Central. The guard unlocked two deadbolts and let Mildred inside.

The front door opened directly onto a reception area, an airy room with walls painted the forcedly cheerful shade of egg yolks. A little table that held a pot of hot coffee and a stack of Styrofoam cups was set up to the left. Mildred entered and waited about twenty minutes before Norma Cruz, the nonprofit's director and founder, ushered her in.

Norma looked to be about 40. She was tiny, just slightly taller than Mildred, and thin. Her black eyes shone brightly behind a pair of glasses perched on the end of her nose. She wore pants, and a shawl was draped gracefully across her shoulders. In the hall outside Norma's office, a six-foot-high tapestry of the Virgin of Guadalupe hung above a small, candlelit shrine. Fresh rose petals were strewn across the altar. Inside, Norma's office was decorated in scattershot fashion with dried roses and framed photographs showing the smiling faces of various women. All were clients of Sobrevivientes. Most were dead.

In 2003, Sobrevivientes was legally recognized as a nonprofit, dedicated to helping female victims of violence in Guatemala. In 2007 alone, according to a U.S. Embassy memo summarizing the foundation's work, Sobrevivientes attended to more than 6,000 victims and their family members. They had also driven investigations that had led to the prosecution and conviction of 30 indivuduals for murder.

The foundation was started after Norma made a terrible personal discovery in 2001. Her daughter, Claudia Marie Hernández, confided to her that Arnoldo Noriega, Claudia's stepfather and Norma's husband, had molested her. Noriega was a powerful leader in Guatemala's Guerrilla Army of the Poor, a rebel movement that had merged with the Guatemalan National Revolutionary Unity Party at the end of the war.

Norma separated from Noriega and brought the issue before movement leaders. She'd joined the rebel army as a teenager in the 1970s, a few years before giving birth, at nineteen, to Claudia. A beloved uncle, a farmer who was a Social Democrat, had been a great influence on Norma, heavily informing her politics. He spoke of the possibilities offered by social equality and land reform. During the war, Norma says, he was mistakenly accused of being a communist by the Guatemalan Army and was shot inside his home. Other members of her family disappeared during wartime. She initially turned to the church for solace and strength and worked as a missionary in the rural region of Alta Verapaz. Norma returned to Guatemala City, questioning her own ability to effect positive social change through a life committed to religion. *I am not going to change the reality of this country by being a nun,* she realized.

And so she took up arms with the Guerrilla Army of the Poor. She learned to handle a gun, fought in combat, and embraced the cause with her entire heart. She was widowed in her early 20s, when her daughter Claudia was still young. A natural leader, Norma was sentenced to five years in exile in Nicaragua because of clandestine activities during the war. Still, through the rebel movement's various schisms and changes of leadership, she remained staunchly dedicated.

In 1987, she returned to Guatemala and became a founding member of the Office of Multiple Services of the Religious Conference of Guatemala, a group that attended to victims of violence during the war. Norma later became director of the Association for Education and Development, which worked to create programs for internally displaced people, and in 1994 founded the House of Services for Agrarian Land Rights to help resolve land disputes. She remained executive director of the organization until 2002, the year her daughter revealed the sexual abuse.

When Norma first brought the charges of molestation to the guerrilla leaders, they asked her not to press formal charges against her husband, fearing political fallout. The cause could be damaged if she went public, they told her. "I come here as a mother!" she replied, shocked. "Not as a member, not as a comrade." To her, the movement leaders seemed more concerned with their image than with justice and accountability. It was a striking contrast to the values she had devoted her life to fighting for.

Disillusioned, Norma came to a difficult conclusion. *Right or left, rich or poor, it's the same for all women. Women always get the short end of the stick.*

She defied the rebel leaders' request and filed criminal charges against Noriega. He was sentenced to jail. During the court proceedings, Norma and her daughter, then seventeen, met a young boy at the courthouse who told them he'd been sodomized by an adult man. Nothing in the Guatemalan penal code referenced man-on-man rape, and the perpetrator therefore faced little in the way of punishment. Claudia was troubled by the glaring injustice. "What can we do to help?" she asked her mother.

"We'll have to change the law," Norma answered without hesitation. The next week, mother and daughter began studying, scouring legal books and learning how to act as lawyers. They pressed for reform, and to their own surprise, were victorious. The penal code was updated.

It was the beginning of Fundación Sobrevivientes. Norma channeled all of her energy into the new organization, which was dedicated to upholding women's rights. The nonprofit set up a wide range of services, focusing primarily on pro bono legal aid and psychological counseling for women victimized by acts of violence. It maintained a maximum-security shelter, with armed security guards and surveillance cameras in an undisclosed location, that could house up to 25 women. A large part of the foundation's work was providing support for those brave enough to take action in the Guatemalan courts in an attempt to bring perpetrators to justice. With each successive campaign, Norma's reputation grew. Soon people began to mistake her for a lawyer, though she'd never been to college and had dropped out of high school. Sobrevivientes became the only private nongovernmental organization in Guatemala specifically dedicated to defending women's rights. Donations came in from the international human rights community, the Guatemalan government, private individuals, and nonprofits like the Global Fund for Women, a key early donor. By 2006, the total operating budget for Fundación Sobrevivientes was about $254,000.

The foundation became known for supporting victims' families after their wives, sisters, and daughters had been assassinated. The national murder rate of women more than tripled between 2000 and 2007. Female corpses frequently showed signs of sexual abuse or mutilation. Sometimes, garbage bags full of dismembered body parts would be found. Local activists began using the word "femicide" to describe the situation. By 2007, Sobrevivientes had a staff of about 35, including six lawyers, four psychologists, one social worker, and additional security and administrative personnel.

In 2006, Sobrevivientes began handling a new kind of case. Women who had lost children, through either fraud or outright kidnapping, began approaching the foundation for help. Many had already tried filing complaints with government institutions, only to see no results. Norma hesitated, unsure if helping mothers find their missing children fell within the general framework of the foundati-on's mission. Yet after conversations with her staff, she determined that depriving a woman of the right to raise her child was indeed a form of violence and oppression.

The foundation made a commitment to help the searching mothers, and the Sobrevivientes legal team began analyzing existing Guatemalan legislation on human trafficking and adoption. Given the lack of safeguards, it seemed remarkably easy to launder children. Manufacturing an "orphan" was both simple and highly profitable. There was a clear need to protect Guatemalan children from the "adoptionists" and their networks.

The first time a victimized woman approached the foundation, Norma commended her for her bravery and assured her that it was imperative to battle against legal impunity. The simple act of visiting the Sobrevivientes office was courageous. Many of those who dared to speak out faced retaliation. One victim's family was killed after she accused her rapist. Norma herself had a 24-hour security detail. Her life had been saved more than once by the quick thinking and intervention of her dedicated driver and bodyguards. Her family had also been targeted. In 2008, international human rights groups like Amnesty International began holding letter-writing campaigns on behalf of Norma and the foundation in an attempt to publicize the threats.

Human rights work is a high-risk undertaking in Guatemala. According to the UN High Commissioner for Human Rights, human rights activists and organizations there were attacked 278 times in 2006 alone. The Guatemalan organization La Unidad de Protección a Defensoras y Defensores de Derechos Humanos (the Unit of Protection Defenders of Human Rights, or UDESGUA), which monitored the safety of human rights groups, tallied 2,028 attacks between 2000 and 2010. According to UDESGUA's 2010 report, Sobrevivientes was the most threatened human rights orga-nization, with 96 registered threats of violence. Many were made via text message to Norma Cruz's cell phone, warning of beheadings and dropping personal information like the plate number and location of her car. The runner-up was the Amatitlán branch of the National Union of Guatemalan Health Workers, which reported 17 threats.

"I have no fear about dying," Norma once told a local reporter after she received an especially gruesome death threat. "In the end, one has to die. What I am afraid of is the Guatemala that does not change."

It was mid-November 2007 when Mildred Alvarado sat down in Norma's office and stared silently at her, unsure of where to begin. A cluttered desk stood between them. "Tell me," Norma told her quietly, leaning forward. "Tell me what happened to you."

Her words made Mildred feel big. She'd been greeted with a hug, and Norma's kindness resonated. Something about the older woman put Mildred at ease. *She is the mother I always wished for,* she thought for an instant, feeling a flash of longing.

She unfolded her story piece by piece, and Norma listened intently, smoking a Marlboro Light. Her presence was warm, and she didn't seem surprised by anything Mildred said. She neither interrupted nor accused Mildred of selling her children. Of all the women who'd come to Sobrevivientes asking for help, Mildred seemed like one of the most timid to Norma. She was extremely shy and reserved, and dignified at the same time. It was clear the young mother was resolutely determined, yet the outlook for her case seemed terribly bleak. First of all, Mildred had handed her toddler, Fernanda, over voluntarily. She might have been confused, but it still didn't look good. A small pile of blank documents, containing Mildred's voluntary signature, existed somewhere. She'd accepted food and rent, which could be viewed as receiving money outright, making her vulnerable to accusations of child selling. Furthermore, Mildred's fractured recollections came out in awkward spurts. Her story jumped from place to place, and parts were hard to follow. She was clearly traumatized.

After about fifteen minutes, Norma called one of her newest staff attorneys, Pilar Ramírez, into the room. At 22, the pretty young woman was fresh out of law school. Pilar had been hired at Sobrevivientes after collaborating on the creation and implementation of Guatemala's first emergency broadcast alert system for missing children, based on the U.S. AMBER Alert system. The Alba-Keneth Alert System was named after two little girls who disappeared and had been found brutally murdered. Both of their bodies showed signs of torture, and Alba had been beheaded and buried in a backyard. Sobrevivientes believed that both kidnappings had initially been linked to illegal adoption networks.

A month and a half before, when Pilar started working for Sobrevivientes, Norma had immediately shown confidence in the young lawyer, dumping nearly forty cases on her desk. As Mildred continued speaking, Pilar tried to conceal her mixed emotions. It was clear that Mildred needed help. She didn't look well, with circles under her eyes, and she had trouble relaying her story in a linear fashion. The documentation Mildred brought showed that she'd already explored almost every possible avenue for help. *But how could she allow so many things to just happen to her?* Pilar wondered. She didn't understand Mildred's history, that she'd been grown up in a family where fearful submission was normalized. *How could she have made such poor choices?*

Pilar glanced at Norma, whose attention remained trained on Mildred. Her boss seemed to believe the young woman. Mildred's hands were folded neatly in her lap. A slight speech impediment caused her to swallow her "R" sounds. As she spoke, she kept trailing off, pausing to stare blankly into the distance, as if lost in her own mind.

For the next hour and a half, Pilar listened intently, curious about what Norma would say next. Typically, her boss tried to take on solid legal cases, ones that seemed possible to win. Not much about Mildred's complicated experience was clear, and much of the case seemed based on the young woman's word. Helping her had the potential to affect not only Norma's reputation, but also that of the foundation. It was a gamble.

But by the end of the conversation, Pilar realized that Norma planned to take the case. Pilar was now Mildred's lawyer.

She considered the case details. First of all, any judge would be hard-pressed to understand Mildred's decision to move in with complete strangers. Other poor women didn't do such foolish things. And the DNA test? Mildred had shown up, of her own accord. It might be impossible to establish that she'd been deceived. Yet the rest of the young woman's account rang true: the network of people working together, Sabrina selling the kids to Coni and Marvin Galindo Bran, the signing of multiple blank pages. Other women had also been tricked into signing blank documents that were later transformed into adoption paperwork.

Finally, it had taken weeks for Mildred to come forward and file complaints about her missing daughters. Why? She said that she'd been terrified, afraid that her children would be killed. But a judge might see only a suspicious lapse of time between when the crimes occurred and when they were reported to authorities.

She wished Mildred had simply said, *I gave them away because I had a crisis. Now I want them back and need your help.* But that hadn't happened. Pilar tried to quash her skepticism as she eyed her new client. *How do I even start to prepare this case?* Though she'd worked on a variety of cases before, this would be her first time litigating. She couldn't imagine a case that could be any more difficult.

Fundación Sobrevivientes was in the middle of its first adoption-related campaign, No Más Cunas Vacías (No More Empty Cribs), when Mildred first came to the foundation. Strollers and empty cribs were propped up in front of the PGN and the Ministerio Público's headquarters to raise awareness about corruption in the adoption industry. Demonstrations were being held in front of various court-houses. Sobrevivientes had grown used to helping women file missing child complaints with authorities who didn't seem to take them seriously. Both the PGN and the MP reacted sluggishly to charges of kidnapping for adoption.

In at least three of the cases Sobrevivientes was helping with, stolen children were suspected to have already left Guatemala with new adoptive parents, despite having been reported missing before their American visas were issued. After a hunger strike, months of advocacy, and pro bono help from Sobrevivientes lawyers, Olga López, Loyda Rodríguez, and Raquel Par were granted access to boxes of immigration records kept by the Guatemalan government. The files contained photographs of children who had left the country on orphan visas. Each of the three women identified a little girl they believed to be her own.

Raquel Par and Marco Batz said that their eleven-month-old daughter, Heidy Saraí, had been kidnapped on April 4, 2006, from Villa Hermosa, San Miguel Petapa. The couple had been married for twenty-two years and had eight children. They lived in the rural region of Chimaltenango. Par and Batz reported the abduction to both the Ministerio Público and the PGN the following day. According to Par, a stranger had given her a spiked drink and then taken Heidy during her bus commute into the capital.

Later, Par identified a child called Kimberli Azucena Jiménez in Guatemalan immigration photos. She suspected that "Kimberli" might be Heidy. Adoption documents provided to Par's lawyers at Sobrevivientes by the Guatemalan Attorney General's office showed that "Kimberli" was in the process of being adopted by an American woman, a single mother from Davenport, Iowa. It was unclear whether the child had left Guatemala, and whether the adoption had been completed.

Olga López, a soft-spoken woman who worked at a piñata shop, reported that her daughter, Arlene Escarleth, had been abducted on September 27, 2006. The baby was 56 days old. López knew the kidnappers, who were relatives of her brother's wife, and believed they belonged to a gang that extorted "fees" from bus drivers. She suspected that they had sold her daughter to an adoption network. Guatemalan authorities initially accused López and her mother of being accomplices to the crime because they were able to identify the alleged kidnappers.

It was hard for López to identify Arlene Escarleth from among the hundreds of photographs in migration records because of her age. She found a few possible matches, including a baby whose name was listed as Cindy García. "Cindy" had been adopted by an American family in Illinois. According to PGN records, the process was facilitated by U.S. adoption agency Palmetto Hope and Guatemalan lawyer Luis Emilio Orozco Piloña. López says she sold her house to pay for a DNA sample to be drawn from her own saliva, in hopes that the American family would agree to provide a sample that could prove or disprove her theory.

On November 3, 2006, Loyda Elizabeth Rodríguez and Dayner Orlando Hernández say their daughter, Anyelí Lisseth Rodríguez Hernández, was kidnapped from their home. The young couple, both twenty-four at the time, had two other children. Anyelí, age two, was their middle child and only daughter. Rodríguez and Hernández reported the abduction to the police the next day. Like

López and Par, Rodríguez later looked through migration records and identified a few children she believed could be her stolen daughter. One child in particular looked like Anyelí — a little girl whose immigration records identified her by the name Karen Abigail López García. According to emails sent by the child's adoptive American parents, Timothy and Jennifer Monahan of Liberty, Missouri, "Karen Abigail" had been referred to them by Celebrate Children International. Marvin Bran had been the facilitator on the case. The man listed on the Monahans' power-of-attorney document was César Augusto Trujillo Lopéz, the same lawyer listed on the Emanuels' power-of-attorney for Fernanda's adoption.

To the three mothers, the worst scenario would be if their missing children, with laundered identities, had been successfully and "legally" adopted out of Guatemala. Once the stolen children became U.S. citizens, it was unclear what would happen next. If the missing children had already been adopted, Norma Cruz hoped that the adoptive parents would collborate with the birth mothers to work out a resolution privately. If the birth mothers were forced to rely on help from governmental organizations in the two nations, such as the American Department of Justice and the FBI and the Guatemalan Ministerio Público and court systems, it would likely take years to obtain answers.

Some missing children that had been given fake identities in order to be laundered as adoptable orphans were found before leaving Guatemala in adoption. Esther Zulamita, the daughter of Ana Escobar, 26, was kidnapped from the family shoe store on March 26, 2007, while Escobar was working. Before leaving, the kidnappers locked Escobar in a bathroom and threatened to rape her. Baby Esther was six months old. Ana filed a complaint with the police the same day; Esther's father, Carlos Rivas, filed a complaint with the courts that May; and the couple filed a complaint with the PGN in July. In August, Escobar approached Sobrevivientes for help. Lawyers there helped her obtained legal permission from the courts to search through nurseries across Guatemala for her daughter. She found the baby in a nursery under the fake name Susy Amarilis Hernández Molina. Escobar was able to identify her daughter because of a uniquely crooked finger.

Esther had been offered to an Indiana couple, Dawn and Ryan Ferry, for adoption by the agency Homecoming Adoptions. Guatemalan lawyers Jorge Mario Sun Santiago and Otto René Gálvez Abril had worked on the case, and the DNA test results for Esther/ "Susy" had been manipulated to "match" her to a woman named Edelmira Hernández Molina, who was posing as the birth mother. A subsequent court-ordered DNA test proved the veracity of Escobar's claim, and Esther was returned. "[The Ferrys] are devastated and completely, totally horrified at the idea that this child was stolen from her mother," the Ferrys' lawyer, Charlie Rice, later told the Guatemalan newspaper *El Periódico*. "They're sad to lose her, but they're very happy that the birth mother recovered her daughter." A doctor and the woman who had posed as the birth mother of "Susy" were charged with human trafficking, conspiracy, and *suposición de parto*, or faking childbirth. A warrant was also issued for the arrest of lawyer Jorge Mario Sun Santiago on conspiracy and human trafficking charges, but according to a July 27, 2008, article in *Prensa Libre,* he had fled.

Another child, whose real name was Dafne Nayeli Camey Pérez, was offered as an available orphan under the name "Yajaira Noemí Muyus" to a couple from Massachusetts. After the required DNA test failed to prove a maternal connection between "Yajaira" and the woman relinquishing her, the child was brought before Judge Mario Fernando Peralta to begin the process of being declared legally abandoned. The adoption stalled when Dafne's mother, who had been searching for her, found and identified the child in Asociación Primavera, the private nursery founded by adoption lawyer Susana Luarca. The child was returned to her mother.

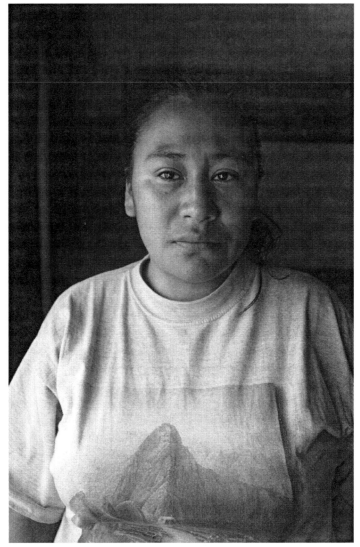

Olga López, mother of Arlene Escarleth, in Guatemala, January 2009. Arlene Escarleth has been missing for five years at the time of this book's printing.

Sobrevivientes's No Más Cunas Vacías campaign captured the attention of the Guatemalan public in late November 2007. In the media, adoption was suddenly a hot topic, and reform measures were being passionately debated. "The Adoptions Law has been mired in Congress for the past 18 years," journalist Carlos Duarte wrote in *La Hora* on November 24, 2007. Sobrevivientes released an impassioned press release in the form of a manifesto, calling for investigations into ten specific cases. Eight involved kidnapped children. One concerned a "disappeared" child, and one a child whose dead body had been found. All of the cases were suspected of being related to adoption.

"All children and teens have the right to be raised and educated with their families, and to be protected by the state from illegal actions that deprive them of freedom," the Sobrevivientes manifesto declared. "In our country, there has been a series of kidnappings of boys and girls under the age of one, who have been seized in a violent way. . . . The authorities have done nothing to stop these violations."

The press release went on to accuse the PGN, the Guatemalan judicial system, and the Guatemalan Congress of "indifference" and wrongdoing. "Those responsible for kidnappings are not brought to justice," it said. "On the contrary, even adoptions with anomalies are given approval to progress, and children whose adoptions originated in felonious acts are allowed to leave the country. . . . This makes officials accomplices to what has occurred." It then summarized the cases, including that of Maria Fernanda and Ana Cristina Alvarado.

"Each of these children [has] mothers and relatives who have been left with a great void in their hearts," Sobrevivientes wrote in closing. "They are living in endless mourning. . . . That is why we ask the Congress to pass the Adoptions Law." The No Más Cunas Vacías campaign was orchestrated to lead up to the Guatemalan congressional vote on the new *Ley de Adopciones* (Adoption Law) on December 11, 2007. Sobrevivientes was hopeful that finally, after a decade of thwarted reform efforts, the country would pass an adoption bill with tighter regulations.

Prensa Libre reporter Lorena Seijo first saw Mildred Alvarado standing quietly alongside the other Sobrevivientes mothers during a demonstration in front of the Supreme Court. It was late November 2007. The women were desperately trying, yet again, to pressure Guatemalan authorities like the Ministerio Público to seriously investigate their cases.

Seijo was working on a story about mothers who'd lost children to adoption rackets but remained determined to find their babies against seemingly impossible odds. Mildred sat down with her and relayed the past year of her life. The resulting article, "*¿Dónde están nuestros hijos?*" ("Where Are Our Children?") ran in the Sunday edition of *Prensa Libre* on November 25. The newspaper was Guatemala's oldest and most respected, with the largest circulation. Above the piece was a photograph of a stroller, sitting empty, in front of a government building. It was one of many props used in the demonstration.

Most of the article dealt specifically with Mildred's case. Seijo noted that the PGN had "identified three private clinics that are dedicated to performing cesarean births to keep premature babies, which are then handed over to the lawyers who manage networks of illegal adoptions." The PGN received forty-five complaints about abducted children in 2007, Seijo reported. The MP received 1,921 similar complaints. It was unclear if complaints between the two government institutions overlapped.

Seijo went on to write that a PGN official had said it was nearly impossible to find stolen children once more than six months had passed. By then, they were almost certain to be living in the United States. At the time the piece was published, Mildred had been searching for fourteen months.

The Ministerio Público's Unidad de la Trata de Personas, or trafficking unit, was created in November 2007, around the time of the No Más Cunas Vacías campaign. First Lady Wendy Berger had requested its formation, and the European Union had provided financial backing. The unit was formed in response to the number of complaints related to adoption "irregularities," including kidnapping and child laundering, that were bogging down the various units that already existed inside the MP. "Adoption cases were spread out across different sections, including general crimes, women and families, minor victims, and organized crime," one prosecutor noted. "There was no continuity anywhere."

A thin, studious man named Álexander Colop was appointed head of the trafficking unit, which fell under the auspices of the MP's organized crime division. Colop had previously worked in the child victims unit, and most recently had overseen a yearlong investigation into alleged kidnapping and baby-selling at Guatemala's public hospital, Hospital Roosevelt. An October 18, 2007, article in *Prensa Libre* by Coralia Orantes mentioned that three social workers had been accused of human trafficking and that 40 separate complaints about child abductions from Guatemalan hospitals had been filed in 2006 alone — but no complaints had ever progressed to court. "Statistics from the Attorney General's Office reflect a high percent of the people who submit DNA tests to give children in adoption are not the children's biological parents," Orantes wrote.

Six investigators and a prosecutor initially were assigned to work under Colop in the new trafficking unit. Many of the new staff had been pulled from his old unit and already knew him . The new unit began work with just one shared computer and no printer. Around the same time, a new section was also created within Guatemala's national police force: La Protección Integral de la Niñez, or child protection unit. A December 20, 2007, article by Luis Ángel Sas in *El Periódico* noted that the new police unit was formed in October 2007 and initially was investigating 15 specific cases of illegal adoption. In each, a child had left Guatemala in adoption through the use of fake documents.

Because of the "delicacy" of investigating adoption networks, Colop had constant security around him. He never knew who a certain lawyer might be connected to, as each individual investigation turned up a web of connections. Although Colop felt his bodyguards were an imposition on his daily life and privacy, having them around was a sacrifice he was willing to make for his work. He changed his routine every day, taking different routes to and from work, assuming that one could never be too careful.

His staff often felt demoralized. "All of the authorities have been involved [in the networks], and that's very frustrating: judges, lawyers, people at registries, doctors, hospitals, everyone is in on it," one investigator admitted. "I mean, adoptions are ultimately a reflection of the society in which they occur. They show how uneducated we are, how little we care. Guatemala got to the point where we sold our children without any remorse; it's all reducing people into objects."

According to a 2008 memo from the U.S. Embassy, 60 percent of the cases initially handled by the new trafficking unit dealt with illegal adoptions. The Embassy noted that a lack of resources limited the unit's ability to prosecute and convict offenders, saying "leaks of information about impending raids and investigations" to criminal targets was a "serious impediment" to Guatemalan law enforcement. For the whole country, just five police officers and one police vehicle were allocated to investigating human trafficking. "The Guatemalan justice system was not able to provide adequate protection for victims and witnesses, which impeded the investigation and prosecution of traffickers," the memo stated. "The overall culture of impunity and violence and fear of reprisal discouraged victims and witnesses from testifying and filing legal action."

A few investigators in the trafficking unit wondered what would happen in the future. What if the children who'd been sent abroad someday returned, seeking answers about where they had come from? It was difficult, and sometimes impossible, to find answers because of the sea of misinformation: fake names, addresses, documents, and relatives. "That's going to be so sad," one investigator said. "There are going to be generations of adopted children in the U.S. who will never know their true origins."

Emily Belle's adoption was nearing completion in the fall of 2007. Betsy and her second-oldest daughter, fifteen-year-old Jill, left for Guatemala on October 25. Since learning that Emily Belle was ready to come to the U.S., the Emanuel household had been in a flurry of preparation, making sure car seats, high chairs, baby clothes, and other details were in order. Betsy hadn't let herself prepare a nursery for Emily Belle because she was afraid that the child might never come to Tennessee. She'd prepared for Jennifer, and then for Fernanda, and deconstructing the rooms had been heartbreaking. Now, finally, a new white crib waited for Emily Belle. Painted pink initials, "E.B.E." were hung from the wall with pink satin ribbons.

The cheapest flight Betsy could find had a seven-hour layover in Houston. She and Jill arrived in Guatemala City late at about 1:00 a.m. Then they missed the shuttle to the Westin Hotel, and found themselves surrounded by a horde of people outside the airport doors. The clamor was incredible: children selling things, people yelling, car horns blaring. Betsy looked down at one begging child and wondered why he wasn't in bed. She was nervous; the airport didn't feel safe. Around them, men called out, offered cab services. It was tempting, but Betsy refused. *Leslie would be so mad if he had to come searching for me in Guatemala!* she thought wryly. Instead, she and Jill got into the next hotel shuttle.

The following day, a foster mother brought the baby to the lobby of the Westin at 10:00 a.m. Emily Belle wore a lime-green jumpsuit and bright white shoes accented in lime. Her short hair was pulled back with a white bow, and tiny stud earrings glistened in her ears. She looked chubby and healthy. The foster mother looked to be in her 30s and wore a pink fleece top and black pants. She seemed sad. She held the baby around the middle, facing the child towards Betsy.

Betsy crouched in front of the pair, stooping to Emily Belle's eye level. The foster mother sat down in one of the lobby chairs, Emily Belle on her lap. The child seemed naturally happy and outgoing and, at age one, could already toddle around. For five long minutes, she appeared thoroughly disinterested in the various toys Betsy held out to her. Finally, Betsy offered her a small blue elephant, and Emily Belle reached out. Betsy took the opportunity to lift the child into her arms. The baby didn't cry or make any other sound. She examined Betsy's face with a serious expression.

For the next ten minutes, the baby rested quietly in her arms as Betsy leafed through the documents the foster mother had brought. Most were in Spanish and made little sense to her.

Upstairs in the hotel room, Emily Belle was surrounded with new toys. Betsy pulled her out of the lime outfit, gave her a quick bath, and dressed her in some of the new baby clothes she'd brought from Tennessee. She was relieved to find no marks on the child's body. Psychologically, the little girl seemed healthy, laughing and smiling in response to Betsy and Jill's attempts to clown with her. "She has a sweet little personality," Betsy wrote on her personal blog, posting a few snapshots of Jill and the baby together on the green hotel bed.

"She is quiet and yet pretty demanding all at the same time. When those arms go up, she wants to be held, and she means it!"

Later that day, Betsy called Marco Tulio Mérida Cifuentes at Adoption Supervisors Guatemala from her hotel room. "Can we find Fernanda?" she asked.

Marco told her that they should wait until the last day of her trip, for the "safety" of Emily Belle's case. He didn't want any trouble with the authorities, he told her, advising Betsy not to draw any attention to herself. Emily Belle's mother was Salvadoran and not Guatemalan, he reminded her. "Get Emily's visa in your hand," Betsy remembers him saying. "Then we'll worry about Fernanda."

Grudgingly, Betsy did as she was told. For the next six days, she took advantage of the hotel restaurant and pool, enjoying the company of Emily Belle and Jill. The Westin even had a "family room" for adoptive parents and their new Guatemalan children, wallpapered in primary colors and stocked with baby supplies, plaid couches, and toys. One day, Betsy and Jill ventured out to the Guatemala City zoo with Emily Belle. The animals there seemed sad, and for a second, Betsy wondered what Steve Irwin would think. She watched the Guatemalan families around them, enjoying their warm interactions. There were children everywhere. Emily Belle scrutinized the other people intently. Betsy wondered if the little girl was looking for her foster mother.

The family who had initially signed up to adopt Fernanda's little sister, Ana Cristina, were also in Guatemala at the time, and also at the Westin. John and Bethany Thompson were finishing up the adoption of a second child Sue Hedberg had presented to them, offered by Marvin Bran, and they were preparing to bring the baby home. The night before their visa appointment, Betsy and Jill took Emily Belle out to dinner with the Thompsons and their new baby at Kakao, a restaurant near the hotel that Sue had recommended. When Betsy arrived at the U.S. Embassy the next day, she found thirty other adoptive families also waiting to get visas for their new children. To her relief, the process went smoothly.

Betsy called Marco again, on November 1, 2007, her last day in Guatemala. She was ready to go to Luz y Esperanza, the hogar where Marvin Bran had supposedly left the Alvarado children. She wanted to see Fernanda with her own eyes. Marco met her in the lobby of the Westin, and they sat at a side table in the lobby. He'd confirmed that two children did indeed live at Luz y Esperanza under the names Maria Fernanda and Ana Cristina Alvarado, but he warned Betsy that they might not be the children she was looking for. Furthermore, the two girls had been kept apart and didn't understand that they were sisters.

Betsy was sure she'd recognize Fernanda from the video clip and the photos Sue Hedberg had sent her. Marco said he'd make the twenty-minute drive to Luz y Esperanza that same day. Betsy begged him to take her along, dying for a glimpse of the child. She'd come up with a plan: to write a check, on the spot, to the nursery director to kick-start Fernanda's adoption. Marco had said it would probably be possible, for about $3,000. He told her that he'd met the orphanage director for dinner a few weeks before and had talked things over.

Marco seemed uncomfortable. Betsy cut him a check for helping "supervise" Emily Belle's adoption. "How much do I owe you for Fernanda's case?" she asked, pausing, her checkbook still open in the middle of the table.

He pushed it gently towards her. "All I did was look into things," he said. "You already had the important information."

For a moment, Betsy was speechless. What was he talking about? He'd claimed he had spent hours in court, poring through records, looking for clues, and had checked at the Embassy and the PGN.

She got a sour feeling when Marco politely but sternly refused to take her along to Luz y Esperanza. It would be better if he went alone first, he said. He'd call her with the details later.

After he left, Betsy waited in at the hotel lobby, watching the minutes pass. Emily Belle was secure upstairs with Jill. Their flight home was scheduled for 6:00 the next morning, and if she didn't go with Marco to the nursery to find Fernanda tonight, she might never get the chance.

Four hours later, at about 8:00 p.m., Marco called. He'd found out that another adoptive family, without children, was in the process of adopting the girls. They'd already visited them five times. "It's best for you to just let it go," he told Betsy. "It's best not to interfere in their lives. Take Emily Belle home and enjoy raising her."

"Marco," she asked seriously. "Did you see them? Are you sure it's really them?"

He admitted that he hadn't. "They were in bed when I got there," he explained. The orphanage director had told him it wasn't convenient.

Betsy hung up in tears. She left Guatemala the next morning, with Emily Belle cradled in her arms and her daughter Jill at her side. As the plane took off, she broke down sobbing.

How can something feel wrong and right at the same time? Betsy wondered. She hated the fact that she was taking the child away from her country, but felt secure in the idea that this was God's plan for both her and Emily Belle.

Outside the plane's window, Betsy watched the sprawl of Guatemala City give way to jagged mountain peaks, and then a bleak expanse of formless clouds. Her guilt and doubt were punctuated by bright streaks of anger. Her gut said Marco had lied to her, and she had the same feeling about Sue Hedberg. *They have to know more,* she thought. *They just have to.*

For most of the trip, Emily Belle rested contentedly. During the last hour of travel, the baby began howling. Betsy felt like the child's screams echoed her own emotional state. As the plane touched down in the United States, she made the decision to tell her story, in its entirety, to the Florida Department of Children and Families.

Before, when she knew that other Celebrate Children International clients were filing complaints, she hadn't wanted to, afraid of jeopardizing Emily Belle's adoption process. Now that the baby was safely in her arms, Betsy was ready.

12. REVELATION

December 2007–January 2008

As the Dealing with the Devil email list grew, the original members decided that it had outgrown its flippant name. A new list name, consisting of a string of initials, was chosen. By fall, the private list had grown to ten members.

The addition of new people was undertaken with care. Every woman on the list would agreed on a new potential member. The women watched the blogosphere, waiting until it seemed clear that another CCI client was experiencing trouble. Then one or two members would reach out to the potential invitee, with a conversational phone call or email to feel them out.

Rachel Robinson sent an email of solidarity to one potential new member: "We are all victims of CCI & Sue Hedberg, " she wrote, ". . .trying to support and comfort each other while working on a plan to stop Sue from hurting any families in the future with her lies, threats, and fraudulent ways."

In September 2007, many of the women on the list filed complaints about their adoption experiences with the Florida Department of Children and Families (DCF), the government agency tasked with licensing Florida's adoption agencies. In one three-week period, DCF received eleven separate complaints about Celebrate Children International. All of the complainants requested anonymity, saying they were "petrified" or "very frightened of retaliation" and of jeopardizing their adoptions by speaking out publicly against Sue. One complainant said she'd "spoken with an attorney in Guatemala who informed her if she went forward with the complaint, there was a 99 percent chance that she would not get her child."

Some of the complainants alleged that CCI used faith as a tactical manipulation, reciting Bible verses, questioning their faith when

185

they asked for information, accusing them of not believing in God. "Sue Hedberg uses intimidation and threats and abuses her power to hurt and scare adoptive parents into silence so they will not bother her," one complaint alleged. "On several occasions, we were told that we did not trust God or have God in our hearts because we inquired as to the status of our case. This kind of emotional blackmail is very cruel and just plain wrong. . . ."

Another complainant said family had paid CCI $24,000 and were afraid to ask Sue what was happening with their adoption. "I was told something that did not make sense," she stated. "When I started questioning her, I received 'whispers' that threatened, 'If you wish to continue with this adoption . . .,' along with threatening emails." Another complainant alleged that Sue was "emotionally abusive" and made comments like "Be glad your child is not dead." Three complainants told DCF that CCI had asked them to undergo psychiatric evaluations.

The CCI clients on the private listserve had also been considering the possibility of a class action lawsuit. Rachel Robinson and Janey Brooks reached out to private Michigan attorney Joni Fixel, a rising star in the adoption community who was trying a new approach to hold adoption agencies accountable for bad behavior: using the Racketeer Influenced and Corrupt Organizations (RICO) Act, which had been written to help the Feds prosecute organized crime.

On October 24, 2006, Fixel had filed a class action lawsuit against Waiting Angels, a Michigan-based adoption agency, on behalf of seven adoptive families who felt they had been victims of fraud and misrepresentation. As the civil case unfolded in the courts, Michigan's attorney general brought a criminal RICO charge against Waiting Angels that resulted in a guilty verdict. The win was groundbreaking: Fixel says it marked the first time that a state had prosecuted adoption agency directors for felony tax evasion. Historically, state authorities, usually an attorney general, had simply closed down problematic adoption agencies, but that meant that the owners could potentially open up shop again under a different name, in a different state, and more or less escape scrutiny. This time, however, the directors of Waiting Angels, Joe Beauvais and Simone Boraggina, were facing jail time. As of August 2011, the case remained in the 6th Circuit Court of Appeals.

From a legal perspective, adoption fraud was fairly easy to identify. Fixel's law practice had downloadable links on its website so that adoptive parents could read others' complaints and understand how litigation proceedings unfolded. Fixel tried to make sure that families understood the limitations of what she could do, such as the fact that she couldn't deal with specific things that had occurred on Guatemalan soil. What she could do, however, was help define certain practices and make sure that U.S. law had been followed. Suddenly being told to pay surprise monthly fees was extortion, and being told that a referral had been lost or that a birth mother had changed her mind was a classic bait-and-switch tactic.

Fixel wondered how long it would take for the U.S. government to do something about the lack of regulation in international adoption. "They're like slugs slithering around," she thought, after learning how agencies began adoption programs in new countries after an established "sending" country stopped sending children in adoption because of trafficking and fraud concerns. "As long as the money's flowing, it's going to keep happening."

Now that Guatemala was on the verge of possibly closing international adoption in order to implement reforms, adoptive parents had been telling Joni that their agencies were offering reduced rates to adopt from Ethiopia instead. She sent a list of questions for the CCI clients to consider, asking each family to write up a one-page synopsis of their experiences with the agency.

Were you sent a referral and asked to send or wire money right away to "hold" the child?

Were you sent multiple referrals that fell through? Did you pay for extra fees (foster fees, apartments, drivers, translators, etc.) that were unsubstantiated?

Did anyone urge you to send money immediately or you could lose the adoption?

Were you encouraged to send or take extra money to bribe local officials?

Did the birth mother return or change her mind within a week of your travel to bond with your child?

Were you told to never discuss the adoption with anyone from another agency or anyone in the country of the adoptive child or you would risk losing the adoption?

Have you ever been threatened or intimidated by an employee of the adoption agency?

To Joni, a deceptive pattern of behavior was clear. Her discussions with the agency's clients revolved around misrepresentation, potential RICO violations, fraud, negligence, and breach of contract claims. Yet every single CCI family was too scared to move forward with litigation. "Even if your adoption is in progress when a lawsuit is filed, the lawsuit WILL NOT prevent the adoption from being completed," she told the CCI mothers in an email to their private discussion list. Despite her assurances, no one wanted to risk it.

On November 8, 2007, Florida DCF licensing specialist Amy Hammett took a call from Betsy Emanuel. She recorded notes by hand. "When Elizabeth made a fuss about the second referral [being lost], Sue told her not to take it any farther," Hammett wrote. "Sue shared w/her that one of her facilitators, Marvin, was threatened by men w/guns who tied his mother up. . . . Elizabeth (Betsy) states Mrs. Hedberg is a master manipulator by crying and quoting Bible verses." [sic] Betsy told Hammett that she wanted to help in any way possible and was available if DCF had questions.

Afterward, Betsy wrote out a detailed account of everything that had happened. The words flowed freely. By the time she had finished, her clarifying letter totaled fifteen pages long. At first, the tone was cool and respectful. Betsy tried to phrase things clearly and simply so that the Florida state officials would understand everything that had transpired with each of the three girls, Jennifer, Fernanda, and Emily Belle. Halfway through documenting the story, though, her emotions took over.

"Why in the world would she ever do such a thing to a child, and to us as a family?" Betsy wrote, referring to the losses of Jennifer and then Fernanda. "I thought I was smart and tough and strong, but this has all brought me to my knees." Before sending the email, she attached digital photos of the children so that DCF could see for themselves what was at stake. *There's no way they'll let this slide,* Betsy thought, feeling satisfied. *Amy Hammett will get to the bottom of everything. It's her job.*

When Betsy filed her complaint, Hammett was in the midst of investigating the eleven complaints about Celebrate Children International that had been filed earlier that fall. At the end of October, DCF had showed up at CCI's offices in Oviedo for an unannounced on-site visit. They'd distilled the eleven individual complaints down into four core issues to be examined: adoption delays, poor communication, Sue's salary, and allegations that Sue requested psychiatric evaluations to silence outspoken or questioning clients.

When asked about delays, Sue blamed adoptive applicants, Guatemalan facilitators, birth parents, and "bad people" operating in Guatemala. She told DCF that potential adoptive parents were all warned that Guatemalan adoptions were "high-risk" and that there was a clear and present threat of failure. CCI had even started asking clients to choose a back up country just in case a Guatemalan adoption didn't work out. "Guatemala had been out of control for the last several years," Sue was noted in DCF's investigation notes as having said. Legally, DCF's jurisdiction ended at the Florida state line.

DCF also looked into CCI's practice of banning clients from contacting anyone in Guatemala. DCF turned to the State Department for help and was told that, ". . . the U.S.-based adoption agency is the adoptive family's agent." The Guatemalan attorney, in turn, was the adoption agency's agent. By that logic, there was no reason for American families to need or want to talk directly to Guatemalans involved in their adoption. DCF asked Sue about the issue anyway. She explained that the policy had been put in place for several reasons. Clients tried to micromanage their adoptions, she said, and the PGN (which she described as "Guatemalan court") was "not reliable" and gave out "wrong" information.

DCF examined CCI's fee structure, and how much money went to Sue. According to the organizational budget for the nonprofit, the executive director was supposed to make an annual salary of $15,000. CCI's tax filings said Sue had earned $209,750 in 2004, $250,500 in 2005, and $269,914 in 2006. Her husband, David, who was not a CCI employee or contractor, was paid $133,500 by CCI in 2005.

When DCF asked for an explanation, Sue said she gave herself a per-child commission plus $1,200 per month. Furthermore, she said, she paid ten "case managers" out of pocket. The case managers were adoptive mothers who'd previously used CCI, and each was paid half of her own commission, or $600, per case. Dave's compensation of $133,500 was called a token gift. Sue said her husband had helped the agency substantially that year.

Finally, DCF asked Sue about her use of psychiatric evaluations. She answered that of 500- to 600 clients, she'd requested psychiatric evaluations for only three in the history of CCI. DCF asked to see the case files for the three families. Sue gave them the files for the Robinsons, the Brooks, and Carrie McFarland. She didn't mention Jillian Richman, who claims to have begged Sue not to make good on her threat of requiring an additional psych evaluation in order for Richman to continue adopting (the evaluation, Richman says, was never ordered). After inspecting some of CCI's adoption files, DCF noted that the business needed to keep better records and document in detail why a client might be asked to undergo psychiatric examinations, if such a situation occurred again.

In the end, the Florida Department of Children and Families' first investigation into Celebrate Children International found that the agency hadn't committed any violations and were in compliance with Florida Administrative code 65:C15, the section that regulated child placing agencies. The code hadn't been updated in twenty years, and if an adoption agency was in compliance, DCF was mandated to provide it with an operating license. If DCF revoked an agency's license, that agency had the right to sue to regain it, a potentially expensive and time-consuming scenario for the state authorities.

"It was a lot of work in unfamiliar territory, in international adoptions," Maria Nistri, program administrator for DCF's central licensing zone, later reflected. Nistri was involved in reviewing Celebrate Children International for licensure and was familiar with her agency's investigations as well. To her, one question loomed. Why did adoptive parents willingly sign such draconian contracts, ceding their basic rights? Nistri wished those who were considering adoption would read more about the process before getting started with it. It seemed that a little research would go a long way.

On the evening of Friday, November 16, 2007, Sue Hedberg fielded questions, as usual, from clients during Celebrate Children

International's weekly online chat. Many knew that an official team tasked with reviewing CCI for Hague accreditation had visited. Because the United States had finally decided to move towards ratifying the Hague Convention on Intercountry Adoption, all adoption agencies offering children from other, Hague-compliant countries needed to undergo a new accreditation process to make sure that their business practices were in line with the treaty's requirements. The Hague Convention was scheduled to go into effect for the United States on April 1, 2008.

Charging excessive adoption fees was prohibited, and the practice of allowing potential adoptive families to choose children via the internet was discouraged. The accreditation process was supposed to help countries sending children overseas in adoption put an end to illicit baby buying and selling by requiring American adoption agencies to take more responsibility for their in-country business partners. In Guatemala, as of December 31, 2007, no new adoptions would be allowed to begin. The entire industry would freeze while new rules were created and implemented.

The evaluation of Celebrate Children International took place over the course of three days, beginning on November 14. One of the investigating team's members was Debbie Schmidt from Catholic Charities. Another was Mikiko "Miki" Stebbing, the accrediting entity liaison in the Office of Children's Issues at the Department of State. The day before the investigation began, Stebbing placed a call to Amy Hammett at the Florida DCF to check in about CCI. Specifically, she wanted to know if CCI had a complaint history. She'd asked Sue Hedberg, who had told her there wasn't one. Hammett provided a rundown of the various allegations. Stebbing confided to Hammett that her office, too, had received complaints about Celebrate Children International.

After their conversation, Hammett emailed Stebbing a copy of the Florida statutes her office was using for licensing guidelines. In reply, Stebbing emailed Hammett more than 100 pages of information about Hague accreditation.

"They were condescending, belittling, mean," Sue told her clients during the November 16 online chat. She said the Hague reviewers had "yelled" at the CCI accountant for writing checks directly to Guatemalan attorneys without getting detailed reports on what the money was used for. "GIVE ME A BREAK!" Sue continued. "NO ONE DOES THAT. . . . Then they told him that this is why the accountant for ENRON went to jail!" She said that the Hague accreditation review had taken the wind out of her sails.

When the first round of evaluation results was over, a total of 220 U.S. adoption agencies had earned Hague accreditation. Eighteen had failed, including Celebrate Children International. The Department of State noted that CCI's failure was owing, in part, to issues including a "willingness to work with unscrupulous facilitators," "failure to know or correct problems with lawyers and facilitators in Guatemala," and "Sue's behavior: unfriendly and not transparent."

But being denied Hague accreditation didn't mean that CCI had to stop working in international adoption. Instead, it meant that the agency could work only in countries that also were unable to gain Hague status — like Ethiopia, a country too poor to implement the kinds of record-keeping procedures and safeguards suggested by the treaty.

CCI had advertised their new Ethiopia adoption program online as early as September 2007, mentioning that Ethiopian children could be viewed in the "Waiting Children section" of the website. It also said that "CEO Sue Hedberg" would be visiting the country for two weeks in September. Ethiopian children cost significantly less than Guatemalan children to adopt, about $12,000 each. In December 2007, CCI received a license from the Ethiopian government to work in adoptions.

Pilar Ramírez, Mildred's young pro bono lawyer from Sobrevivientes, pored over the hard copies of the complaints her client had filed with various authorities in Guatemala. She was impressed. Although Mildred trusted Victor Hugo Mejicanos from the PGN's denuncia unit, Pilar, having dealt with him before, did not. Talking to him was probably a waste of time. She decided that the best bet for reviewing the *denuncia penal,* or criminal charges, at the Villa Canales branch of the Ministerio Público was to show up in person.

Mildred and Pilar went to the office together. Mildred had never brought anyone with her before, and Ariel Guevara seemed shocked to see a young *capitalina*[17] lawyer who could pass as a contender for the next Miss Guatemala pageant standing alongside her. He quickly invited the women to sit down.

"Prosecutor Guevara," Pilar began sweetly, "can you please bring us up-to-date on what's been happening in my client's case?"

He began, carefully, bringing her up to speed. He explained how Mildred's complaint had been passed from court to court and how the proper jurisdiction had finally been established after months of bureaucratic shuffling. Coni and Sabrina had both been arrested but had posted bail. Nothing could be done to speed the pace of Guatemala's justice system. Therefore, the complaint was considered to be in process. Pilar asked if it would make sense for the complaint to be handled by the MP's new trafficking unit based in the capital, as Coni was facing charges of *trata de personas,* human trafficking, in addition to aggravated kidnapping.

Guevara readily agreed. Handling a case like Mildred's made him nervous. He worked and lived in Villa Canales, an area known by authorities and the general population as a *zona roja,* or red zone, because of its high crime and violence. It wasn't uncommon for Ministerio Público staff to be killed by people they were investigating.

Over the past three years, about fifteen judges and lawyers, including some MP staff, had been killed. Many assassinations were carried out in public places, in the daytime, in clear view. On March 4, 2005, Carlos Estuardo Marroquín Santos from the Ministerio Público's corruption unit was murdered after investigating cases against former bureaucrats and the military. An MP assistant prosecutor, Desiderio Martin Tojín Silva, was gunned down in August 2007 while investigating a murder case that implicated police officers.

Court officials, witnesses, and judges were also targets. The second clerk of the Villa Nueva Peace Court was killed on June 20, 2005, in Villalobos, the small shantytown where Mildred had lived with Marjorie. He was shot while in the area to inform an accused criminal of the charges against him. In 2007, a judge in Quetzaltenango, Fausto René Maldonado Torres, was stabbed to

---

[17.] From the capital.

death after accusing other judges, prosecutors, and public defenders of corruption and refusing to take a 15,000 quetzales bribe.

On November 30, 2007, on the anniversary of Fernanda's disappearance, Betsy sent Sue a letter. It seemed almost certain that Fernanda, as well as Jennifer, would grow up under institutional care, without the love of a family. "One year ago today marks the loss of Maria Fernanda for our family," Betsy wrote. "We still do not understand the strange explanation you gave us. Sue, whatever happened to Maria Fernanda and her case?"

When the agency director replied, she asked Betsy if the Emanuels were still interested in adopting Jennifer. Sue ignored the questions about Fernanda, as well as the fact that Betsy had already made it clear that her family didn't have the extra $19,000 CCI required to adopt Jennifer.

On December 11, 2007, the Guatemalan Congress finally passed the Adoptions Law, paving the way for the country's ratification of the Hague Convention. The new law theoretically created the infrastructure necessary for Guatemala to implement the treaty, months ahead of the United States.

Editorials for and against the decision cropped up in Guatemala's newspapers. "Obtaining children to give in adoption has become the target of a pack of hunting hounds inspired by an underlying principle: The children of the poor are better off in the hands of rich people. . .," Guatemalan novelist and lawyer Carol Zardetto wrote in an opinion piece that ran in *El Periódico* three days after the new law was passed. "Swept along by this wave of dollars and euros," Zardetto continued, "everyone involved was left blind. Boundaries vanished. The day came when the children who were not given voluntarily were stolen. Mothers rented their bellies. Unmarried girls were pressured and humiliated, or used by their men for a few thousand quetzales. . . . The market prevailed: He who has money can get what he desires. . . ."

Adoption lawyers like Susana Luarca spoke out against the reforms. The Guatemalan media reported that she was poised to file an injunction against the new legislation with the Constitutional

Court, on the grounds that the bill contained errors and was unconstitutional in nature.

With the new law in place, no new adoptions could be started until after "the reform" took place. As of December 31, 2007, the adoption industry would be frozen indefinitely, until additional safeguards could be created and implemented. Adoptions initiated before that cut-off date would be allowed to proceed.

Celebrate Children International and some other American adoption agencies offered their clients Guatemalan children up to the last minute. On December 22, nine days before the Guatemalan adoption freeze was to go into effect, the CCI website was still advertising Guatemalan infants and toddlers. A few older children from orphanages were also offered as "available," including nine-year-old Jennifer Yasmin Velásquez López, who sat at the bottom of the list.

Betsy panicked when she saw the listing. The wording was identical to that in the advertisement she'd first seen two years before, when she'd found the girl on Precious.org. She was sick with doubt and began to reconsider the decision not to continue with Jennifer's adoption. Had she given up too soon?

The sudden burden of responsibility felt like a punch to the gut as she realized that Jennifer would be sentenced to a childhood in an orphanage unless someone signed up to adopt her by December 31. Her emotions took over, and she quickly called Florida DCF, withdrawing her complaint against CCI.

A day later, common sense took over. What if the listing was a lie and Jennifer wasn't really available? What if she'd already been adopted? Even if the child was truly available, what was to stop her referral from getting "lost" again? There was no right answer. It was just too risky, Betsy decided. Annoyed with herself, she decided to resubmit her complaint.

The day before the cut-off date for adoptions, on December 30, 2007, *El Periódico* ran an infographic about the barrage of new adoptions that had been filed ahead of the new rules going into effect. "THE FINAL DAYS," the headline read, floating over an image of a worried woman in white plucking a baby from a shared crib. On Friday, December 28, the newspaper reported, a grand total of 164 new adoption cases had been filed for processing before the deadline with the attorney general's office. Australia, Estonia, Israel, and

Puerto Rico had each registered one new adoption case. Ireland had filed two, and Guatemala three. The United States had filed a total of 155.

A few weeks before the new law went into effect, tragedy beset the family of Carla Girón, the woman who had come to the Escuintla courthouse asking to begin abandonment proceedings for Mildred's daughters. Five members of Carla's family were murdered. The bodies were found with slit throats in the Guatemala City home of Carla's sister, who was one of the people killed.

When the massacre happened, Carla was in the United States visiting her boyfriend, Jim Harding, who ran the adoption agency World Partners Adoption, Inc. At the time, Carla had been caring for a baby in the middle of an adoption process to a California couple, the Azhderians, who were using an agency called A Field of Dreams. Carla had left the baby, Jhossy, in Guatemala with her sister when she left for the U.S. The baby, too, had been murdered.

Carla's teenage nephew was arrested and charged with the killings of his mother, his father, two siblings, and baby Jhossy. The Guatemalan press seized on the gruesome story. The authorities didn't investigate possible connections between the killings and the adoption networks Carla and her stepmother, Miriam Bonilla Monterroso, were involved with. Instead, the Ministerio Público pointed to the teenager's drug use, antisocial behavior, depressed attitude, and "emo"-style taste in music and clothes as evidence and motive. The boy's blood was also found at the crime scene.

On the morning of January 21, 2008, Betsy Emanuel awoke early in her Tennessee bedroom, heart fluttering. It was 5:00 a.m., and she'd tossed and turned all night. Leslie, her husband of twenty-nine years, remained asleep. She crept into the bathroom, curled up on the floor, and broke down in silent, racking sobs.

Although Emily Belle had been home for two months now, she just couldn't stop wondering what had happened to Fernanda. She'd contacted the State Department, the Department of Children and Families, and the U.S. Embassy in Guatemala. No one had any answers. Leslie was worried about the toll the stress was taking on his wife's health.

Betsy was charged with an electric feeling of helplessness. Her staunch faith had kept her going through the adoption ordeal, and she believed that Fernanda was being watched over. Everything would be revealed in time, she felt, yet she was tired of waiting. The past year of prayer and searching for answers had yielded few leads, let alone concrete details regarding the child's safety and well-being.

Lying on the bathroom floor, Betsy began to pray, her body heaving with sobs. *Please God,* she pleaded. *Release me from this child. Take the love out of my heart.* There seemed to be only two answers: Either she had to somehow stop caring about Fernanda, or she needed to understand exactly what had happened. Neither option seemed likely.

When the alarm clock went off at seven o'clock, Betsy eased to her feet, worried that Leslie might catch her coiled pitifully on the bathroom floor. She splashed water on her puffy eyes. *I can't wait any longer,* she thought.

In the kitchen, Betsy quickly fixed herself a cup of coffee before the kids got up. There weren't many possibilities. If Fernanda turned up in Guatemala, there was a good chance she'd be in an orphanage like Jennifer. If that was the case, another family might be in the process of adopting Fernanda, unaware of the Emanuels' failed attempt.

Coffee in hand, Betsy went downstairs into the old broom closet Leslie had lovingly converted into a makeshift office for her. Clicking through the blogs of other Celebrate Children International clients, she looked to see who, if anyone, might have accepted a referral for Fernanda. Nothing came up. She Googled the names of the people associated with Fernanda's adoption: Marvin Bran, CCI's adoption facilitator. Sue Hedberg, the agency's director. Alfonso Close, one of CCI's attorneys. Mildred Alvarado, the mother who was supposed to have relinquished the child. Guiding her browser to Guatadopt.com, Betsy typed Fernanda's name into a new search field.

To her surprise, a news article popped up. It had been published two months before, in the November 25, 2007, edition of Guatemala's *Prensa Libre.* The first line read, *"El dolor que siente una madre cuando pierde a un hijo es indescriptible." The pain that is felt by a mother when she loses a child is indescribable.*

Betsy skimmed the piece, trying to tease out meaning from the jumble of Spanish words. None of it made sense. Then, recognizing the name Mildred Alvarado, she froze. Could it be the same Mildred Alvarado? Rereading the text, Betsy picked out Fernanda's name. It had to be the same child. Betsy felt a hard pit form in her stomach. She carefully copied and pasted the article, sentence by sentence, into an online translator.

Young mothers travel the streets and to state institutions, crying for justice and the return of their children, stolen by networks dedicated to international adoptions.

 Mildred Alvarado, a young woman living on the outskirts of Guatemala City, was described as having the "perfect profile for a victim of organized crime groups: a single mother, little economic means, and little education." The article detailed Mildred's ongoing search for her two young daughters, 2-year-old Fernanda and baby Ana Cristina. Ana Cristina, an infant, had been cut from Mildred's womb while the young woman was unconscious. Fernanda had been kidnapped in August 2006 by a woman who was supposed to be providing temporary care for the child. For almost a year and a half, Mildred had been clinging to the flickering hope that her daughters would somehow be found, unscathed, and returned to her.

Betsy sat perfectly still, slowly realizing that she'd been given an adoption referral for her Fernanda at the same time, in August 2006. The coincidence was stunning. Betsy struggled to catch her breath, turning the new information over in her mind. She'd been adopting a stolen child.

With her heart in her throat, she reached for the phone.

13. TWO MOTHERS, NO ANSWERS

February 2008

Mildred was making noodles and cream, her favorite lunch, when the phone rang. It was Norma Cruz from Fundación Sobrevivientes. She dropped her spoon in surprise. "Mildred," Norma said, her voice warm, "I have news for you."

Reporter Lorena Seijo from *Prensa Libre* had called Sobrevivientes. An American had called the paper's headquarters after reading her article featuring Mildred. Although "*¿Dónde están nuestros hijos?*" (*Where Are Our Children?*) had been published months before, the American had just found it online. The woman claimed to have information about the missing children.

When Betsy first tried to call Guatemala after finding the article, she had a hard time communicating. The newspaper's phones were answered, unsurprisingly, in Spanish. The suddenness of discovering that Mildred, too, was searching for Fernanda made Betsy feel the urgency of every passing hour. Betsy was sure she could help Mildred find the children. When she initially called the *Prensa Libre* offices in Guatemala City, the only English speaker there was a young man named Hector, who apparently worked in the mailroom. It took days and multiple calls before Betsy got through to Lorena Seijo. "I only want to help this mom," Betsy told her, explaining that she'd been offered the stolen children as adoptable orphans. Seijo left Betsy's number with Sobrevivientes.

Words failed Mildred. She sat down, listening silently as Norma spoke. As Mildred listened to the calm voice, something told her that the girls were OK, alive and unhurt. Her heart told her that they were still in Guatemala.

"Can you come to the foundation?" Norma asked. "We have pictures, and you have to see if they're your daughters. The American sent them. She thinks they're still in Guatemala."

When Mildred found her voice, she told Norma she'd be there as fast as she could.

At Sobrevivientes, Mildred sat down in a black folding chair. The room was crowded with women, many of whom had brought their children along with them. It was much busier than the first time she'd visited, a few months before.

She'd left her own Mario and Susana alone at home in her frantic dash to get to the Sobrevivientes office. Mario was thrilled with the news and had immediately knelt on the floor, praying urgently for "my 'Nanda," as he called Fernanda. The six-year-old missed his little sister dearly.

Mildred squirmed in the hard metal chair. Time crept by. In the Sobrevivientes waiting room, three different posters were taped to the front of the receptionist's desk. The largest showed a string of smiling, ethnically diverse women against a lavender background, standing beneath the words "You Have the Right To Live Without Violence. You Have The Right to Be Happy."

The two other posters were simple 8.5 x 11 computer printouts. One advertised a phone number the public could call with information about the kidnapped children of Olga López, Loyda Rodríguez, and Raquel Par. The second featured a color photograph of Raquel's toddler Heidy wearing a flowered *güipil* (or *huipil*, a traditional Mayan blouse embroidered with flowers). The baby was pale-skinned, and her short black hair was pulled into two pigtails erupting from the top of her head. The caption beneath her read "Reward: Missing Child."

Mildred crossed and uncrossed her feet, debating whether or not to pour herself a cup of black coffee. She usually took her coffee with heaping spoonfuls of sugar, but now, her stomach felt too excited to handle the sweet liquid.

After about a half-hour, Norma peeked into the reception area, locking eyes with her. She was suppressing a smile. Upstairs black-and-white printouts spread out on a conference table awaited Mildred. They were photos printed from emails sent by Betsy Emanuel, the American who had tried to adopt Fernanda. Mildred saw her girl and again lost her voice. She started sobbing so hard that Norma, concerned, called downstairs to one of the foundation's psychologists.

In the images, Fernanda wore a jean jacket and a smart-looking dress. She clutched an expensive doll, the kind whose cost was equivalent to months of Mildred's rent. She smiled in some of the pictures. Fernanda looked more like a child now than the toddler Mildred had known eighteen months before. Her hair had been cut into wispy bangs, and her expression was an intense, expectant stare. Another photo, a close-up shot of her face, looked to have been taken at an earlier date. Fernanda was biting her bottom lip and gazing wide-eyed into the camera. She looked uncertain and apprehensive.

"Yes," Mildred told Norma with absolute certainty, "that's my girl."

She glanced at the other photos spread across the table. They were of an infant wrapped in blankets. In one picture, the baby's tiny hand was stretched upwards, as if to wave hello. She was apparently Mildred's youngest daughter, Ana Cristina.

How do I know she's mine? Mildred thought. *She could be anyone's baby.* She was surprised to feel no connection to the child in the pictures. Surely, her maternal instincts would have been triggered if the baby were really hers. Daunted and overwhelmed, she refocused her attention on the pictures of lovely Fernanda.

Norma continued asking questions, but they were lost on Mildred. She was drowning in the photos of Fernanda. The sudden, real possibility of regaining her daughter was paralyzing, and she was having trouble staying emotionally present and engaged.

Norma explained that they were going to call the American adoptive mother, Betsy, with the help of another American, Sue Kuyper, who happened to be working in the office. Kuyper was program director for the Network in Solidarity with Guatemala (NISGUA), an American human rights group that sometimes worked with Sobrevivientes. NISGUA ran the Guatemala Accompaniment Project, which recruited and trained American "accompaniers," volunteers who stood side-by-side with vulnerable witnesses in high-risk cases, like those testifying in trials against former Guatemalan Army officials accused of genocide and crimes against humanity. NISGUA volunteers also accompanied local activists, leaders, and other threatened human rights defenders (individuals, communities, and organizations) as needed.

When Kuyper, whose home was San Francisco, California, first met Mildred, she felt an instant connection to the young woman. Her own daughter had been born just days before Ana Cristina and Kuyper couldn't help but think about how quickly her daughter's appearance had changed through her first year of life. Her heart broke for Mildred. How could she expect to find a child she'd never seen?

When Betsy's phone rang, she was reading a children's book aloud to Emily Belle, enjoying the quiet moment while the rest of her kids were downstairs. Betsy didn't recognize the number on the caller ID. Hesitating, she wondered whether the call was important. Then she picked it up.

"Elizabeth Emanuel?" a female voice said. "This is Sue Kuyper. I'm here in Guatemala with Mildred Alvarado. Can we ask you a few questions?"

The three women were sitting around the desk in Norma's office, Kuyper at the end, with Norma on her left, chain-smoking, and Mildred on her right, motionless. Mildred seemed dazed, dissociated from the events that were unfolding. All three had tears in their eyes.

Betsy sank down into Emily Belle's rocking chair, her heart racing, her knees weak. She slid the baby onto the floor in front of her, handing her a few toys to play with. "Of course," she stammered. "Please."

The translator's voice, low and raspy, was much stronger than that of Mildred, whom Betsy could hear speaking quietly in the background. "Mildred would like to thank you for coming forward," Kuyper began. "She would like to thank you for helping her."

There was a long pause as Kuyper waited to hear what Mildred would say next. The young woman's voice cracked, then went silent.

No, no, Betsy thought frantically. Her heart was beating uncontrollably. *I should be thanking her. Sue Hedberg was wrong. She loves her children, I know she does. I can tell.* She heard Mildred start to weep. A powerful wave of sadness washed over her, and within seconds, Betsy had also broken down in tears. *Fernanda has a mother who loves her,* she realized. *She isn't my daughter. She never was, she never will be.* Mildred wasn't some drug-addicted wreck, as she'd been led to believe. The sound of Mildred's voice drove the reality home.

Sue Kuyper swallowed hard, struggling to keep back her own tears as she listened to the two women cry. Mildred rocked back and forth, her arms wrapped around her body. *She's in so much pain,* Kuyper thought. *It's like she has to keeper body moving to hang on.* When both Mildred and Betsy had regained their composure, the conversation slowly started again.

Betsy explained, in spurts, how Sue Hedberg had told her that Mildred's daughters were orphans in need of a home. Unlike Mildred, whose dignified and reserved nature tended towards silence, Betsy released her emotions in a rush of words. She told them how she couldn't afford to adopt both children, how Sue Hedberg had said Mildred didn't care if the girls were separated. She said that Marvin Bran had brought the girls to Celebrate Children International. She even shared the secret part of the story, about how she'd hired private investigator Marco Tulio Mérida Cifuentes and Adoption Supervisors Guatemala.

Betsy paused to catch her breath. At her feet, Emily Belle began to wail. Jill, her teenage daughter, came in and saw the serious look on her mother's face. She scooped the baby into her arms and carried her out of the room. Betsy collected herself and refocused on Mildred, imagining that the young woman was terrified.

"Sue, can you please tell Mildred how proud I am of her, how brave she is for telling her story to the newspaper?" she said. Her own voice trembled slightly, and she wished she could just wrap her arms around Mildred. "Please tell her that I love her children, that I love them so much, and that I've been praying for them every day. . . ."

Sue Kuyper translated carefully. There was a brief pause. "Betsy," Kuyper said, "Mildred would like to know if you are still going to try to take her daughters to the United States."

"Oh no, no! " Betsy said. She started to explain all over again, more slowly this time. She felt a shared sense of victimization with Mildred, and an intense anger towards Sue Hedberg.

Kuyper took careful notes. When Betsy mentioned that Marvin Bran had put the children in a hogar called Luz y Esperanza, Kuyper interrupted excitedly. She sent Mildred down the hall to get Pilar.

The young lawyer came in and got on the phone, asking rapid-fire questions in Spanish, only to realize that Betsy didn't understand.

"How does this woman know about the baby?" Pilar wanted to know. The fact that the American had seen Mildred's youngest daughter before the child's own mother was perplexing. Who had taken pictures of the newborn? Where had they been taken? Since Betsy received the digital images so quickly, it might mean that the people who'd abducted Ana Cristina and Fernanda had a pre-existing relationship with an American adoption agency.

It was the kind of miraculous breakthrough that held great potential. With Betsy's willingness to help, there was a better chance of recovering the children, if they hadn't already been adopted to someone else. Everyone at Sobrevivientes started grinning. *At last,* Pilar thought. *Something to go on. Something real.*

Pilar drew up a list of questions to be translated and sent to Betsy. Her main concern was establishing Marvin Bran's involvement with Mildred's children. The Ministerio Público kept saying that they wanted to go after him, but he hadn't been charged with anything. Until Betsy called, Pilar and Sobrevivientes hadn't known he was so heavily involved. Now it seemed, he was the key link to the American adoption agency. Betsy had sent them a video showing Marvin Bran, Fernanda, and Sue Hedberg in the same room. It seemed like irrefutable evidence that Marvin and Sue had worked together on Fernanda's adoption.

The progress was invigorating. News about the break in Mildred's case quickly spread to the other women being helped by Sobrevivientes. Olga López, Loyda Rodríguez, and Raquel Par shared Mildred's excitement, even though all of their children remained missing. Now, at least, there were leads. The daughters of all four women had been abducted around the same time, in the fall of 2006. If Mildred's girls were indeed still in Guatemala, it was possible that the others were, too.

After talking to Norma and Mildred, Betsy emailed Benita Noel, a producer for NBC in New York. Betsy had gotten Noel's months before from another adoptive parent who'd been a source for the seven-part *Dateline* series "To Catch a Baby Broker." The program, which focused on Guatemalan adoption, aired for the first time just days before Betsy found the *Prensa Libre* article about Mildred. She thought the reporter might be able to help.

"To Catch a Baby Broker" described the operations of an adoption network centered around Thanassis "Teo" Kollias, one of Guatemala's most infamous facilitators. Teo was the "baby broker" NBC had set out to catch on that episode. On-air reporter Victoria Corderi even went undercover, posing as the director of a new American adoption agency, to try to catch Teo lying. The news show was specifically attempting to solve the kidnappings of Candida, Claudia, and Enma Galicia, three young sisters from Jalapa, Guatemala.

Dateline hired a private investigator, Pablo Hernández,[18] to trace the girls. But the report left out a key piece of information: Carla Girón's involvement in the case. She was the one who had offered Candida to the American agency Adoption Blessings Worldwide for placement. It was unclear what agency she'd offered Claudia to. "She asked not to be mentioned at all because of 'reprisal,'" Hernández said. "She knew her middlemen were involved in shady things . . . Carla knew her own people weren't clean."

Both Candida and Claudia Galicia were eventually returned to their parents. After the *Dateline* piece aired, Hernández said, the Galicia girls' father was beaten so badly he lost an eye. The youngest Galicia girl, Enma, remains missing. Hernández believes that she may have been brought to the U.S. in an abandonment adoption through the use of a fake identity. "I just don't think they would have killed her," he said. "The criminals know that unless there's someone digging around, things will be fine and no one will talk. To kill her would have been a loss of money."

When Benita Noel received Betsy Emanuel's email, she replied immediately. Her experience working on "To Catch a Baby Broker" had been moving. "Would you mind if I forwarded this to Kevin Kruetner at Guatadopt?" she wrote back. "I think he would be the most knowledgeable/capable person to help you."

Betsy felt weariness overcome her when she read Noel's response. Though she liked Kevin and knew he was highly knowledgeable, she didn't completely trust GuatAdopt, and she hesitated. The site's advertising came from adoption-related businesses, and Guatadopt.

---

18. The name has been changed to protect anonymity.

com's other moderator, Kelly Caldwell, had previously worked as a Guatemala program coordinator for the adoption agency Children of the World, a business that had at one time partnered with Teo, the man named by *Dateline* as a baby broker. "I just need to know what officials, or who in Guatemala, will care enough to help this woman find her children," Betsy told Noel.

The NBC producer then offered to contact someone she said might be able to help investigate. "He may not do it for free," she told Betsy.

"Thanks, but I just paid $30,000 for an adoption that began at a fee of $17,000," Betsy answered, annoyed. "I'm not really interested in paying more people to extort or profit from these poor women and children who are so obviously being victimized by people in that country AND this one!"

Noel sent Betsy an apology later that day. "I have had a really busy day and have only just now been able to read through everything and fully comprehend all of this," she wrote. "This is all unbelievably disturbing. I am so sorry for all you've been through, and I'm deeply troubled by what has happened to this poor mother. I'm not sure how much help I can provide, but of course I will do anything I can. . . ." She said that another producer friend would send along the names of a few contacts at Casa Alianza, an NGO, and at UNICEF. Noel also called GuatAdopt's Kelly Caldwell asking for advice. Caldwell steered her towards the Ministerio Público.

In the end, Betsy went ahead and sent an email to Kevin Kreutner. He advised talking to Adoption Supervisors Guatemala's Marco Tulio Mérida Cifuentes. Betsy pressed him for more ideas, and Kreutner mentioned that he might be able to put her in touch with the "right" Guatemalan authorities. "I just want to make sure we're not making a mistake," he wrote. He received a massive amount of email from adoptive parents, pertaining to all sorts of issues. Sometimes, when they seemed serious or involved possible fraud, he'd put his time into helping sort things out, only to have the adoptive family drop the matter. Like many Americans who adopted children from Guatemala, Kreutner believed the media blew adoption corruption out of proportion, seizing on the goriest accounts. He felt it was nearly impossible to decipher the truth from media reports as they focused on the sensational. A few cases could be used to paint the whole industry as corrupt.

The day after Mildred saw the photos, she paid a visit to Victor Hugo Mejicanos at the denuncias unit of the PGN. He was supposed to have been helping her, but he hadn't. Mildred was angry. How could he not have told her that Fernanda and Ana Cristina were being adopted? There had to be paperwork filed with the PGN. Surely, he could have found it if he'd tried.

Mildred confronted him. Of all the officials she'd seen, he was the one who acted from the start like he believed her, always offering a few cents for bus fare to and from the capital. She'd cleaned his office floors with vigor.

"I trusted you," she told him. Even in anger, her voice was quiet. "You were supposed to help. And you betrayed me."

"No, no, Mildred," Mejicanos said. He was almost pleading. "I swear to you, you have my word. I didn't know there were adoption files. No one told me. I'll try to find out more, and of course I will let you know."

This time, she didn't believe him.

Sue Kuyper emailed Betsy on Friday, January 25, 2008, after Mildred and a Sobrevivientes staffer had spent the day searching Zone 4 of Guatemala City for the nursery Betsy had described. "Unfortunately, they were not able to locate the hogar today," Kuyper wrote. "It seems not to exist officially. Norma asked me to ask you if there was any way you could get in touch with the lawyer to see if he has more information."

Betsy's stomach lurched. Had Marco lied to her about visiting Luz y Esperanza? Had she given Mildred wrong information? "I feel so sick, I could just die," she told Janey Brooks later that night. She'd been keeping both Janey and Rachel Robinson abreast of everything as it unfolded. "I can't believe I've given them false hope."

She called Marco Tulio Mérida Cifuentes that same night to ask for the address of the nursery where he'd claimed the girls were. He refused to give it to her. "The birth mother terminated all rights," he said repeatedly. He seemed unhappy and asked Betsy to leave his name out of future conversations with Norma Cruz and anyone from Sobrevivientes. The abandonment decree for Fernanda's adoption was "sealed," he explained. Betsy couldn't believe how uncooperative he was being. Marco said he'd call back on Monday, and Betsy hung up, fuming. *Doesn't he realize how important this is?*

Pilar crafted a letter asking for an *exhibición personal,* or order of judicial permission, to enable Mildred to go inside specific nurseries to search for her daughters. It was approved within a few days, granting permission for Mildred to look for Fernanda and Ana Cristina in more than twenty different private nurseries. The majority of the nurseries had names that sounded divinely inspired: Fundación de Niños de Jésus. Hogar Nuestro Señora de la Piedad. Hogar Luz de María. Foundation for the Children of Jesus. Our Lady of Piety Nursery. Light of Mary Nursery.

"The nurseries were all very secret," Norma Cruz recalls. To her, it seemed as if they were *granjas de niños,* baby farms. "We filed 100 habeaus corpus appeals in 2007 to get into them. . . The family court judges don't like me, because they are in on the baby trade, and they made the process very difficult."

First on the list was Esperanza Juvenil, or Youth Hope, in Zone 2 of the capital. Mildred set out, flanked by Olga López and Ana Escobar. López and Escobar had been searching together for months for their own daughters, and had grown close. Mildred, feeling like an outsider, kept to herself. López found her to be quiet and shy, but felt a respect for Mildred because she saw that the young woman worked hard, cleaning and doing laundry for others to pay for the travel expenses her continued search for her daughters incurred.

In many of the nurseries, babies and children were segregated by age. Some of the centers were clean and well-kept; at others, up to a hundred tiny wards were in poor condition, infested by lice and scabies. The searching mothers were repeatedly devastated by the "bad" nurseries, wondering if their own children were suffering.

As they entered a hogar, children often ran to them, swarming around their legs in a frenzied cluster. Their small hands would reach upwards, clutching at the women's pant legs with surprising strength. The women would be forced to pry their tiny fingers away. Even the babies seemed to cling when lifted. Each time, it was difficult to leave. The searching mothers wondered if they'd missed a child, or if their own missing son or daughter had been hidden before they arrived. Oftentimes, they fell, fast and furiously, in love with certain children in the nurseries, hugging babies to their chests. They frequently left in tears.

Betsy waited all day Monday, refreshing her email repeatedly. Why wasn't Marco Tulio Mérida Cifuentes calling? His reluctance to help seemed suspicious. Was he in league with Sue Hedberg? Was he representing another family in adopting Fernanda or Ana Cristina? She left him a message, hoping to quell her growing suspicions.

Janey Brooks and Rachel Robinson prayed along with Betsy, from miles away. They, too, couldn't believe that their trusted private investigator was refusing to help. "Still nothing from Marco! 2:57 pm AND COUNTING!!" Betsy told her friends at midday. "I HOPE MF IS THERE!!!" Janey responded. "She just has to be. . . ."

Sue Kuyper called at about 6:30 that night with bad news. The girls weren't at Esperanza Juvenil. Betsy wrote to Mérida yet again. Her patience had evaporated. "All I need from you is to know where Maria Fernanda is," she said. "You knew where she was when we spoke in November, and again in December. . . . I have been trying to talk to you about this for a week now. I tried to tell you on Friday that her birth mom is looking for her. I know you said she has lost her rights, but it seems that both children were forcibly removed from her, Marco, and if that is true, this needs to be corrected before Fernanda leaves the country. . . ."

Then she switched tactics, thinking that an appeal to Mérida's morality might go farther. "Mildred Alvarado is a real person, and she needs a chance to be heard on this," she wrote. "Marco, if you can help, you should. . . . A judge has already said they can look for Mildred's children, but no one knows where to look. . . ."

Finally, at the end of the email, Betsy confronted him directly. "Can you help or not?" she wrote bluntly. "Are you by some chance representing the other family [adopting Fernanda]? Or is there a reason that I am not aware of that you would not want to help? Where is Luz y Esperanza? Who did you talk to about us when you went that night? If I stay quiet, Marco, that makes me part of the lies! I will not be part of Sue and Marvin's lies!"

To her surprise, Mérida called immediately. He promised to look into things and call back in the morning. He didn't. For the next half-hour that morning, Betsy hit redial repeatedly, listening to busy signal after busy signal. When a receptionist finally picked up, she explained that Marco was in a meeting. "Can I have him call you back?" she asked.

"Sure," Betsy said. She was weary. With the excitement of connecting with Mildred, she'd been certain things would move forward fast. She didn't want to contact the U.S. Embassy yet because she was afraid of having to reveal her family's relationship with Adoption Supervisors Guatemala. Betsy imagined that that would lead to a terrible chain of events. Sue Hedberg might find out she had used the private investigators and perhaps retaliate by causing trouble with Emily Belle, even though her adoption had culminated months before.

When Mérida called back, he was typically cordial and polite. He spoke to Betsy for over an hour, promising to meet with the lawyer who was now handling the adoptions of Fernanda and Ana Cristina to a new U.S. family. He didn't say when, and he didn't give any names. To Betsy, it seemed like he was afraid to get involved, and he clearly didn't want his name associated with the case. He told her that the other family had already signed power-of-attorney forms and that since the case was considered an abandonment, there was no need for DNA testing.

Norma Cruz had met with officials at the U.S. Embassy who said they didn't have any current adoption paperwork on the Alvarado sisters, and that there was no other documentation on them other than the adoption pre-approvals that had been issued to the Emanuel and Thompson families a year and a half before. It didn't appear as if the children were being adopted to anyone else, at least not under their real names, unless the U.S. Embassy was lying.

Days later, Betsy was still waiting for Mérida. She wasn't sure whose side he was on. He might be her and Mildred's best friend, the person who held the key to finding Fernanda and Ana Cristina. Then again, he could be their worst enemy, tipping off whoever else might be involved with the children.

She decided to contact the U.S. Embassy. On January 30, Betsy sent John Lowell, the consul general of the U.S. Embassy in Guatemala, a detailed email summarizing her adoption experience with Celebrate Children International and what had happened with Mildred's children. He didn't write back.

On the second day of February, a dozen hopeful CCI clients from across the U.S. spent the day in unified prayer for their adoptions. At least six CCI families accepted referrals for Guatemalan children in December, before the new Hague rules went into effect. Sue had placed children up until the last possible moment, and three of her clients were now matched to referrals without documentation. It was unclear whether the adoptions would succeed.

The Joint Council on International Children's Services continued to lobby on behalf of "children in need of permanent families" and the adoption agencies in their membership, which handled 75 percent of the world's international adoptions. Thousands of frustrated Americans caught in Guatemalan adoption processes wrote letters and emails and were making phone calls to elected officials at home and abroad.

At the end of January, Guatemalan President Álvaro Colom received another adoption advocacy letter, this time from Minnesota Senator Norm Coleman, co-chair of the Congressional Coalition on Adoption and a member of the Senate Foreign Relations Committee. Coleman addressed the Guatemalan president on behalf of his constituents adopting from Guatemala, asking him to "support pushing forward the reform relating to the adoption system. . . . I am sure you'll agree with me that the ideal situation is one in which these children who are in need of loving families be united with them as quickly as possible." In closing, Coleman wrote that he hoped to have a "strong friendship" with President Colom, and he offered his "good offices as a U.S. senator" to assist him in efforts to get a new adoption system up and running.

Lorena Seijo, the reporter whose article had brought Betsy and Mildred together, wrote a follow-up piece. On February 4,

2008, *Prensa Libre* published the article under the blazing headline "Embassy 'Approved' Adoption of Stolen Children!"

"The U.S. Embassy approved the adoption of Maria Fernanda and Ana Cristina Alvarado, two Guatemalan sisters who were stolen in 2006, although the girls' mother had already lodged a complaint with the Ministerio Público," the article began. Betsy was identified by the pseudonym "Sindy." The article blamed the U.S. Embassy for issuing pre-approval for the Alvarado girls after they'd been reported missing.

It implied that the Embassy should have checked with the MP to make sure that the children weren't among the many reported missing. In response, U.S. Embassy spokesperson Scott Smith said he couldn't comment on specific cases. Instead, he offered assurances that the Embassy's goal was to "ensure that all adoptions were in compliance with the laws of both Guatemala and the United States." Lorena Seijo went on to note the involvement of Celebrate Children International, Sue Hedberg, Coni Galindo, and Marvin Bran. Coni was "the head of the criminal organization," Seijo wrote, and faced up to forty-two years in prison if she was convicted of human trafficking. She also mentioned that the children were believed to still be in Guatemala. Next to the full-page article ran two of the color photographs of Fernanda and Ana Cristina that Sue Hedberg had emailed to Betsy.

The *Prensa Libre* piece sparked uproar among CCI's clients, who easily identified "Sindy" as Betsy. Blowback came quickly, and passionate emails in defense of Sue Hedberg and CCI started landing in Betsy's inbox. Some CCI clients, especially those whose adoptions were being handled by Marvin Bran, felt "their" children were now endangered by the heightened attention. Even some of the women on the private listserve, whom Betsy considered friends and allies similarly disappointed with CCI, were upset.

Lorena Seijo's article published in Prensa Libre, February 4, 2008.

"Adopting is my ONLY chance at having a daughter," Carrie McFarland angrily told Betsy. "[Your going public] has the end result of jeopardizing the 150 cases in process with CCI — my case included!"

The idea was deeply troubling. hat night, Betsy lay awake, imagining that she'd robbed hundreds of orphans of the chance to "come home." The Embassy must have flagged all of CCI's cases. But a small voice in the back of her head kept on questioning. *Don't these families want to know where their kids come from? What if their babies were stolen, too?*

On February 4, when the damning article came out, Betsy tried contacting the U.S. Embassy again. She forwarded the email she'd previously written to John Lowell. "If a crime did occur, all who were involved in taking the children away from Mildred Alvarado, handling their documents and presenting them for adoption as legal, should be prosecuted in both Guatemala and the United States," she wrote.

This time, Lowell wrote back within hours, saying that Department of State staffer Gerrie Fuller had already informed him of the situation. The Embassy had been "actively investigating this case since we received the information forwarded to us last week," he explained.

Betsy sent him scores of supporting documents, including the video clip showing Sue Hedberg, Marvin Bran, and Fernanda together. "Is it possible that the [girls'] names were changed?" she asked. "I am very worried that if photo matching isn't done on Maria Fernanda, she could still be in an adoption process under another name."

Lowell told Betsy that the girls couldn't be adopted under new identities, since the "old records in the system have been flagged to note the mother's decision to get them back." But if the girls had been laundered with new names, how would the Embassy be able to catch the fraud?

Celebrate Children International staffers began quitting in February 2007. Most didn't know that the Florida Department of Children and Families had investigated the agency, but some harbored suspicions. "Most kids came home for the right reasons, but some didn't," said one former Guatemala case manager who had worked at CCI for five years. "You always wondered if the lawyers and facilitators were telling the truth. I never really knew how it all worked, how they would get the kids. Sometimes I tried to piece things together. But to be honest, I don't want to know." Many of the employees were adoptive parents, and former CCI clients, themselves.

Independently, four of the agency's former employees offered the same story: Sometimes it was better not to know. Each of the staffers harbored concerns, especially about CCI's work in foreign countries. They say they had almost no access to information that could have proved or disproved their concerns, as Sue Hedberg controlled so much of the work flow at the adoption agency.

One CCI staffer says that in mid-February, she received a panicked phone call from a board member asking about the *Prensa Libre* article that had linked Celebrate Children International to alleged child traffickers in Guatemala. The staffer hadn't heard about the article. She hung up and skimmed it online, shocked.

Sue was in Guatemala at the time. When the staffer called her to ask what had happened, Sue told her that *Prensa Libre* was the equivalent of a Guatemalan *National Enquirer*, a sensationalist rag with little credibility. Sue was adamant about not wasting time discussing the kidnapping allegations. The article was quietly copied and passed around the CCI office. Some employees reacted with disbelief, and others felt that their worst fears had been confirmed. The staffer who had fielded the original phone call was unsatisfied with Sue's explanation and quit less than a week later. Ethical concerns hadn't been the only thing pushing her towards resignation; she said she'd also grown increasingly concerned about CCI's bookkeeping, suspecting that a kind of shell game was being practiced with the agency's accounting. It seemed Sue handled a number of "private cases," or independent adoptions, that were kept off the books. Things didn't seem quite right.

Five CCI staffers quit that February. Some say they had signed non-disclosure clauses when they were hired, prohibiting them from talking about the agency. One former staffer claimed that everyone left because of ethics concerns. Another said it was because Sue's behavior towards her staff was, at times, harsh. "The girls at the front desk would cry," said one ex-employee.

"I loved and cared about Sue," says CCI's former Haiti program manager, who built the agency's Haiti adoption program and managed it for over two years. "As a sister in Christ, I wanted her to make better choices." Within three years of its inception, CCI's Haitian adoption program had grown into the second-largest in the U.S., she says, behind only that of Bethany Christian, a much larger adoption agency. Through a partnership with For His Glory Adoption Outreach, a Christian ministry that worked with the Maison des Enfants de Dieu orphanage in Haiti, CCI was able to place children with U.S. families. The former Haiti coordinator says she quit because she wasn't making enough money from her part-time wages. "It was an eye-opener for me to experience the wrath of Sue," she says sadly. Even today, she adds, she remains conflicted about her work with the agency. "[Sue] made lots of threats to me when I left. I didn't understand that about her until I experienced it myself, though I had heard stories."

Another CCI program coordinator had no regrets about leaving, saying she wished only that she'd done it sooner. The stress of working at Celebrate Children International had affected her physical health, she believed. She says she spent countless nights lying awake in bed, unable to sleep after having been berated at work. She was responsible for coordinating a program in a country where CCI wasn't licensed to do business, and therefore had been working with another agency that held a license there. "It was at the point where I almost went off the deep end," the former staffer explains. "I got strange feelings about what was going on."

Not all who worked at Celebrate Children International left unhappily or had suspicions about the agency's business practices. Some long-term staff, like Taiwan program manager Julie Erwin, worked with Sue Hedberg for over ten years with no complaints. "We've had hundreds of clients adopt," she said. "They're all happy."

Many CCI clients spoke of wonderful experiences with the agency. "Sue Hedberg returned my calls promptly and worked hard on our behalf," said Laynah Sheets, an adoptive mother of four Guatemalan children. "She is extremely dedicated. . . . I brought my baby boy home eight months after my case began, and if it hadn't been for Sue, it would have been much longer." Jessica Richter, a client from Wisconsin who adopted biological Guatemalan siblings, found CCI's director to be helpful and knowledgeable. "Sue and [her] attorney allowed Adin's birth mother to foster him for his first three months," she said. "Both of our babies came home young, and we credit the great attorney [Elmer Belteton] and our great God for such speedy processes."

Other clients, like Carolyn Pringle, had mixed emotions about their experience. "Sue has different sides to her," says Pringle, who lives in Winter Park, Florida. "It's odd. She can be short and flip, very nervous, very busy. Everything is very hurried. Sometimes you'd feel like you were bothering her. Sometimes she'd be very sweet — especially when she was dealing with the children. . . . I don't know if I can say I was satisfied, but they did meet their contractual obligations. I would have liked for them to be more forthright. I found out many things through other adoptive parents."

Beth Hunt, an adoptive mother with fourteen children, also had a positive experience adopting from Guatemala with CCI. "Since then, having heard so many awful things about CCI, despite our great experience, I have had some doubts. I can't understand how the same Sue Hedberg who we think of so appreciatively could be the person other people have described so negatively."

Jennifer Crist, a volunteer assistant humanitarian aid coordinator at Celebrate Children International, says "I think the thing to be mindful of is the number of families and adoptions Sue has done, versus the number of complaints filed. I have seen Sue work her butt off and get no sleep. Most adoption agencies just have in-country staff and don't even travel to countries where they work to personally make sure that regulations are being adhered to. Sue was there so much, always trying to find things out."

On February 6, 2008, Norma Cruz and a small group of mothers, including Olga López and Ana Escobar, met with Gudy Rivera, the president of the Comisión del Menor (Commission for Children), to ask for help in finding the missing children. Rivera proposed a thorough review of all pending adoption cases.

The same day, Guatemalan newspaper *La Hora* reported that a total of 3,000 adoptions were currently in process, and a total of 500 children had been reported stolen. The correlation between kidnappings and adoption was implied but unproven. The article mentioned that Sobrevivientes was helping with ten cases.

The mothers continued searching the nurseries to try to find their children. One afternoon at the Sobrevivientes office, Olga López, who'd lost her infant daughter Arlene Escarleth, turned to Sue Kuyper. Olga, who was in her late twenties, worked at a piñata shop to support her two other children. She'd been searching for fourteen months now and had sold her house to help defray the expenses she incurred during her search.

"Do you think she looks like me?" Olga asked, holding up a photo of a girl she'd seen at one of the nurseries, a baby she hoped might be her own. Her voice was soft.

Sue Kuyper shook her head slowly, unsure. Olga gingerly folded the picture, eyes downcast, and tucked it back into her pocket.

14. HOGAR LUZ DE MARÍA
February 2008

The courtyard inside the private nursery Hogar Luz de María, January 19, 2009.

The fact that two children under her care were featured in *Prensa Libre* didn't sit well with nursery director Dinora González Palacios. When Fernanda and Ana Cristina Alvarado arrived at her Guatemala City nursery, Hogar Luz de María (Light of Mary), seven months earlier, she hoped their adoptions would progress as usual, like other abandonment cases.

Instead, the children had been identified in the newspaper, with color photos, as kidnapped minors. It would look terrible if the authorities raided Hogar Luz de María and seized the sisters. If that happened, Dinora knew she might be implicated by association.

Carla Girón had dropped the sisters off at Luz de María, which cared exclusively for children aged six and under, on August 27, 2007, as children who were in the process of being declared abandoned, Dinora said. Carla and Dinora were friends and sometimes business partners, as they worked in the same industry. It was about a year after Fernanda had been taken, and eleven months after Ana Cristina had been seized at birth. That spring, Dinora had worked with her friend Carla on the adoptions. An American adoption agency director, Tedi Hedstrom, of the shuttered Tedi Bear Adoptions, was interested in adopting the older girl, Fernanda. Tedi was now the director of Adoption Blessings Worldwide, another adoption agency, and she considered both Carla and Dinora to be friends. She regularly facilitated adoptions for children that Carla and her associates brought forward.

"This is the little girl that we met in Guatemala and fell in love with," Tedi mass-emailed to a group of friends and Adoption Blessings Worldwide clients on April 10, 2007, months before Dinora says the girls arrived at Luz de María. Attached to the email, a batch of digital pictures with file names including the date "February 2007" showed Mildred's missing daughter in what appeared to be someone's home.

"Our wonderful facilitator, Carla, is in the process of having her declared abandoned along with the help of one of our other great facilitators, Dinora," Tedi wrote. "The judge could agree to the abandonment or disagree. . . . We ask that you would all pray with us that Maria Fernanda comes home, and that she is protected and safe until that day! Most of you are aware that we have 19 children and that the Lord gave me the number 20 as a stopping point for our family. Maria Fernanda would be our twentieth child."

In one photo, Carla Girón sat behind Fernanda, a hand on each of the toddler's arms. They appeared to be in a house. Carla perched on a wooden chair, next to a kitchen table standing on a red and yellow linoleum floor. Fernanda's black skirt had pink flowers embroidered on the hem, and she wore a pale pink blouse with pearly floral buttons. Her dark hair had been cut into bangs. Carla held one of Fernanda's arms aloft, as if to show off her clothes. The child's smile looked tentative.

Dressed in pinstripe pants, a dark knit top, and shiny black boots with heels, Carla herself was smiling so hard that a vein was visible in her forehead. A pair of glasses sat atop her head, holding back straight dirty-blond hair. In the series of nine pictures, which according to camera metadata were taken the same day, Fernanda wore four different outfits: a pale-blue windbreaker, a pink-and-white print dress, a pale-green romper, and a pink gingham button-down with cheerful yellow-and-pink-striped pants. In one image, the child was brushing her teeth and looked surprised by the camera. Her eyes were big and round. In one photo, Fernanda appeared delighted, her eyes crinkled shut, mid-laugh. Another showed her somberly staring at something outside of the frame, her small hands clasped together.

The location where the photos were taken is unknown. Although Tedi's email implied that Dinora was involved with the Alvarado children as early as April 2007, Dinora maintains she first met them at the end of August 2007, when Carla Girón brought them to her nursery. At the time, Ana Cristina was a few months shy of her first birthday, and Dinora said she was difficult, crying nonstop for three to four days. She also had trouble eating. Fernanda cried too, Dinora said, begging for "Mama Carla." Nannies at the nursery flocked to the new arrivals, doting on them and marveling at their beauty.

Hogar Luz de María, a two-story structure surrounding an open courtyard where children mingled during the day, was in central Guatemala City. The courtyard's bleak grey walls were painted with cartoon characters: Winnie the Pooh and bumblebees, Piglet hatching from an Easter egg, Eeyore the donkey wreathed in flowers. Blue picket fencing kept children cordoned off in sections that appeared to be broken up by age group.

Upstairs, the nursery's sleeping areas were broken up according to age. In a room with a pale-green wall, infants slept two to a crib. The single room held eleven cribs. Sticky notes attached to headboards identified the babies both by name and by the case number corresponding to their judicial file. In another upstairs room, nine larger wooden cribs stood in neat rows. All the rooms were immaculately clean.

Dinora ran the hogar with her sister, Claudia Briola González. Hogar Luz de María had opened just three years earlier, in 2004. Dinora, a slender, well-dressed woman who appeared to be in her thirties, was the director. She'd worked with adoption lawyers Susana Luarca and Alma Valle Mejia and spent five years as director of another nursery before moving to Hogar Luz de María.

Some of the things Dinora had seen troubled her. It was common for birth mothers to be tricked or deceived. She had heard of cases where pregnant teenagers, largely uneducated and naive, came from rural areas to Guatemala City, taking jobs as live-in help for wealthier families. They would be taken to a hospital to give birth, and both the babies and all related documentation would be seized, leaving no proof that the births had even happened.

For this to happen, though, a birth mother would have to be unwilling or unable to object. If a birth mother showed up at an abandonment hearing, a judge could decide to restore custody of the child in question to her instead of to the hogar or lawyer who had asked for the hearing. One story in particular haunted Dinora: She remembered learning of a young mother who had been killed in a sugarcane field after her child had entered an adoption process.

Dinora took pains to operate her own nursery fastidiously, reviewing the paperwork of every child who came to Hogar Luz de María. Many of the children had been ordered to the nursery by Judge Mario Fernando Peralta, the Escuintla judge whom government investigators had nicknamed "Danny DeVito" and who was suspected of accepting bribes in exchange for issuing abandonment decrees.

Hogar Luz de María housed 20 to 30 children at a time and worked with U.S. adoption agencies including Wide Horizons for Children, Open Door Adoption Agency, and Adoption Blessings Worldwide. On their website, Wide Horizons for Children stated they'd placed over 250 children from Hogar Luz de María in the U.S. Wide Horizons also placed children from Hogar Luz de Fatima, another Guatemala City nursery where Judge Peralta often sent "abandoned" children.

Dinora's nursery had a colorful website and an active Facebook page she updated frequently with her Blackberry. Having an online presence helped to attract donations, and also helped adoptive parents stay informed about what their potential sons or daughters might be doing at the nursery. Occasionally, kids from Luz de María went on field trips to places like the Guatemala City zoo.

The nursery's website, HogarLuzDeMaria.org, was in Spanish and English. There, Dinora listed a Miami post office box under her own name, where Americans could mail charitable donations. The nursery's Guatemalan banking information was also posted for those wanting to make wire transfers. On their "Donations" page, Hogar Luz de María's monthly operating expenses were listed as about $10,000.

The *Prensa Libre* piece was concerning. Dinora certainly didn't want her own name in the paper connected to adoption fraud. In the first week of February 2008, in order to preempt a possible raid by authorities searching for the Alvarado sisters, Dinora decided to bring the girls' documents to the Sala de la Niñez. The Sala was the court responsible for distributing cases among Guatemala City's three family courts. Dinora wanted a judge to reaffirm that the children were supposed to be in her care. The Sala passed the files to the Juzgado Tercero de la Niñez y Adolescencia (the Third Court of Children and Adolescents), presided over by Judge Ricardo Gómez Damman. Coincidentally, Gómez' court was the one that had received the files on Mildred Alvarado's complaint about her daughters' abductions.

Following protocol, Judge Gómez reissued a decree he'd ordered three months before, on November 21, 2007, asking court officials to serve the children's mother with information about the next step: a hearing for those involved or interested in the case to come forward and make themselves known. The order, reissued on February 13, 2008, confirmed the original hearing date of February 25 —nearly a year after the date on the snapshots of Carla Girón and Fernanda.

The authorities and Guatemalan citizens generally regarded Judge Gómez as an honest man, someone who placed children's interests over those of adoption lawyers. Although his court was supposed to be handling Mildred's complaint, there was no simple way to cross-check a report about missing children against the files of children who'd been brought in for abandonment hearings. There were computers at the court, but not everything was digitized. Mildred's complaint might have been taken by one of the law students working in the court's crowded reception area, escaping the judge's attention. The complaint might then have been buried under one of the stacks of files piled atop the desks scattered throughout the building. In any case, the coincidence went unnoticed.

The pediatric medical records related to the Alvarado sisters that were sent to both the Emanuel and Thompson families by Sue Hedberg had originated in the office of Guatemala City pediatrician Dr. Napoleón Castillo Mollinedo. To Dr. Castillo, the children were just two more coming in and out, brought in by frequent clients the Galindo Bran family, whom he'd gotten to know well over the years.

Coni Galindo Bran's daughter, Kimberly, was the one who usually brought the children in for exams. Occasionally, Coni's son, Marvin, or even Coni herself would come in. Dr. Castillo calculated that the Brans had brought hundreds of children to his private office, located in a rough part of Zone 1 in Guatemala's capital. He kept track of the children on a digitized Excel spreadsheet dating back to 2005. Before that, his office kept records by hand, in a thick bound book.

During the height of the adoption craze, Dr. Castillo, a tall man with striking light-green eyes, seized the opportunity to make money. The Galindo Brans weren't the only adoptionists who brought children to his practice. Eight or nine others, who handled even more adoptions than the Galindo Bran family, brought children to him for exams and vaccinations.

Business grew so rapidly that Dr. Castillo rented an additional office, adjacent to his examining room. That way, he could see a child in each, saving time by simply moving back and forth through the doorway. He instated a new policy for billing: Instead of charging per child, a process that left everyone drowning in paperwork, he allowed adoption facilitators bringing "volume" through his office to keep a tab, paying in a lump monthly sum. The facilitators with "volume" also received a slight per-child discount.

Sometimes cuidadoras offered doctors bribes, asking them to provide fabricated medical records without actually seeing children. Dr. Castillo says he always refused to take such bribes and that working with adoptionists left him feeling uncertain. Still, as the years passed, he'd stopped questioning much of what he saw. The Galindo Brans, he said, "didn't overflow with love" for the kids they brought in for examination. "They took average care of the children," he said, "perhaps a bit worse than the other facilitators." They left buying medicine for sick children to the very last minute, the pediatrician said, and then only when it was absolutely necessary. "The children brought in by the Brans weren't abused," Dr. Castillo remembers, "although not buying medicine is certainly abuse."

On a child's first visit to his office, Dr. Castillo would ask about his or her background and felt he had no choice but to take the answers provided to him by cuidadoras at face value. Every time one of the women hesitated, he felt chilled. More than half the children examined at his office didn't have proper paperwork, such as a birth certificate. Sometimes their names would change. It wasn't his responsibility to investigate, the pediatrician told himself; he was just there to make sure that the kids were being cared for.

Mildred Alvarado's daughter Ana Cristina was brought in to see Dr. Castillo when she was four days old, on September 11, 2006, according to his memory and his patient database. The woman who brought her in, Ruth Monroy, told him that Ana Cristina had been born in Cobán, Alta Verapaz, five hours outside of Guatemala City. Over the next five months, he saw the baby five times. The last time was February 12, 2007. The address listed for Ana Cristina and the woman tasked with caring for her, "Ruth Amarilis," was a crumbling house within a slum in Zone 1. When asked, a wheelchair-bound man living at the address in August 2010 said he'd never heard of Ruth Amarilis. No neighbors had, either.

Dr. Castillo also saw Ana Cristina's sister Maria Fernanda a total of five times, starting on August 22, 2006. That was the day after Marvin Bran offered the girl to Sue Hedberg, who in turn offered her to Betsy Emanuel, just hours later. The address listed on Fernanda's medical records was Coni's house in San José las Rosas. The woman accompanying Fernanda to Dr. Castillo's office was noted as "Kimberly" in the pediatric records, with no given last name. Dr. Castillo says "Kimberly" was Coni's daughter.

Diana Pérez[19] couldn't believe her good fortune. When the nursery she worked at was raided, she'd narrowly escaped arrest. She

---

[19.] The name has been changed to protect anonymity.

thanked God over and over. It was as if her deceased grandmother, whom she believed to be her guardian angel, was watching over her. When the authorities arrived, all fifteen of the babies and children that Diana had been paid to care for had already been evacuated and relocated. It seemed too fortunate to be a coincidence, Diana thought. Her bosses, Carla Girón and Coni Galindo Bran, must have known about the raid.

Afterward, Coni was apparently unruffled. Perhaps it was because she was used to having her houses raided, Diana thought — after all, it had also happened back in November 2006. That time, a woman named Mildred Alvarado had filed a complaint and showed up with the police in search of her stolen daughters. Although the stakes of this raid were high — there was an entire unlicensed nursery that had been set up, with the help of Carla Girón, in one of Coni's homes—it had failed to uncover anything illegal. The day before, Carla had dispersed the fifteen children across Guatemala, handing them off to various cuidadoras to be cared for in their homes. Diana was racked with guilt. She loved the kids she cared for and worked hard to help them, especially the older girls who'd been abused. It had taken Diana months to bring some of the severely malnourished babies back from what seemed like the edge of death.

Many of the children's origins were unclear to Diana. She knew Fernanda and Ana Cristina Alvarado, who lived in the nursery briefly in early 2007, to be "problem" girls (children with problematic adoptions). Diana was under the impression that Carla Girón had given the sisters to Coni Galindo Bran, in lieu of money, to settle a debt. The two frequently worked together, Diana believed, trading money and adoption cases. The smaller one, Ana Cristina, was always crying. The two girls didn't seem to know that they were sisters.

Diana began taking care of children for Carla Girón just after Christmas 2004. A "contact" named Hilda had met Carla and Diana at a McDonald's, handing over a malnourished 9-month-old boy who weighed only about nine pounds. Diana understood that Carla worked in adoption with a core group of five people — Alejandra Ortiz, Freddy Ariel Maldonado, Pablo Alejandro Méndez, Karla Ordoñez, and a man known as Oscar — plus various jaladoras and finders. The associates established an office in Zone 9 of Guatemala City, where cuidadoras sometimes picked up baby supplies and petty cash for taxis to and from appointments, like DNA sampling and court hearings.

As time passed and Diana proved herself to be a kind, hard-working caretaker, the number of children Carla gave her increased. Once, Diana found herself caring for six children in her home. Carla paid 800 quetzales ($100) per child per month, though, Diana and other cuidadoras noted, she wasn't punctual with payments. Diana had introduced Carla to other women in the neighborhood interested in making money by temporarily taking an extra child into their homes. Seven women worked as cuidadoras for Carla in San José las Rosas, the gated community where Coni Galindo Bran and her son lived. Many of them believed that Carla was an attorney, and Diana says that Coni Galindo Bran did, too, referring to Carla with the formal title *Licenciada*, a term used to address professional license holders like lawyers.

Most of the children came from sad situations. One little girl, Glendy, was starving. Her birth mother was paid 5,000 quetzales ($635) to give her up, Diana remembers. During the first week, Diana repeatedly found Glendy eating garbage. The little girl would eat an adult-size meal and still seek out trash to consume. Diana started hiding the trash can. Another birth mother gave up seven of her children consecutively in adoption, two of whom Diana cared for. Sometimes, Carla rotated the children among her cuidadoras; Diana remembers being given a sick child to nurse back to health, only to be asked to pass the baby to another caretaker once the baby was stable. Then Diana would get another sick child. After just four months, she said proudly, the first malnourished boy she'd ever cared for had more than doubled in weight.

Birth mothers generally received 11,800 to 39,000 quetzales ($1,500 to $5,000) per child, as far as Diana knew. She and the other cuidadoras compared notes and gossiped frequently, sharing tidbits of information from various places, including from the birth mothers themselves. Women who sold their children weren't fit to be mothers in the first place, Diana thought. The price of a child, it seemed, was often a point of contention. A woman was often promised more money than she was given, and when the full amount didn't materialize, she might try to back out of an adoption in protest, demanding her child back. Diana had heard from Carla that a woman might sell the same child more than once, to different adoptionists, after backing out of an original plan.

In early 2007, Carla told Diana that she had a new idea. She wanted to set up her own nursery. That way, she could save money by paying one or two caretakers to look after a bunch of children instead of paying various women to care for one or two babies each. Around San José Las Rosas, Diana says, the project became known as "the baby house." American adoptive parents referred to the nursery as "Carla's baby house." The Americans sent supplies and donations to help the nursery get started, since it would be housing children they thought of as their own. "We weren't really sure if it was happening or not," notes Katie Tuel, one American adoptive mother. Still, many chose to believe the best-case scenerario.

Because Coni Galindo Bran had two homes in San José las Rosas, Diana says, Carla asked if she could set up a nursery in one of them. After the police raided her home on November 29, 2006, searching for Mildred Alvarado's daughters, Coni moved up the block into a house one door down from her son, Marvin Bran, and his wife, Mariela. The raided house was left vacant until Carla rented the space and set up her nursery there in early February 2007.

According to Diana and other adoption facilitators who worked with Carla Girón, Coni Galindo Bran was one of the jaladoras, or "baby finders," who provided "adoptable" children. They also allege that Coni kept pregnant women at her home, who were then brought to her brother-in-law's medical clinic in Guatemala City to give birth and subsequently relinquish the babies. Carla and her associates would then sometimes handle the infants' adoptions. Diana estimated that typically, five to ten pregnant women at a time lived at Coni's house. "When the mother was dumb — or not dumb, more like simple, unable to think complex thoughts — then they would tell her the baby had died," Diana remembered. "But they wouldn't give her the body. They'd have her sign blank papers, and the child would be put up for adoption." Faking a baby's death saved money, since the mother wouldn't have to be paid off.

Carla asked Diana Pérez to run the baby house. Diana was reluctant; before agreeing, she laid down a single rule: Carla had to hire more staff. Fifteen babies and children were simply too many for one person to handle. To her relief, Carla promised to bring four professional nurses on board. Diana thought the medical help was needed, as some children were seriously malnourished and some suffered from bad diarrhea. A few of the older ones would cower like abused animals. One girl had burns all over her body from her birth mother allegedly throwing boiling water on her, and another had the pattern of a stovetop burner branded into her backside. The girl's mother, Diana was told, had sat the child on a hot stove as punishment for urinating on herself. Another girl, age nine, had been raped. One boy's deformed ears had never separated from his head. Another baby had somehow survived only on water, not milk. Overall, Diana felt, the lot of them were in poor condition.

She divided the children into sections by age, struggling to learn their names and quell the spread of lice. As February became March and March became April, Diana kept asking Carla about the additional help she'd promised. She was exhausted. Her sister often helped out, and the two women would arrive at the baby house early in the morning and leave at about 9:00 pm, when two other cuidadoras came in to work the night shift. One of Carla's business associates remembers having a conversation with Diana during which she exclaimed, "I'm going crazy here with fifteen babies!"

The number of children wasn't the only issue. Carla was notoriously cheap with supplies. Other caretakers who worked for her say that they were given just enough resources to keep the children alive, but no more. "She'd give us two packs of diapers and one box of milk, and that was supposed to last a baby the whole month," recalled one cuidadora. "There were lots of malnourished children. And if they hadn't found a family for a baby, you'd take him to the doctor and he'd say, 'Don't bring him back until he has a family that can pay for his vaccines.'" Cases that belonged to Carla and her associates were often taken to pediatrician Dr. Roberto Tobar in Guatemala City. Tobar was afraid to talk about adoption or Girón. Cases handled by Coni Bran Galindo and her family went to Dr. Castillo.

Finally, Diana got fed up. The fifteen children were suffering, and it wasn't fair. She had come to doubt Carla Girón's promises. American adoptive parents had given Diana contradictory information when she delivered children to them during their visit trips. She realized that Carla lied to them frequently, about everything from a baby's health down to what type of formula he or she was given.

At about 6:00 one evening in late April 2007, Diana snapped. "Look for replacement caretakers, because I'm done here," she remembers telling her boss. "I'm tired. I can't do a good job with so many children, all of different ages. Either you bring in more help right now, tonight, or take the children away."

The next morning at about 10:00, Diana watched, surprised and sad, as taxis holding five other cuidadoras pulled up in front of the baby house in San José las Rosas. Children were distributed among the cars and then taken away. Two children were left behind, and Diana took them into her own home. Hours later, at about 5:00 pm, the newly vacated nursery was raided by a team that looked, to Diana, like the police. Diana wondered if Coni or Carla had been tipped off. She'd heard rumors that Coni's family had connections inside the local branch of the Ministerio Público and that one of Carla's friends, attorney Amadeo Guerra, was the son of a magistrate.

American adoptive mother Nancy Steadman[20] says she got a call from Tedi Hedstrom, the director of Adoption Blessings Worldwide, informing her about the raid. The child she was trying to adopt, Teresa, had been living under Carla's care in San José las Rosas. She remembers being told that it was a "nighttime raid" and that the children were being held at an undisclosed location because of "poor paperwork." In a 2007 email sent to another client, Hedstrom wrote, "Please pray for the Steadman family . . . [and] their referral of Teresa, who Carla lost due to her being I believe a stolen child. . . ." Later the Steadmans wondered if Teresa had ever really existed. They had no real evidence that she had. They filed a complaint with the Florida Department of Children and Families.

Another American adoptive mother remembers the raid happening on the 10th or 11th of February, not in April, as cuidadora Diana Pérez says. "They were in the process of raiding a bunch of homes, these corrupt cops," the American explains. "The kids would disappear." She wasn't sure how the Guatemalan child she adopted had made it through the process. "His name kept changing, his birth date kept changing," she recalled. "Apparently, they had the files mixed up. . . . On his DNA test, the dates don't match. There was another kid's picture on his passport." Back in the U.S., she says, she reported the irregularities to the U.S. Embassy and the Secretary of State. "I

20. The name has been changed to protect anonymity.

thought maybe they had an investigation going on," she says, noting that no one ever followed up with her. "Maybe because things were so corrupt and things were closing — maybe they just didn't care anymore."

Reflecting on her work in adoption processes, Diana says she can't understand how God allowed the adoption industry to manifest as it did, bloated by lies, half-truths, and swindles. "I don't know if I'm guilty or if I have responsibility," she says. She finds solace in the fact that she tried, hard, to love every child who'd come under her care. Still, finding the words to talk about everything that transpired remains difficult. Diana loved and believed in the concept of adoption. Yet the children, she says, were treated like animals: bartered, bought, and sold.

Pilar Ramírez, Mildred's lawyer, was taken by surprise when she got a phone call from the Third Court of Children and Minors. Ever since the *Prensa Libre* article featuring Mildred, everyone at Sobrevivientes had clung to the hope that whoever had the children would bring them forward. The newspaper piece had been big news, consisting of a whole page with color pictures of the missing children. Whoever had the kids must be scared. And now, finally, real information had surfaced! Pilar tried to control her excitement, reminding herself how much work lay ahead. Anxiously, she realized that she'd have to make Mildred understand why they couldn't just go and pick up the girls. Judge Gómez would decide whether or not to restore custody at the hearing.

Pilar called Ariel Guevara, the investigator from the Villa Canales branch of the Ministerio Público, who provided a street address for Hogar Luz de María, the nursery where the girls were reported to be. Guevara warned against trying to visit. In a formal statement to the court, Dinora Palacios, the woman who ran the hogar where the children had been staying, and her business partner and sister, Claudia Briolas, asked the judge to prohibit visits to the Alvarado children by "the supposed mother" and "the entity supporting her claim" (Sobrevivientes). They were concerned about "the image" of their nursery and about how the Alvarado case could bring "unimaginable problems" for the rest of the children in their care. They didn't elaborate on what that might mean.

Pilar and others helping with Mildred's case at Sobrevivientes had questions: Why hadn't the hogar brought the Alvarado girls forward in November, after the first *Prensa Libre* article mentioning them came out? Did they think they could give the girls in adoption despite Mildred's missing-child complaints?

After talking to Pilar and Norma, Mildred called an old friend from the auto parts shop who used to drive a taxi. She read him the address of Hogar Luz de María: 10 Avenida 13-85, Zona 12. "That's Colonia Reformita," he told her.

It was just blocks from the market at the bus terminal where Mildred used to sell food. Her mind raced with excitement. *I can go there,* she thought. *I can get up a wall, or fence, or whatever is there. I know I can.* She remembered shimmying up trees as a girl in the country and imagined that scaling a wall could be done with similar ease. She'd climb over and rescue her girls on her own. Then no one else would be bothered, anymore, with any of it. No one would ask her, ever again, if she'd sold her daughters, or laugh at her plight, or tell her to give up. She just wanted her children back and to be left alone.

Besides, then there would be one less case for the authorities to handle. They hadn't helped much, anyway. Fighting for justice the way Norma Cruz and Sobrevivientes did, failed to hold much appeal for Mildred. She just wanted to get on with her life. Public attention made her uncomfortable.

When she told Patricia her idea, her sister just looked at her, shaking her head sadly. "If you do it, you'll ruin everything," she said. She convinced Mildred to wait.

The next day, Norma told her the same thing: Hold on just a little longer. She seemed confident the children would be returned. A Ministerio Público investigator had visited Hogar Luz de María, Norma said, and told her that the children were in good health. He'd examined their arms and legs for bruises and hadn't found any.

Still, Mildred remained fixated on the obvious possibility that her children could be moved and hidden in another nursery.

After Pilar reviewed the paperwork that Hogar Luz de María had turned in, she began trying to piece together what might have happened with the children. Perhaps Marvin Bran had initially tried to get the children adopted as relinquishment cases with Celebrate Children International, but had ran into problems after Mildred began speaking out. Perhaps Marvin or his mother had sold, given, or traded the Alvarado girls to Carla Girón, who then tried to open abandonment proceedings for them before Judge Peralta in Escuintla.

Though the actual chain of events remained fuzzy, certain facts were now clear. Judge Peralta had issued orders sending Fernanda and Ana Cristina Alvarado to Hogar Luz de María for care back in August 2007. According to nursery director Dinora González Palacios, the children had been there ever since, until the *Prensa Libre* article allegedly inspired her to bring them forward to the judge. Dinora's motivations were unclear; either she wanted to help the children, or she'd realized there was no way the adoptions could keep "walking" through the Guatemalan bureaucracy. Mildred had filed too many complaints with too many institutions, and now the American Betsy Emanuel had provided color photographs of the girls.

Then, as luck would have it, the judge randomly selected to handle Dinora's request for guidance about what to do with the Alvarado sisters was none other than Judge Gómez, who was also overseeing Mildred's missing-children complaint. The coincidence seemed too good to be true.

Late in the afternoon on Valentine's Day, Betsy Emanuel learned that Fernanda and Ana Cristina had been located. She cradled the phone in one hand, leaning against her dresser as she listened to Sue Kuyper, the same woman who'd translated her conversation with Mildred. Kuyper assured her that the children were safe and gave her a quick summary of what would happen at the upcoming hearing. Betsy hung up and bowed her head to say a quick prayer of thanks.

Then she emailed John Lowell at the U.S. Embassy, wondering if he'd heard the news. Betsy figured that the hardest part — physically locating the girls — was over. Now the authorities would step in and uncover what had transpired with the abductions and subsequent thwarted adoptions of the children. "We want to see this crime corrected," she wrote to Lowell, "and those who said nothing but had knowledge of this tragic situation punished to the fullest extent of the law in both countries."

The U.S. Embassy was the only institution with the power to help, Betsy thought. She asked Lowell if it was possible to retro-actively nullify the Embassy's pre-approval of the Alvarado sisters' adoptions, since they hadn't been voluntarily relinquished and were never authentic orphans. She also asked if he could check to see if either child had been offerd in adoption to another unsuspecting family. "At $25K or more for each adoption, these girls may simply be a commodity at this point," she said.

Lowell replied quickly. Betsy read his email twice, with a growing sense of dread. He didn't seem to know that the Alvarado children had surfaced. "How did you learn of this?" he asked.

Betsy sighed. If she had learned the news from her home in Tennessee, how could the general consul of the U.S. Embassy in Guatemala not have heard? A week earlier, on February 6, she'd felt genuinely reassured by John Lowell. She thought he'd been serious about looking into the case. He'd even promised to tell her if the children were located.

So much for that, she thought. *At least they're safe.*

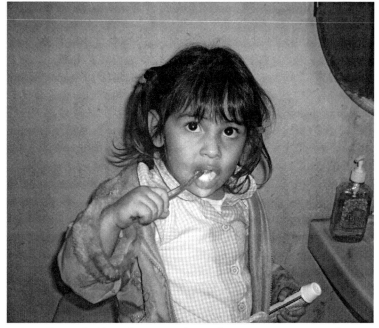

Maria Fernanda Alvarado, in an unknown location, sometime in early 2007.
Photograph courtesy anonymous.

15. CUSTODY

February 25, 2008–May 2008

With the court date nearing, Pilar started preparing Mildred for the big day. Though Norma seemed confident, the success of getting the children back rested squarely on Pilar's small shoulders. She'd been at Sobrevivientes for only a month and was now handling one of its most high-profile cases. Rootman Pérez, another young Sobrevivientes lawyer, was working with her on Mildred's case. Between them, they had lots of theoretical knowledge but almost no practical experience. It would have been funny if the stakes hadn't been so high.

As it was her first time litigating, Pilar decided that caution was the best policy. Neither she nor Rootman had ever worked a child protection case before. Pilar was afraid of being surprised by something unexpected in court, so the two lawyers studied the judicial structure and reviewed old decisions until they felt prepared for any scenario.

To make matters worse, there was the distinct possibility that their plaintiff could be a loose cannon at the hearing. In the week leading up to the court date, Mildred sat through three separate mock trials at the Sobrevivientes office. Pilar and Rootman drilled her with questions, asking her about every part of what had happened. They wanted her to stay calm, to understand the ambience of a courtroom. They tried to get Mildred to understand that they were on her side, even if it didn't feel like it. They needed her to understand that she would feel attacked but that she had to remain composed.

Pilar got a sinking feeling in her stomach as Mildred shyly repeated her story in a monotonous, flat voice. How would she react to being in the same room with her daughters? Stress was practically radiating from her body, and she was just practicing. In response to some questions, Mildred laughed nervously.

"No," Pilar scolded her. "You have to answer seriously. They may ask you this: 'Again: Why don't you want to care for your girls?' "

Mildred cleared her throat, struggling to maintain her composure. She'd told Pilar many times that she had always wanted her girls. Being questioned on this again and again was irritating. "No," she answered. She grinned anxiously to quell the anger. "No!"

Pilar tried again. "You must answer," she said. "You can't do this at the hearing."

Sometimes during a response, Mildred would trail off mid-sentence, seemingly lost more in space than in thought. Sobrevivientes had paid for psychological tests in order to determine if there might be a physical or chemical cause for her lapses, or some kind of undiagnosed mental illness. The tests had found that Mildred was poorly educated and mildly depressed. She was honest but easily manipulated.

Pilar worried that the lawyers for Hogar Luz de María or Judge Gómez would push her to the breaking point. She was dignified but fragile, and at a certain point in the questioning, she had the potential to fall apart. Pilar could envision Mildred in court, pushed to the point of emotional exhaustion. If she was asked how much she got paid in exchange for her children — a question that might well come up — Pilar could easily imagine her snapping and yelling, "No, Judge!"

Pilar swallowed her feelings of doubt. She'd racked her brain to come up with ways to bulletproof the case, but it all came down to the judge. That was outside her control. She'd done everything she could, even seeking out help from the Guatemalan Congress and the Congressional Commission on Children and Families. The head of the commission, Gudy Rivera, had promised to appear to show his support. The media had also been informed of the hearing.

Pilar ran through the inconsistencies in the case for the thousandth time. Mildred had been tricked into relinquishing Fernanda. She'd signed blank papers. The baby's kidnapping was a little easier to prove, as Sabrina's mother-in-law had paid for the C-section and signed her name to the hospital receipt. But what about the DNA test? And worse, how to account for the month between when the baby was taken and Mildred filed her complaint?

Oh, my God, how will I explain it? Pilar wondered. *What can I say? Your Honor, I believe her, just because I do.*

They'd decided to ask Judge Gómez to return the children immediately, that same day. For such a request to be granted, Mildred had to make a good impression in every way. Otherwise, the waiting would continue while the judge ordered an investigation into whether she was fit to parent. Given the pace of the Guatemalan judicial system, the wait Could take months, if not years.

"Listen, Mildred," Pilar said. "What are you going to wear to the hearing? You need to look good. Do you have nicer clothes?"

"No," Mildred replied, offended. She took pains to appear clean and presentable. "Look, I'm poor. I wear what I have."

"No, no," Pilar said. "I don't mean to make you feel bad. We just need you to be presentable. You need better shoes."

Mildred looked down at her sneakers, the only pair of shoes she owned. She figured she could get 20 quetzales ($2.50) from Patricia to buy a pair of used black shoes. Pilar instructed her to wear black pants, along with her newest sweater, which had crisp red-and-white stripes on it.

"Do you want me to do your makeup and your hair?" the young lawyer offered. Pilar's own glossy black hair and makeup were meticulously done. "I can do it here at the office before the hearing."

Mildred shuddered. "No, no way," she said, imagining the news cameras Pilar had warned her about. "If my father ever saw me wearing makeup, he'd kill me." She tried to say it lightly, yet the thought of enduring a beating made her feel light-headed. Wearing makeup was the last thing she wanted to do.

Mildred barely slept the night before the hearing. She woke at 3:30 in the morning, dressed, and waited. Pilar had told her to be at Sobrevivientes at 8:00 so that they could arrive at the courthouse by 8:30 for the hearing, which was expected to begin at 10:00.

Instead, Mildred left Villa Nueva at 5:00 am, to arrive outside the locked Sobrevivientes building at 6:00. The city streets were ghostly calm, the usual glut of rusted cars and heavy smog a distant memory. Before leaving, Mildred had made coffee, but found she couldn't drink it. She was too nervous.

She paced up and down the street, between Sobrevivientes and the Partido Patriota headquarters up the block. At about 7:30, she realized that the cleaning woman, Salvita, was already inside.

"So early!" Salvita said, eyeing her with kindness. "Why didn't you ring the doorbell?" Mildred shrugged sheepishly.

Inside, Salvita poured a cup of coffee and handed it to Mildred. It was burning hot, but she downed it quickly. Her nerves jangled. The harder she looked at the clock, the slower it seemed to move.

Pilar arrived late, blowing through the door a little after 8:30, accompanied by the other Sobrevivientes lawyer, Rootman. Mildred got into Pilar's small red car. "I'm so sorry," Pilar said. "Let's go!"

At the court, a PGN car was already sitting outside. Members of the Guatemalan press began to arrive. Because the kidnappings had been in the national newspapers, it seemed that everyone was waiting to see what would happen next with the case. Soon a Sobrevivientes van packed with Sue Kuyper, Norma Cruz, and three other mothers, Olga López, Loyda Rodriguez, and Raquel Par, arrived. Salvita tagged along, too.

The courthouse looked like any other single-story house on the block. The nondescript building blended in well in Zone 1, the oldest section of the city. Everyone milled on the crumbling, crooked sidewalk.

Outside, Mildred saw Mejicanos, the man who headed the PGN's denuncia unit, get out of a white car. She looked at him quizzically. *What is he doing here?* She'd stopped cleaning his floors when she realized he hadn't been doing much to help her.

His expression was hard to read.

That morning, Victor Hugo Mejicanos had received a call from his boss, Mario Gordillo, personally asking him to make an appearance at the hearing, despite the fact that another PGN lawyer was assigned to Judge Gómez's courthouse on behalf of the PGN.

Mejicanos felt as if the PGN's image rested on him. The situation was delicate. If the PGN, on behalf of the country of Guatemala, declared that the children shouldn't be returned, there might be public outrage. *Everyone will jump on us,* Mejicanos thought. *But if we say yes, without any conditions, it will also look bad.* He began trying to think of a compromise. He still found Mildred's story confusing.

Glancing around, he saw Norma Cruz behind Mildred, along with a small entourage from Sobrevivientes. Norma was a political force, someone with the influence to exact change. She was a fierce and determined fighter. Plus, the media adored her. Crossing her would be a political move and had to be done with the utmost care.

Mejicanos strode over to Mildred. "I'm here to support you," he said quietly. "And I'm going to try to make sure everything goes well for you and that the girls are turned over today." Mildred nodded and made her way inside.

A PGN recommendation was no real comfort, because the judge ultimately made the final decision.

In the small reception area, Mildred saw Fernanda and Ana Cristina sitting quietly on the laps of two women. They were about six feet away from her, and she recognized the girls instantly. A surge of joy coursed through her body, but she felt afraid to look directly at them. Ana Cristina wore a fresh yellow jumpsuit, and Fernanda had on a smart denim romper and a bright-red sweater dotted with tiny hearts. They were grown up now, Mildred thought to herself. Fernanda looked like a girl, not a baby. She was now a few months shy of five years old. Ana Cristina was already one-and-a-half, almost a toddler. Both children had plump cheeks and shiny hair. They appeared to have been well cared for. Both were extremely quiet and very still. They looked vacant. Neither child seemed to notice or recognize Mildred.

Norma Cruz clutched her hand, and Pilar and Rootman hovered nearby. Mildred had been warned not to approach the children, but the room was small. Again, she was seized by the terrible urge to grab Fernanda and run. It seemed so simple. Mildred quickly ran through the possibilities in her mind; the police and the court security guards weren't even outside yet. There was a chance she could get away with it. Carla Girón and the woman next to her seemed to be glaring at her.

"Pilar," she said, looking at her lawyer. "Are you sure we will get them today?" Pilar assured her that it was possible. Mildred asked again a few minutes later, tears welling up in her eyes. She glanced, briefly, at Fernanda, then returned her gaze to the tile floor. She was afraid that if she looked at her daughters again, she'd lose control, and she didn't want to cause a stir. Tears began rolling down her cheeks, and she repeated Pilar's stern instructions in her head: *Stay calm, Mildred. Stay calm.* It didn't work, and she started sobbing.

Judge Gómez sat at the front of a courtroom cluttered with a long oval table and a few desks. Nothing about the décor seemed particularly official; the simple room looked like a generic office space. Gómez was a graying man of medium height, with an even expression. He looked to be about 60. He terrified Mildred, and she avoided looking at him. He sat behind a table.

Only those with a direct stake in the custody of the Alvarado children were allowed into in the courtroom. Mildred, Pilar, and Rootman sat together, as did Dinora González Palacios, Carla Girón, and César Augosto Trujillo. Trujillo was the lawyer whose name appeared on many of the ower-of-attorney forms for Celebrate Children International clients adopting Marvin Bran babies. He was also the Galindo Bran family's personal lawyer, the man who had presided over the marriage of Marvin to his wife, Mariela.

Dinora told the judge that Carla Girón had dropped the children off at Hogar Luz de María, in accordance with the orders of Judge Peralta in Escuintla. She said she hadn't realized anyone was looking for the children until she saw the *Prensa Libre* article "Where are my children?" earlier that month. Yet the article she cited had been published in November 2007, not February 2008. The follow-up piece, "U.S. Embassy Approves Adoption of Stolen Children," was dated February 4. Mildred's story had been in the media for months before Dinora said she'd learned about it.

Judge Gómez looked at Mildred. She'd been weeping through-out the hearing, which was stretching into its second hour. "Did you give your daughters up for adoption?"

"No," she said. The tears continued to run down her face, but her voice was strong.

"Did you receive money for them?" he asked.

"No," she said. "I did not. I swear to God that I did not." Once again, she broke down in tears.

The questions continued. At one point, it seemed to Pilar that Judge Gómez might be leaning towards issuing an order for the children to be kept in provisional care in another nursery rather than returning them to Mildred. His questions were hard for Mildred to answer: What was your relationship with Sabrina? Why did you give up Fernanda voluntarily? You never suspected Sabrina worked in adoption? Why did you sign the documents? Mildred was trembling, and her voice kept breaking.

Judge Gómez was frank but compassionate. Mejicanos asked a few questions on behalf of the PGN, which was acting on behalf of the Guatemalan government. When Mildred grew flustered, Judge Gómez told her to take her time and to consult with her counsel. "That's what lawyers are for," he said kindly.

Later, César Augosto Trujillo, the man whose name had been on Betsy Emanuel's power-of-attorney form, presented the notarized relinquishment forms. The documents, one for each girl, stated that Mildred had consented to give the children to Carla Girón on December 12, 2006.

A smile of relief tugged at the corner of Pilar's mouth. It was almost too good to be true. To counter, she presented the missing-persons reports Mildred had filled out with various authorities in November 2006, a full month before the relinquishment papers had been created. Mildred had reported the girls missing more than thirty days before Carla Girón claimed their mother had voluntarily relinquished them. Across the room, Pilar noticed, the other women did not look very happy.

When Judge Gómez issued his decision, Mildred didn't understand it. He'd stated, quite clearly, that she was allowed to take Fernanda and Ana Cristina with her, that day. "Are you sure?" Mildred asked Pilar repeatedly. She couldn't believe it.

Outside the courthouse, Sue Kuyper, the American Sobrevivientes volunteer, waited with other supporters, unsure of what was happening. Norma paced back and forth, smoking Marlboro Lights and cracking jokes to ease the tension. Sobrevivientes had prepared placards with blown-up photographs of Olga, Loyda, and Raquel's missing children, hoping to take advantage of the media attention on Mildred's case.

After what seemed an eternity to Kuyper, someone from inside the hearing ran out of the courthouse yelling. Mildred had been granted temporary custody, pending a DNA test to make sure she was really the children's biological mother. A chorus of delighted cheers erupted.

As they left the courtroom, Mildred lifted Fernanda into her arms. The child stared at Mildred with wide eyes. Next to her, the Sobrevivientes lawyer Rootman carried Ana Cristina in his arms. As they stepped outside, people swarmed around.

Sue Kuyper called Betsy in the United States, holding her cell phone in the air to let her hear the cheers as Mildred emerged from the courthouse, beaming. Rootman had passed Ana Cristina to her, and she now balanced a child on each hip. The children looked dazed.

Olga López, whose daughter Escarlett had been missing for over two years, tried to smile in spite of the tears rolling down her cheeks. Her placard had fallen to the ground. In one fist, she clutched a small, faded photo of her abducted four- year-old. Norma swiftly took her aside, offering words of comfort and encouragement.

Local media gathered around them. "I thank all of you for your support," Mildred said to a bouquet of microphones. "This is the happiest day of my life." Her chin was raised, and her face glowed with defiant joy despite her tears. She was fully aware that she'd beaten near-impossible odds. "I hope you will support all the mothers who still search for their children," she continued, looking around at the press. Her smile faded as she locked eyes with Olga. "They deserve the same support. . . ." Her voice trailed off, overcome with the gravity of the moment.

Norma Cruz stepped up to say a few words, Mildred standing proudly beside her, the two children heavy in her arms. Mildred had last held Fernanda, now almost five, when she was two. When she'd taken little Ana Cristina into her arms, the child had stared at her blankly. Mildred had tried to stem her emotions but couldn't help crying. Ana Cristina's first teeth had already begun to come in.

Through the phone, Betsy could make out Mildred's voice, spea- king and then crying. Betsy sobbed along with her from Tennessee, listening to the sounds of Spanish words she couldn't understand. It felt as if the last eighteen months of confusion, sadness, and frustration were suddenly and finally crashing to a halt.

Recupera a sus hijas

...ando y Ana Cristina fueron entregadas por un juez a su madre

POR LORENA SEIJO

La emoción colmó la sede de la Sala de Audiencias del Juzgado Tercero de la Niñez y la Adolescencia, a las 10.30 horas de ayer, cuando se conoció la resolución que devuelve a Míldred Alvarado sus dos hijas.

Las niñas fueron raptadas en agosto del 2006 por una red de adopciones internacionales.

Ayer terminaron 20 meses de ininterrumpida lucha, durante los cuales Míldred Alvarado nunca perdió la fe de recuperar a sus pequeñas, María Fernanda, de 4 años, y Ana Cristina, de año y medio, que fueron secuestradas por una mafia de adopciones ...les.

Míldred no pudo conte...

Míldred Alvarado sonríe junto a sus hijas, María Fernanda y Ana Cristina, en la sala de juegos de la Fundación Sobrevivientes.

Foto Prensa Libre: ÓSCAR ESTRADA

El negocio de las Facilidades para el

Guatemala es de los pocos países donde se adopta en escasos meses

Míldred Alvarado con sus hijas, Ana Cristina (izquierda) y María Fernanda

Implicados en el caso de Míldred

Guatemalan newspaper clips show Mildred Alvarado with her daughters after they were returned via court order by Judge Gómez in Guatemala City in February 2008.

244

It was a wild ride back to the Sobrevivientes office for Mildred and her daughters, crowded into the van with Norma and others from the foundation. A police officer managed to close the van door, but the press surrounded the vehicle, restricting its progress.

"Lose them," Norma instructed the driver. The driver managed to take off, weaving a complicated route back to Sobrevivientes. Inside the van, everyone tried to interact with the two children. Sue Kuyper found it disturbing how quietly passive they were. She got the feeling that the kids could have been handed off to anyone, with little difference in their reactions. Fernanda studied Mildred's face. Norma radioed the Sobrevivientes security team to prepare for their arrival. When they pulled up to the building, a few intrepid reporters were already waiting for them.

The last thing Mildred wanted to do was deal with journalists. As she started to get out of the van, a man thrust a microphone in her face. "How do you feel?" he demanded.

"Why are you here?" Mildred asked him earnestly. She felt as if her bones were melting from the stress. "I feel like I can barely stand anymore, I'm so nervous."

"We support you," the journalist said. "We share your joy."

Mildred looked at him for a beat before replying. The circles under her eyes were dark and deep. "No you don't," she said flatly. A strange fierceness tinged her voice. "No one can understand this like I do."

Inside the Sobrevivientes office, there was a brief celebration. The foundation's staff gathered around, congratulating Mildred and admiring the children. Fernanda began to speak, calling Norma *abuelita*, or grandma. "How about a kiss?" Norma asked the five-year-old.

"No," Fernanda announced. "I will give you a kiss if you give me Pollo Campero.[21]"

"Well," said Norma, with a serious smile. "We can arrange that."

Later that day, an armed detective from the police department arrived to escort Mildred, Fernanda, and Ana Cristina home to Villa Nueva. After a few minutes, he pulled over. An unmarked car

[21.] *Pollo Campero* (Country Chicken) is the crown jewel of Guatemalan fast food, and to many, their fried chicken is a source of national pride.

appeared next to them, and the family climbed in. The driver took a long, complicated route in case they were being followed. It seemed unnecessary, Mildred thought. If Marvin and Coni wanted to find her, she was sure they could. Fernanda and Ana Cristina fell asleep during the ride.

Patricia rushed out to meet them when she heard the car approaching. Mildred got out, handing her sister a bag of donated clothing Norma had given her. "Are they OK?" Patricia asked hesitantly. She wasn't sure what to expect after a year and a half without the girls. "Is there anything wrong with them?"

"No," Mildred answered. "I checked them at court." She lifted Fernanda from the car, then Ana Cristina. Before he left, the police detective told Mildred to wait a week before going out in public. *That's OK,* Mildred thought to herself. *We need time to get used to each other again anyway.*

Inside the two-room apartment, Susana and Mario hugged Fernanda and looked at Ana Cristina skeptically. "This is the girl they took from us," Mildred explained. "This is your sister. A miracle has occurred, and we got her back." Ana Cristina began to cry. Mildred held her, rocking and humming. For the next week, the child screamed, refusing to eat or sleep. She was inconsolable. When left alone, Ana Cristina would remove her diaper and eat her own feces. As for food, unlike Mildred's other children, who had all eaten everything, including hot chiles, from a young age, Ana Cristina refused even plain bean soup.

The lush plumpness soon vanished from the toddler's cheeks. *How do I know she's really mine?* Mildred thought, exhausted. She felt no connection to the child and was still waiting for the DNA test to confirm that the girl was indeed hers.

To make matters worse, the death threats begun anew. Eleven-year-old Susana, her oldest, was threatened. When a car tailed Susana home from school one day, Mildred took all of her children out of school. The family tried not to leave the house. Sobrevivientes sent a social worker to Mildred's home in an attempt to help the family recover from their trauma. The organization also sent food and more clothes. Ana Cristina continued to refuse food and never seemed content. At almost two, she still couldn't walk. She didn't like to be touched or held, preferring to lie on the ground in a far corner, alone. Mildred had never known such an unhappy child. When Pilar visited, she wondered if the toddler might have pediatric anorexia.

Fernanda's memories of the past two years of her life trickled out slowly. Fernanda didn't call her little sister by her name. Instead, Ana Cristina was just "Titi," a nickname meaning "sister." The five-year-old told her mother about how she'd been hit for being "bad," and how she'd seen Titi get hit for crying. She sheepishly admitted that she, too, had hit Titi, like the grown-ups did. Fernanda revealed that she'd been hit frequently by other children, and that she would strike them back, only to be punished with further blows from the adults.

Both children, Mildred realized, were used to a different kind of life, a more luxurious life. Fernanda threw tantrums, demanding chicken from McDonald's or Pollo Campero, food that was well beyond Mildred's budget. Both children's transition back to simple home-cooked meals — tortillas, beans, rice — was difficult. Mildred tried her hardest to help Ana Cristina adapt, but nothing she did seemed to make a difference. Fernanda picked at her fingers until her cuticles ripped and bled.

Mildred continued to travel into Guatemala City about once a week to visit her lawyers at Sobrevivientes. The Ministerio Público's investigation into the kidnapping of her children was ongoing despite the fact that the children had been returned. Norma continued to be surprised by Mildred's fierce dignity. The young woman refused to accept any money and only grudgingly accepted donated clothes. She told Norma she was afraid that Judge Gómez might change his mind and reverse his order, deciding that she was unfit to parent. A court-ordered social worker occasionally showed up at Mildred's apartment to check on the children. Both girls had lost weight in the months following the hearing, Norma noticed.

A month or so after Fernanda and Ana Cristina had been returned, Mildred showed up at Sobrevivientes to talk to Norma. She'd met a man she liked. Solemnly, she asked Norma for permission to go out with him.

"Of course you can!" Norma told her, surprised. Many of the women Sobrevivientes worked with felt obligated and bound by gratitude, yet the plaintive sincerity of Mildred's question pained her. "You don't need my permission! You have a right to live, Mildred."

"Yes, Doña Norma," Mildred replied, quietly. "I don't want to do anything wrong that could make them take away my girls."

Mildred called Norma one afternoon in advance of a trip to Sobrevivientes. She asked for permission to bring homemade tamales to sell to the various people who worked at the office. "Of course," Norma told her. "I'll send a van to pick you up."

Before Mildred arrived with her four children in tow, Norma gruffly issued a warning to every member of her staff: "Even if you're not hungry, you will buy every single *tamalito* (little tamale)," she said. "Every last one."

To Mildred, going to Sobrevivientes was a constant reminder that there were criminal proceedings creeping forward against Coni Galindo Bran and Sabrina Donis, the woman she'd lived with in Villa Canales. Both women remained free on bail. Mildred worried about running into them and wished that the entire situation would just go away, even if it meant that they were never held accountable. She just wanted to be left alone now that she had her girls back.

At night, the nightmares of rape, which had remained with Mildred since her childhood molestation, finally eased. Dreams of strangers stealing her children took their place.

*The Alvarado children together at home in Villa Nueva, Guatemala, in 2009.
Left to right: Susana, Fernanda, Ana Cristina, and Mario.*

16. THE PERFECT CRIME

February 2008–June 2008

Betsy Emanuel was hell-bent on figuring out how, exactly, her family had ended up accepting an adoption referral for a child that had been stolen. The outrageousness of the situation consumed her. To her, it was plain and simple hypocrisy that Celebrate Children International professed to operate according to Christian morals and family values. She felt like a fool, and she resented how much power Sue Hedberg had wielded over her during the adoption process. She hated that the other CCI clients she'd grown so close to had been scared into submission, just as she had when Sue Hedberg had re-offered Jennifer for adoption. Two years had passed since Betsy had first contacted CCI about adopting from Guatemala. She realized she'd still never met Sue Hedberg face-to-face. *I could probably walk right into her office, and she wouldn't know who I was,* Betsy thought, slightly amused. *What would I say?* She wandered around the daydream for a moment. *I'd look her straight in the eye and ask: Sue, what really happened to Jennifer? Why was finding Fernanda "too dangerous"? What did you know?*

A wave of anger coursed through her. What *did* Sue know, and who, if not Betsy, would ever find out? How many other "irregular" adoption processes had CCI orchestrated? Moreover, shouldn't Mildred be compensated, somehow, for all of her pain and suffering? It was situations like this one that ruined adoption for those children who were authentically in need.

Unsure of where to turn next, Betsy tried John Lowell at the U.S. Embassy again. Two of her previous emails to him, dated February 18 and 21, had gone unanswered. The silence increased Betsy's anxiety. She tried for a third and final time on February 28, 2008, to get in touch with Lowell. "You are no longer responding to my emails," she told him bluntly. "If the U.S. Embassy cannot enlighten us as to the best path to follow in our quest for an investigation of this case, then we'll check with the U.S. Department of State and the Department of Homeland Security. . . ."

To her surprise, Lowell wrote back the same day, saying he'd met with Norma Cruz two weeks before to discuss the case. The U.S. Embassy was following the case very closely, he told Betsy, including what had happened at Mildred's recent custody hearing. "We were pleased to see that decision," Lowell wrote. "She was obviously entitled to regain her children. Let me assure you that we have shared the information you provided and information available to us from several other sources with a number of appropriate authorities."

For a moment, Betsy stopped reading, wondering what he meant. Appropriate authorities? Who were they? No one had contacted her about any kind of investigation. Perhaps one was already underway.

The following line of Lowell's email snuffed out her optimism. "I regret, however, that I cannot provide details about that," he said.

Norma Cruz found John Lowell and his staff at the U.S. Embassy to be inconsistent. She believed that Lowell had intimate knowledge about adoption fraud and suspected that certain people inside the U.S. Embassy in Guatemala City were taking bribes related to the processing of adoption cases. Norma was infuriated about Lowell's not helping with the other searching mothers' cases. If evidence pointing to the U.S. Embassy's issuing adoption approval for Guatemalan children previously reported missing should materialize, Norma wanted to sue them. Sobrevivientes had provided photos of the missing children of Olga López, Loyda Rodríguez, and Raquel Par to Lowell months before. Now Norma suspected that the children had been adopted into the United States anyway, despite Lowell's assurances that that couldn't happen.

Over the next four months, Betsy reached out to whomever she thought might be able to help. She tried the nonprofit Ethica, the Joint Council on International Children's Services, the Council on Accreditation, and the U.S. State Department's Office of Children's Issues. She found that trying to talk to the State Department was like speaking to a brick. Betsy started to imagine what Mildred had gone through in her quest to get the attention of the Guatemalan authorities. Her own efforts to solicit help from the American authorities felt futile.

"I feel very discouraged with the seemingly little interest our government has taken in this case," she told Gerrie Fuller, the adoption unit chief at the Department of State. She copied John Lowell at the U.S. Embassy on her note. "If you do know of any other officials we should share our concerns or information with, please let us know. . . . We want to see some accountability for the unlawful offering of these children to us. . . ."

Fuller told her he'd communicated her concerns to "the relevant office." He advised Betsy to try contacting local licensing officials, the Florida Department of Children and Families. He also suggested contacting the Better Business Bureau.

It's like they think Fernanda was a piece of furniture that was never delivered, Betsy thought, outraged. Instead, she called Amy Hammett, the lead licensing specialist at the Central Florida Department of Children and Families. Hammett listened with concern. Allegations of child trafficking were serious, and Betsy's account of the attempted adoption and subsequent return of the Alvarado children in Guatemala prompted her to open yet another investigation into Celebrate Children International. Betsy re-sent the 15-page account she'd furnished to Hammett's office months before, in November 2007, along with a variety of Spanish-language news clips detailing Mildred's plight.

On April 8, 2008, Hammett called Sue Hedberg to inform her of the allegations. Sue said she had "absolutely no concerns" regarding trafficking and told DCF that her agency had done nothing wrong. All of the children she placed came from lawyers, she said, whom she knew very well. Though Hammett didn't say who'd made the complaint, Sue correctly guessed that it was the Emanuel family.

An in-person meeting was scheduled for April 14. DCF officials were to visit the CCI offices to talk to Sue Hedberg, and Betsy sent Hammett a few recommendations in advance of the meeting in a clumsy attempt at guidance. "I see no point in just asking Sue Hedberg if she knew the girls were kidnapped," Betsy explained. "I think she'll just say no. It was Sue's job to know that the birth mom was in total agreement with the placement. We trusted that if she had been licensed by the state, someone would know if there were problems with her agency."

Betsy became more impassioned as the note continued: "I'm sorry," she wrote, "but if offering children who have been forcibly removed from their mother for adoption, so that the involved parties can financially profit, isn't wrong, then the State of Florida needs to take a hard look at the codes on the books!"

Even as she typed the words, Betsy doubted DCF's capacity to investigate. Their fall 2007 investigation into Celebrate Children International, spurred by eleven individual complainants, hadn't uncovered anything new. It seemed as though DCF had taken Sue's version of events at face value. For example, when Sue had said she'd only requested three psych evaluations on clients in the history of her agency, DCF apparently didn't check on the veracity of the statement. If they'd done their homework, Betsy believed, they could easily have found more than three examples; she personally knew of five clients who claimed Sue had instructed them to undergo psychiatric testing. She closed her note to Hammett by urging DCF to follow the money trail.

At 9:00 on the morning of April 14, Amy Hammett and Stacy Lewis, a second DCF licensing specialist, dropped by the offices of Celebrate Children International. They were there to hear Sue's account of what had happened in the Emanuels' adoption. According to notes from the meeting, Sue started by describing the general Guatemalan adoption process. As far as the Alvarado children, Sue said that the birth mother was lying about the kidnapping, being sedated, and "having her children taken away."

Marvin Bran had returned the children to Mildred, she told DCF, and Mildred had then tried to give them to another lawyer. She made it clear that she didn't "assume responsibility for where the children come [from]," but nonetheless went "out of her way to ask" about their origins. Furthermore, Sue continued, CCI had no remaining cases with Marvin. She said that every case she'd done with him, except those of the Alvarado children, had been successful.

When Amy Hammett told Sue that a custody hearing had been held in Guatemala and that the judge had ruled in Mildred's favor, Sue brushed it off. "Mrs. Hedberg stated that the judge probably felt pressure," Hammett wrote in her notes. "Mrs. Hedberg indicates that

Guatemala is a very anti-adoption culture and UNICEF will assist birth mothers with getting their children back, even if it means they lie about the circumstances. Mrs. Hedberg would not be surprised if UNICEF was involved with this case and assisted the birth mother with creating a story that her child had been stolen."

Sue then launched allegations of her own against Betsy Emanuel, saying Betsy was looking for a "perfect child" and had wanted Fernanda because she was "virtually Caucasian." Hammett dutifully recorded a summary of the conversation in her notes. Betsy was "a very needy person," Sue told DCF, whose email communication was "long and constant." With all of her other clients, she didn't have time to read Betsy's emails or address her "needs." It wasn't her responsibility to find out why a child had become unavailable for adoption, Sue said, though it was usually because a child had died or a birth mother had changed her mind.

When asked about the charges against Coni Galindo Bran and the pending arrest of her son, Marvin Bran, Sue played it down. "When asked, Mrs. Hedberg indicated that being arrested in Guatemala is not like being arrested in the U.S.," Amy noted. "She indicates both are currently free."

DCF officials reviewed the CCI's records related to the Emanuel family. There was no documentation of phone or email communications between Sue and Betsy, and nothing was mentioned in the files about the family's first two referrals, Jennifer and Fernanda. When the officials asked for printouts of all email communication between CCI and the Emanuels, Angela, Sue's assistant, said that CCI's printer was out of toner and offered to forward the emails instead.

Before the meeting ended, Sue made one last point to DCF: "Guatemala is a violent culture," she said. "Women are murdered every day, and their bodies are picked off the street. Now that adoptions are closed, many children are going to die."

In the meantime, Celebrate Children International's new adoption program in Ethiopia had begun to succeed. On April 1, 2008, two weeks before the DCF investigation into the Emanuels' complaint began, CCI brought the first of what would be 30 Ethiopian children adopted that year into the United States.

"Ethiopia's people, though poor, are some of the friendliest anywhere," the CCI website stated. "It is very pro-Western and is a relatively safe place to travel for you and your family." On the Ethiopia program page, a warning told potential adoptive parents that CCI wasn't taking adoption applications for "female children under the age of 3 years old," owing to the "long line of families already waiting" and the uncertainty of the program's future.

Since the inception of the Ministerio Público's human trafficking unit in 2007, investigators and prosecutors working on adoption cases there had been trying to follow the money. There was no other way to investigate the adoption networks. One of the more seasoned prosecutors in the unit had arrived at the sobering realization that relying on witness testimony in Guatemala was just too dangerous. Witnesses disappeared or changed their stories under pressure. He'd started to build his prosecutions exclusively from documents. On his personal blog, he listed his occupation as "defender of lost causes."

Within the Ministerio Público, the Alvarado case was first assigned to prosecutor Mynor Pinto, then passed to Claudia Soto Rodríguez. Both were amicable, friendly, and overworked. Each of their desks overflowed with stacks of file folders, and Pinto kept case evidence locked away and hidden inside his cubicle. Trafficking unit chief Álexander Colop and prosecutor Julio Barrios were also familiar with the Alvarado case, as was Óscar Rivas, a prosecutor from another section of the MP. Rivas and the organized crime and extortions unit were also looking into the activities of the Galindo Bran family organization because of another case: that of Loyda Rodríguez's allegedly kidnapped daughter Anyelí.

Loyda, one of the searching mothers who was being helped by Sobrevivientes, had identified a picture of a child she believed to be her daughter: Karen Abigail Lopez García. "Karen Abigail" had already left Guatemala in an adoption to an American couple, Tim and Jennifer Monahans. The Monahans were Celebrate Children International clients, and Marvin Bran was the adoption facilitator who'd offered "Karen Abigail" to Sue Hedberg as an adoptable child.

According to emails sent by the Monahans to Guatemalan attorney Susana Luarca, Karen Abigail Lopez García had failed the July 2007 DNA test to establish her relationship to the woman posing as her birth mother. Later, like Mildred's children Maria Fernanda and Ana Cristina, "Karen Abigail" was brought before Judge Mario Peralta in Escuintla for an abandonment hearing. Judge Peralta issued an abandonment decree and assigned custody over "Karen Abigail" to the nursery Asociación Primavera, founded by Guatemalan attorney Susana Luarca. "Karen Abigail" flew to Liberty, Missouri, with the Monahans aboard a Continental airlines flight on December 9, 2008.

The Ministerio Público obtained 2007 correspondence between Luarca and the Monahans about the adoption of "Karen Abigail." Even before the results of the failed DNA test emerged, the Monahans had called Adoption Supervisors Guatemala, the same investigative firm the Emanuels had hired to "check" on the status of their adoption. According to notes written by Jennifer Monahan, the Monahans spoke to attorney Luis Aragon. "He tells me and Tim that their agency has several cases open on Sue and Marvin Bran, and that they have a stormy relationship. . . ."

After the Monahans learned that the child they were adopting had failed the DNA test, they hired another private investigator in hopes of finding out what had happened. Their investigator, Wilbert Reyna, told them in an August 2007 email that the child's "inscription of birth is based on lies and false statements," claiming that the fraudulent birth mother was Karen Abigail's aunt and that the child's real mother was "an alcoholic and a prostitute." The investigator told the Monahans that he thought Marvin Bran was a "cheater." Later, the investigator told the Monahans that there was "no point to pursued this investigation" [sic] because, in part, of the safety risks involved. He claimed to have been threatened by Coni Galindo Bran and advised the Monahans that even if they tried to adopt a different child with CCI and the Galindo Brans that "the odds are high somewhere along the way something illegal would come out again."

Rodolfo "Rudy" Rivera, a Spanish-speaking American lawyer and adoption agency director based in Missouri, once met with Coni Galindo Bran and Marvin Bran in the lobby of the Radisson hotel in Guatemala City. "Marvin Bran was bad news," he says. "His mother was what they call a jaladora, a finder, a foster care lady. My gut made me feel uncomfortable with them."

Prosecutors at the Ministerio Público continued trying to unravel the cases involving Bran. Before any charges could be filed against him, Bran showed up preemptively to give the government investigators his side of the story. He'd hired one of Guatemala's most famous defense lawyers, Fernando Linares Beltranena, a conservative attorney known for representing powerful people like military officers and alleged narco-traffickers. Linares himself had worked in adoption, placing Guatemalan children with American agencies in the 1980s, and believed that adoption was essentially good and noble.

"Marvin is astute," Linares says of his former client, "but not intelligent. He was an adoption pimp, involved because of his mother. . . . She'd put the word out into the world [for babies], to the regional hospitals and intermediaries. It's the same as if you wanted to buy a green Ford pickup truck; you'd get the word out." Linares explains that Marvin offered a deposition because he thought it would make him seem friendly and cooperative to the Ministerio Público investigators, who in turn might make him a protected witness in exchange for a deposition about his business partners, including Susana Luarca and Sue Hedberg.

But the MP didn't make any such offer. According to Linares, who stopped representing Marvin shortly thereafter, his client wasn't a "big enough fish." According to MP prosecutors, no such deal was offered because Marvin lied under oath to them. Regardless, Bran did provide the authorities with emails, documents, and other information about his former business partners.

Through the spring of 2008, the Ministerio Púbico wasn't the only authority investigating irregular adoption cases. The International Commission Against Impunity in Guatemala (known by the Spanish acronym CICIG) was, too. Prosecuting human trafficking in adoption had been on the commission's radar since the independent organization began working in Guatemala in December 2007.

CICIG was created under a formal agreement between the United Nations and the government of Guatemala to help identify and dismantle deep-rooted corruption in government and postwar clandestine security apparatuses. CICIG helped high-profile cases through Guatemala's existing criminal justice system, often working with Guatemala's Ministerio Público as special prosecutors or technical advisors, providing resources and advice. An April 2011 article in *The New Yorker* referred to the commission's work as "blasts of radiation on a cancerous organism."

CICIG's staff consisted of lawyers, analysts, judges, investigators, prosecutors, and security personnel hand-picked from around the world. Because of the dangerous nature of their work, CICIG staff worked inside a compound protected by bomb-detection devices, high opaque walls, and armed guards. All visitors had to undergo a security check and couldn't bring electronic devices, including cell phones, inside.

"From the beginning, the commission assumed illegal adoption cases were organized crime and high-impact cases," says Carolina Pimental, a CICIG analyst. "There were several facts that supported the initial hypothesis, including the financial incentives, the amount of false documents, the authorities involved, and the fact that the kidnapping networks were a part of international illegal adoption activities."

During the Alvarado investigation, MP prosecutors formally requested an arrest warrant for Marvin Bran for alleged human trafficking and conspiracy charges. Judge Magda Corina Martínez Cabrera, the Mixco judge who had jurisdiction over the request, refused to grant it. Because a criminal case was already underway against Coni and Sabrina, she ruled that it was too late to add Bran to the process. The timeframe for investigation was over, she said, and demanded that the Ministerio Público build a new case against Bran.

Claudia Soto Rodríguez, the Ministerio Público prosecutor who remained responsible for Mildred's case, planned to ask a different judge to approve arrest charges for trafficking and conspiracy against Bran. She also wanted to bring charges against two more attorneys who were involved with the Alvarado children: Amadeo Guerra and Saul Vinicio García, who both, apparently, had been trying to start adoptions for Mildred's children with different American families.

As the investigation unfolded, the Ministerio Público discovered that Saul Vinicio García, an evangelical pastor and attorney, had notarized documents that said Mildred had voluntarily given Ana

Cristina in adoption on September 10, 2006, and had relinquished Fernanda a month later, on October 13. Similar documents notarized by Amadeo Guerra claimed that both children had been relinquished December 12, 2006. MP officials didn't know that César Augosto Trujillo — the lawyer who had married Bran and his wife, served as the Galindo Bran family's personal lawyer, and was listed on Betsy Emanuel's power-of-attorney document from Celebrate Children International — was involved in Fernanda's adoption. On the Guatemalan side of the investigation, Trujillo's name didn't appear on any documents, although the lawyer frequently worked with García. Between 2002 and 2007, researchers say, the two worked together on the adoptions of at least 60 different children, some of whom were cared for by the Galindo Bran family.

When Saul Vinicio García found out that he, like Marvin Bran, was being investigated, he also turned himself in to the Ministerio Público. García claimed that Trujillo was the one who'd actually filled out all adoption paperwork. He said he received 2,500 quetzales (about $320) per adoption to sign paperwork, and that he did nothing else. Ministerio Público investigators said that García claimed to have met Bran at his church when the young man attended one of his services. García told investigators that Bran had introduced himself as a law student who worked in adoption and said he needed the help of a notary. García claimed he had operated in good faith but had been manipulated, and insisted that he didn't read any of the paperwork that Bran paid him to sign. When he left the MP offices after giving his deposition, García left a stack of bibles behind on the prosecutors' desks, including those of trafficking unit lead investigator Julio Barrios and unit chief Álexander Colop. "I said to him, 'You, as a pastor, should know that there are divine laws, and then there's the law,'" Colop recalls.

As the Ministerio Público's investigation into the theft and attempted adoption of Mildred Alvarado's children continued, paperwork corresponding to the ongoing efforts filled three thick three-ring binders. The MP typically used simple binders to collate case files; a criminal case could take three to four years to be resolved, from start to sentencing, and could fill multiple binders. Some, but not all, information was stored electronically. In the first two years the trafficking unit existed, 2007 to 2009, just one case made it to sentencing. The case, which Sobrevivientes had worked on, involved the abduction and subsequent murder of a nine-year-old girl from Chiquimula. The criminals had allegedly tried to sell the child for 19,000 quetzales (about $2,400) to an adoption network, though the Guatemalan press reported that the attempted sale might have been for the child's organs.

Ministerio Público prosecutors believed that Sabrina Donis, the young woman Mildred had temporarily lived with, was in touch with a "contact" inside a health clinic where Mildred had received free prenatal vitamins while pregnant with Ana Cristina. When seemingly vulnerable women passed through certain clinics, "contacts" inside could be paid to pass on their information. Once a target was identified, she would be approached with offers of aid or money. The MP charged Sabrina with human trafficking in addition to aggravated abduction, but a judge allowed only the kidnapping charges to stand.

"Many people in Guatemala get off the hook because trata, human trafficking, is both legally and culturally understood as sexual exploitation, not trafficking babies for adoption," says Mynor Pinto. "It's hard for us to convince a judge to use human trafficking charges at trial, which has harsher penalties — whereas with abduction, they can get off with a slap on the wrist."

Investigators discovered that Dr. Miguel Paniagua, the surgeon who performed Mildred's C-section, had signed a birth certificate for Ana Cristina that claimed she'd been born at home instead of at his clinic. When asked about this discrepancy, Paniagua said he didn't remember the case.

According to medical records from Dr. Mollinedo, the Guatemala City pediatrician who examined and vaccinated children for the Galindo Bran family, about 60 individual children were brought to his office by the Galindo Brans between 2005 and 2007. He said he believed they were one of the smaller operations.

No one has been able to determine where Fernanda and Ana Cristina were held during long periods of their abduction. Marvin's sister, Kimberly Bran, seems to be the first person that cared for the sisters. She can be seen sitting in the room with Sue Hedberg, Fernanda, and Marvin Bran in the video that was sent to Betsy Emanuel in September 2006. In the clip, when Sue Hedberg asks who is taking care of Fernanda, Marvin says "Her," possibly referencing Kimberly. Later, Fernanda seems to have been cared for by Carla Girón. According to the Ministerio Público, Leticia Choc Sactic, a cuidadora in the Galindo Brans' neighborhood of San José las Rosas, also cared for Fernanda at some point. Carla Girón's former business associates say the Alvarado children were kept apart for most of the time and that at one point, Fernanda lived three hours outside of Guatemala City.

Pinto says Sue Hedberg's "dealing" of Fernanda is a key piece of evidence. "With Sue, we would have charged her with child trafficking and money laundering," Pinto says. "With the video, she's linked."

Yet charging an American with a crime was complicated. For the United States to extradite a U.S. citzizen, that citizen would first have to be found guilty of equivalent charges in the United States. A Guatemalan attempt to prosecute an American for human trafficking in connection with adoption would fail, as the the U.S. Trafficking Victims Protection Act of 2000, which was reauthorized in 2005, defines "severe forms of trafficking in persons" as either for the purpose of sex, "in which a commercial sex act is induced by force, fraud, or coercion, or in which the person induced to perform such act has not attained 18 years of age" or labor, meaning "the recruitment, harboring, transportation, provision, or obtaining of a person for labor or services, through the use of force, fraud, or coercion for the purpose of subjection to involuntary servitude, peonage, debt bondage, or slavery."

The providing of babies to adoptive families didn't fit into the framework. Despite Pinto's bluster, he knew that prosecuting an American like Sue Hedberg was basically a pipe dream. Prosecuting Guatemalans was hard enough. Trying to bring charges against Sue Hedberg wasn't worth wasting precious time and resources. To even place a phone call to the U.S., a Guatemalan prosecutor at the Ministerio Público first had to get a department supervisor to agree to pay for it, and then arrange for translation, another expense. An international investigation would be incredibly costly and difficult.

Trafficking unit head Colop says Sue Hedberg was an American adoption agency director whose name just kept popping up in "irregular" cases. "She would appear over and over in the adoptions, as if she had a monopoly on it," he said. "She knew the business."

When adoption money would come in from the United States, Colop notes, adoption organizations like the Galindo Bran family operation would take payments to a *cambista,* or money changer, who converted the checks to quetzales and took a commission. The checks from adoption agencies would come in the mail or by UPS. Some in the Ministerio Público trafficking unit didn't understand why the U.S. government wasn't prosecuting U.S. adoption agencies for money laundering. Some seemed to be clearly profiting by accepting payments of up to tens of thousands of dollars for "orphans" whose origins were unknown.

Victor Hugo Mejicanos, the man who headed the PGN's denuncia unit, didn't help Mildred for obvious reasons, says one of his former superiors. When he looked into the case, the supervisor found that Mejicanos had never entered Mildred's complaint in the computerized PGN system. That meant the adoption files on her kids had been allowed to keep "walking" without pause.

Bribery within the PGN was no secret. In a fact-finding report published in May 2007 by Ignacio Goicoechea, the liaison legal officer for Latin America for the Hague Conference on International Private Law, it was noted that "allegations of corruption [have been] made about PGN officers requesting hidden payments to process adoption files." Certain Guatemalan adoption facilitators, according to adoptive American parents, even offered "expedited PGN processing" for an additional fee.

In her 2010 adoption memoir, *Mamalita,* adoptive mother Jessica O'Dwyer openly discussed her own attempt to bribe the PGN. "It was as if we both knew we were involved with something illicit and slimy," she wrote, referring to another American adoptive mother who was also in the process of trying to figure out how to bribe the Guatemalan attorney general's office. "But if we didn't discuss it, it didn't exist." Ultimately, O'Dwyer writes, she did not pay a bribe.

Another adoptive mother, Becky Prior[22], says she successfully paid a bribe of $3,000 for a 24-hour turnaround when the PGN

22. The name has been changed.

was reviewing the file on the girl she hoped to adopt. The adoption facilitator who helped her, she says, was Karla Ordoñez, a young woman who worked with Celebrate Children International as well as Adoption Blessings Worldwide and other U.S. agencies. "She had a friend at [the] PGN who pushed the file through," Becky explains candidly. "We saw Barrios [the head of the PGN], and I met him. Karla gave him money when I wasn't there. Part went to Barrios, and part to her friend." Typically, a PGN review took weeks, if not months. Becky adds that she and Karla had tea in Barrios's office, and then thanked him for his help.

Ordoñez, however, says she has never met Barrios in person and knows nothing about bribes. "I always tried to be honest," she insists. "I have nothing to hide. No one was ever open to talking about fees."

Raquel Par, one of the women being helped by Sobrevivientes, holds up a photo of her missing child in the plaza outside Guatemala's National Palace in April 2011. At right, an empty stroller is covered with "Wanted" posters featuring Marvin Bran. Photograph courtesy of Fundación Sobrevivientes.

Fundación Sobrevivientes' Cunas Vacías campaign successfully raised awareness about anomalies in Guatemalan adoption processes, but for the searching Sobrevivientes mothers, awareness alone wasn't enough. Their complaints were creeping through the Guatemalan judicial system, and the investigations that were supposedly underway were yielding few results. In late April 2008, Norma Cruz and four of the women whose children remained missing decided to step up their fight. They decided to go on a hunger strike.

About three years had passed since Loyda Rodríguez, Olga López, and Raquel Par had lost their daughters, and a year had passed since Ana Escobar had lost hers. Mildred's victory had been bittersweet for them. Loyda had watched Mildred's reunion thinking, *When will that day come for me? When will I get my girl back?*

The four women, accompanied by Norma Cruz, planted themselves in front of the entrance to the National Palace and began their hunger strike. It lasted eight days, with the five participants sustained only by water and *suero* (whey solution). Their demands were simple: They wanted the PGN to grant them access to PGN adoption files for 2006, 2007, and 2008. They were requesting the opening of specific investigations by the Consejo Nacional de Adopciones (the National Council on Adoptions, created as a result of the Hague Convention) into the whereabouts of each of the girls the women believed to be their stolen children. Because at least three of girls believed to be identified were already enrolled in adoption proceedings, the women were also asking the PGN to revoke those adoptions that were already underway.

Mildred didn't participate. Her sister Patricia had to work, and she wasn't going to bring her four children along to sit through the strike, day in and day out. She continued to stop by Sobrevivientes regularly to talk to the lawyers who were continuing to handle her case.

The hunger strike participants slept on the ground at night, covered by blankets. Loyda kept imagining that those populating the park at night were thieves or hired assassins. Olga, too, worried that "adoptionists" would send someone to harm them for speaking out. The first few days without food were the worst; the women felt light-headed and dizzy. By the fifth day, the hunger had subsided. The women sat and weaved blankets. Raquel knitted a blouse. Norma, who was almost 50, said she could feel her body deteriorating, but she refused to quit. Without her "officializing" presence, the women would be less credible. Many people passing by stopped to offer kind words, and more than a thousand signed their names in a book of support.

On May 5, 2008, eight days into the strike, the governmental Committee on Children and Families, the PGN, and the National Council for Adoptions announced that they would allow the four mothers to review the files and photographs from their offices, and that they would suspend all pending adoption proceedings for at least a month while they reviewed them and checked for anomalies. The strike had worked. Congressional representative Gudy Rivera, the chairman of the Committee on Children and Families, told the press that there were signs that DNA tests had been manipulated and that in-process adoptions needed to undergo review to ensure legitimacy.

At a press conference and during meetings directly after the strike, Norma had trouble thinking clearly. She spoke only when she absolutely had to, feeling as if her body was suffocating. A doctor scolded her, telling her she was foolish to have given up eating. Norma hadn't even considered giving up, thinking about how the mothers of kidnapped children sometimes went days without food in order to pay the costs incurred in searching for their children.

The day after the hunger strike ended, Congressman Rivera's sister Rosalinda was arrested at a clandestine nursery that housed nine children. Along with four others, she was charged with trafficking and conspiracy in relation to the 2007 kidnapping of a baby. Sources say the head of the Ministerio Público, Juan Luis Florido Solís, tried to quash the investigation, going so far as to fire Mynor Pinto, one of his own prosecutors, for bringing charges against the congressman's sister. Florido was later ousted from the Ministerio Público amid allegations of corruption, and Pinto was rehired. Congressman Rivera told the press he hadn't seen his sister in three years and wouldn't "lift a finger" to help her.

One day in late June 2008, Betsy Emanuel was sitting at her dining room table, sorting through her mail. Her family had just gotten back from vacation along the Alabama coast, and the stack of mail was piled high. Betsy was excited to see an envelope from the Florida Department of Children and Families. Inside was the final report on the findings of the state investigation into Celebrate Children International. As she started skimming the six pages of documents, her excitement subsided.

The investigation had found that Celebrate Children International and Sue Hedberg had done nothing to violate the Florida administrative codes governing the operation and regulation of adoption agencies. Over the course of a four-month investigation, DCF had found no evidence of wrongdoing.

"It was a very difficult process for us, because [the alleged crime] was international and not on U.S. soil," said Maria Nistri, one of the DCF officials involved in the investigation, during a subsequent interview. "It got really gray dealing with the overseas stuff. Somebody would say, well Guatemala this, PGN that. . . . There was always an abstract entity in an unreachable place, and we couldn't confirm the information. And neither could the complainant!"

DCF tried to enlist help from other institutions involved in adoption, including the Department of State's Office of Children's Issues and the Council on Accreditation (COA). Who was responsible for what remained murky. DCF staffer Amy Hammett tried asking the U.S. Embassy in Guatemala for help, inquiring whether or not American adoption agency directors were responsible for knowing whether children they offered for adoption had been kidnapped. She also was requesting information about "the extent of Celebrate Children International's involvement" in the Alvarado case. No one responded. After three attempts to contact the U.S. Embassy via email, Hammett apparently gave up.

She didn't have much luck getting information from anyone else, either. Richard Klarberg, president of the COA, told Hammett that he needed permission from the Department of State to speak about the agency — despite the fact that the Department of State had directed Hammett to Klarberg in the first place. The COA was the entity responsible for reviewing and accrediting international adoption agencies in compliance with the Hague Convention. DCF knew that Celebrate Children International had failed to gain accreditation, but the local authorities didn't know the reasons behind the denial.

The State Department's Office of Children's Issues steered Hammett to Stephanie Kronenburg, a staff lawyer specializing in visa and immigration fraud. On May 21, 2008, Kronenburg wrote to Hammett that Children's Issues had received "several messages" about the Alvarado case, from "a number of sources." She said that there were points that would "compel one to investigate CCI further." "Let me straighten a few other things out before you look any further," she wrote. "The investigation won't go on realistically if there is misplaced responsibility for critical actions."

She launched into a whirlwind description of problems in Guatemalan adoptions, laying out complicated issues in blunt language. "The American government didn't oversee "the official manner" in which foreign children were found to be legally adoptable, or how they'd become available for adoption in the first place. The U.S. Embassy had been "trying to curb baby-selling and baby-stealing," Kronenburg said. "Switching children during the adoption process happens often enough around the world that it is a major concern." It seemed impossible to hold an American adoption agency responsible for the work of its in-country associates.

Adoptive parents could believe they were adopting a healthy child only to discover the child they'd brought home had special needs. Kronenburg said switching also happened with "pretty" and "not so pretty" children — American families would begin an adoption for a "pretty" child only to end up with one who looked nothing like they picture they'd been given. Baby-switching also enabled adoption agencies and "arrangers" who didn't want to refund fees to smoothly finish an otherwise difficult case, Kronenburg explained, as when a baby died mid-process. The dead child could be replaced with another baby, and the adoption could continue under the deceased child's name. The adoptive parents might never know their original child had died.

Kronenberg also laid out a few points she thought might help the State of Florida's investigation. "If a birth parent is induced, bribed, or threatened in any way to give up a child, the child is not an orphan and the [Guatemalan] government needs to catch the people behind the illegal adoption," she wrote. She advised Hammett to find out what was used to "encourage or induce" Mildred to show up for the DNA test.

It was a lot of information for DCF to take in. Far from clarifying things, Kronenburg's email only raised more questions. Amy Hammett printed out the email and penciled questions in the margins: *How would Florida go about investigating this? Does CCI prepare the file, or does the lawyer?*

Eventually, a conference call was arranged among DCF staffers and Department of State officials to discuss "concerns" about Celebrate Children International. According to notes taken by a DCF staffer, the State Department said that child trafficking "would not be under their jurisdiction." It wasn't under DCF's jurisdiction, either, unless the trafficking had occurred on Florida soil. Then again, a child illegally adopted into the United States wouldn't be considered trafficked, anyway, even if he or she had been kidnapped.

When the DCF asked again why CCI had failed to earn Hague accreditation, the State Department responded with a list of ambiguous issues, including concerns about how the agency conducted business in Guatemala, a lack of honesty when dealing with adoptive parents, a failure to know about or correct problems with partners in Guatemala, and a willingness to work with unscrupulous adoption facilitators.

DCF ordered CCI to take three corrective actions, including a written explanation of the Emanuel family's lost referrals. The resulting three-page explanation detailed the chronology of both Jennifer and Fernanda's thwarted adoptions. Jennifer, CCI said, had been "moved to an orphanage due to her birth mother changing her mind." After the child's mother died, Sue said she'd visited

Jennifer three times. The Emanuel family had voluntarily declined to continue her adoption after she'd been re-established as legally adoptable via abandonment. As for the Alvarado children, CCI said that their mother had "changed her mind and reclaimed the children." They said "armed men" may have "demanded the child back with violence," and it was "clear to Sue that the circumstances were possibly too traumatic for Marvin Bran to talk about."

In closing, CCI said the allegations made by Betsy Emanuel and the newspapers in Guatemala about the Alvarado children being stolen were "impossibilities." Sue didn't "see how it is possible that the circumstances presented are possible or realistic given the safeguards against child abduction in the Guatemalan adoption laws."

Reading the explanation, Betsy felt her blood pressure rise. *This is it? The entire investigation?* She was astonished. The Florida Department of Children and Families had not only failed to ascertain accountability, they'd apparently taken Sue's own word as concrete evidence, without independent verification. Betsy wasted no time in shooting a scolding email to DCF. "At this point, there is nothing preventing this from happening again in the countries where CCI works now!" she told them.

In May 2008, about a month before DCF issued its final report on the Emanuel family's complaint, *The New York Times* published a story noting that 15 percent of American adoption agencies had recently closed their doors. Many hadn't been able to obtain Hague accreditation, so their ability to work in many countries around the world was limited. Guatemala's temporary freeze on new adoptions, which took effect on December 31, 2007, the day after the new Adoption Law was implemented, meant that many agencies saw their profits plummet. Ninety percent of the 235 children whom Celebrate Children International had reported placing with American families in 2007 had been from Guatemala. Now no one knew when the small country might reopen to adoptions; estimates ranged from months to years. Like many other agencies, CCI by 2009 seemed to be on the brink of financial failure. Minutes from a February 20, 2009, board meeting at CCI read, "Sue agreed to take a pay cut to stay open."

The minutes also show that the agency considered dipping into charitable donations meant for children who were supported by monthly sponsorships. "Sponsorship is $30.00 a month," the notes read. "Maybe we would keep $5.00 at CCI for supplies/office space, and send $25.00 to Guatemala." Only two other full-time employees remained at the agency, and the company's "available funds" totaled $15,257.

Celebrate Children International had started laying the groundwork for an Ethiopia adoption program well in advance of Guatemala's closure. Notes from a July 11, 2006, board meeting show that although the agency was still working on getting a license to operate in Ethiopia, it had already hired a "full-time employee" and set up an office there. Ato Dereje Yeshidinber, CCI's new Ethiopian employee, worked with U.S.-based Ethiopia program manager Debbie Wankel to start the program. The first order of business was putting together a budget. Yeshidinber managed to get a hold of a copy of Christian World Adoption's budget for CCI to examine. "CWA is helping us more than they know, I'm sure!!" Debbie joked to Sue in an email contained in the agency's state licensing file. Dereje explained at the time that after submitting CCI's budget, the agency wouldn't be "forced to follow our plan 100 percent." CCI received its first Ethiopia operating license on December 10, 2007.

By 2009, the agency had relationships with six different orphanages in Ethiopia. At least four of them identified as evangelical Christian, including Elolam Care for Children, Ethio Tinsae Orphan and Widows' Service, Emanuel Orphans Development Association, and the Kamashi Orphanage and School. Contracts between CCI and each of the orphanages show that the institutions provided children to the adoption agency in exchange for monetary donations. CCI's contract with the Emanuel Orphans Development Association stated that CCI would pay one million birr (about $60,000) over the next three years. In October 2008, CCI signed a contract to work adoptions with the 500-bed Kamashi Orphanage and School in the Benishangul-Gumuz region, one of the poorest areas of Ethiopia. The orphanage was built in 2006 by Blessing the Children International, a Michigan-based missionary organization. Blessing the Children had "planted" 1,000 evangelical churches across Benishangul-Gumuz. Keith Strawn, the organization's director, helped Sue and CCI nail down the details of their proposed Ethiopia program. Contractually, the Kamashi orphanage agreed to "assign children to CCI for adoption."

"All our orphan centers are run by evangelical Christians, which should help us to believe that they are honest and ethical," Sue reassured one potential Ethiopia client in an email.

Celebrate Children International offered Ethiopian children to its own clients as well as to those from two other American adoption agencies that didn't have licenses to work in Ethiopia — one agency in Texas and one in South Carolina. By July 10, 2010, according to statistics provided by the agency to the state of Florida, CCI had placed a total of 211 Ethiopian children in the United States, and it had 70 pending adoptions. Sue, back on full pay, now traveled frequently to Africa to check on cases. Meeting minutes from a March 14, 2010, CCI board meeting reported that the Ethiopia adoption program had been "very profitable to date."

According to research group Transparency International, Ethiopia ranked even more corrupt than Guatemala. Celebrate Children International wasn't the only adoption agency supported largely by placing Ethiopian children: The Department of State reported that the African country sent six times the number of orphans to the United States in 2008 as in 2004. "Our concerns are if the [adoption] program grows too quickly, then they [the Ethiopian government] won't be able to regulate it," one U.S. government official close to the situation said from Addis Ababa in 2010. "Then they will be open to problems of child trafficking and other negative influences."

But others, like Cheryl Carter Shotts, say that such abuses have already been happening for years. Carter Shotts, the founder of Americans for African Adoptions, began working in Ethiopia in 1986. Her agency, she notes, no longer operates there because of rapidly changing practices — including a dramatic mark-up on the price of children. "People saw Zahara Jolie," she says, referring to the adopted daughter of celebrity couple Angelia Jolie and Brad Pitt. "Ethiopia was flooded. I've heard rumors of agencies paying $100,000 or $200,000 to get a license to work there. I don't know if the Embassy knows about any of it. The joke is that now Ethiopia's biggest export is children."

Through 2009 and 2010, allegations related to adoption fraud in Ethiopia began to circulate. One dramatic TV broadcast, "Fly Away Children," gave a name to the practice of locating children for adoption: "harvesting." In January 2011, a delegation from the U.S. State Department traveled to Ethiopia with the mission of reviewing the country's adoptions program "in light of growing concerns about its operation and oversight."

Afterward, the State Department's presentation of findings noted that "vulnerabilities" in the Ethiopian adoption process included document inconsistencies, a lack of diligence on the part of adoption agencies in trying to learn the "true facts" about a child's availability, a lack of proper intake records at orphanages, payments "per capita for children" from U.S. adoption agencies to Ethiopian orphanages, and a lack of information regarding the whereabouts of birth parents. According to the findings, Celebrate Children International's Ethiopian adoption program was the the fifth-largest among 27 American adoption agencies working there. CCI handled the adoptions of 250 children, whereas the largest agency handled a reported 346, and the smallest just four.

A high-ranking official from the U.S. Embassy in Ethiopia, speaking in 2009 on condition of anonymity, said that the Ethiopian government didn't have the funding or resources needed to "police" the intercountry adoption process. In 2007, when he began working at the Embassy, he said he realized that local people working for U.S. adoption agencies frequently didn't understand what an "orphan" was. "Certainly there's vulnerability," he said. "It's naïve to think children aren't going to be bought and sold. You have to plan for it."

On December 5, 2010, the International Commission Against Impunity in Guatemala (CICIG) published a groundbreaking report. Starting in March 2009, the organization collected information on 3,332 "transition" adoptions that were being processed under Guatemala's December 31, 2007, Adoption Law, with what was supposed to be heightened scrutiny. Once the new law was in place, all of these adoption cases were supposed to be reviewed for legitimacy.

But approximately 900 cases hadn't been brought forward for verification. "It is suspected that there are ghost cases, manipulated files, and stolen children," wrote Gema Palencia in a July 5, 2008, *Prensa Libre* article examining the Guatemalan government's difficulties with the review process. There weren't enough resources to investigate the more than 3,000 adoption cases. Additionally, no one seemed able to say whether the 900 missing children with adoption files really existed or had somehow been erroneously created through document or administrative mistakes.

The CICIG report was meant to clear up the confusion, as well as to provide an unbiased, independent analysis of how the Guatemalan government had handled the reforms. Leading up to the report, CICIG had already been providing technical assistance and counsel to the Ministerio Público on cases related to illegal adoption. On December 28, 2008, the organization had become an official complementary prosecutor on the Rosalinda Rivera case.

The findings of the 115-page CICIG adoption report were stark. The numerical discrepancy in the adoption files had largely been due to the disorganization of the government institutions involved in the review. Despite the added protective measures and reform measures, Guatemalan children were still being bought and sold in adoption. "In many cases," a CICIG press release noted, "there are multiple and clear indications that the illegal procedures were promoted by transnational organized crime." The report noted the involvement of state officials, saying they played a key role in the facilitation of illegal adoptions.

The four CICIG staffers who worked full-time on the report created a complete dataset related to the 3,332 transition adoption cases that were in various stages of completion as of January 2008. They culled and digitized data from stacks of hard documents gathered from various sources, including the PGN, the National Council on Adoptions (CNA), the Guatemalan Immigration Bureau, the Ministerio Público, and interviews with government officials. "One of the most challenging tasks was the search for reliable information from public institutions, particularly the PGN," notes one CICIG analyst. "The process of collecting and contrasting information revealed a number of instances of repeated and contradictory information."

In some cases, CICIG found, the photograph of a single child appeared in more than one adoption file. The organization unearthed cases in which children whose adoptions had never gained approval from the PGN had been given passports anyway. In other cases, a single child's identity was used in the adoption documents prepared for "two or three sets of adoptive parents." Other children, the report said, left Guatemala on private flights, and there was no information about where they had gone or who had taken them.

A March 2009 memo on human trafficking from the U.S. Embassy in Guatemala noted that human traffickers in Guatemala had "reportedly altered their modus operandi after Guatemala passed a restrictive national adoption law" in December 2007. "Pregnant Gutatemalan women were transported to other countries, such as Spain, where the women gave birth and where adoptive parents registered the babies as their own," the U.S. Embassy cable stated. "The Public Ministry (Ministerio Público) reported that traffickers utilized various violent and non-violent methods to carry out illegal adoptions, including camouflaging them as legal adoptions."

Between 2008 and 2010, CICIG found, 90 percent of all children who left Guatemala in adoption had been relinquished, and in many cases, illegitimately so. Some relinquishments were not made voluntarily, one CICIG investigator said, or had been made by women who were not the true biological mothers. More than 60 percent of the transition adoptions contained abnormalities, including "theft and the illegal purchase or sale of children, threats and deception to biological mothers, and forgery of documents to carry out 'adoption processes. . . .'" Guatemala's participation in international adoption in 2008–2010 was a "lucrative form of human trafficking," CICIG noted, saying that adoption was sometimes used as a "mechanism" to deliver children to those requesting and paying for them. At the report's end, a list of suggestions for investigating and prosecuting illegal adoption activity was included, including the use of Guatemala's Law Against Organized Crime to prosecute the networks. As of May 2011, an estimated 325 adoption processes with signs of possible criminality remained under investigation by the Ministerio Público. At least six Guatemalan government officials were being investigated for "charges of dereliction of duty and trafficking in persons for irregular adoption purposes," and more than twenty-five public notaries and five adoption lawyers were also under investigation.

"CICIG expects the complete fulfillment of the recommendations," one of the organization's legal officer said. "Every mother whose child was stolen has the right to know what happened."

In early 2010, Mildred met an older gentleman, Guillermo Cabal.[23] His own wife was gone, and his children were grown. He was quiet and soft-spoken, like Mildred. Instead of wearing jeans and T-shirts like the younger generation of Guatemalan men, he dressed in carefully pressed button-down shirts and slacks. Guillermo had lived in Villa Nueva his whole life and could remember when it was still countryside spotted with farms, back before the crush of people looking for work had turned the land into a patchwork of crowded slums. For forty years, he had driven truckloads of gasoline across Guatemala, delivering loads of fuel to various gas stations. He had been living alone in a modest home he owned in Villa Nueva.

Mildred's children took to Guillermo quickly. When he smiled, his eyes crinkled at the corners, and he had a direct, honest gaze. To him, Mildred was a good woman. In August 2010, the Alvarado family moved in with him. At Mildred's request, Guillermo bought three chickens to keep in the home's walled courtyard.

For the first time in years, things felt calm. The children smiled freely, and returned to school. Even Ana Cristina, who would stare at the wall, motionless, for hours and cried when touched, began to improve noticeably. At age four, she began to walk. Occasionally, she giggled. The small developments gave Mildred hope. She continued working as a cleaning woman, hoping to save enough money to open her own business selling homemade food.

Mildred allows herself to feel cautiously hopeful about the future. "I used to pray to the Virgen de Guadalupe to return my girls," she said to me in 2010, not long before she moved in with Guillermo. "Now I pray to her to help me raise them; I pray for their character. There is no cereal here. You don't see a box of milk. But God gave them to me, and I fought to get them back. I love them, and I should be with them."

[23.] The name has been changed.

The Alvarado family in Guatemala, 2011. Back row, from left: Guillermo Cabal, Mildred Alvarado, Mario, Susana, and baby Adriana. Fernanda and Ana Cristina are in front.

The Emanuel family in Gallatin, Tennessee, 2010. Back row, from left: Betsy, Leslie, Burton, Bo, Jackson, Lee, and Jill. Front row from left: Hannah, Matthew, and Emily Belle. Photo courtesy Ashley McMahon.

EPILOGUE

At the time of this book's publication, new adoptions between Guatemala and the United States remain suspended. No one knows when the country might reopen. Approximately 300 cases from 2007 and 2008 are still being underway; according to the International Commission Against Impunity in Guatemala, 20 percent have been referred to the Ministerio Público in order to be investigated for criminal fraud.

Penal proceedings against Coni Galindo Bran and Sabrina Donis continue within the Guatemalan justice system. Both women are free on bail. They maintain that they don't know each other. Coni says she has never met Mildred, and that "no one in her family has ever worked in adoption." Both women claim that that Mildred sold her children into adoption, but not to them. Neither offered explanations of how or why they believed this. According to Rony Cruz de Bautista, Sabrina Donis' former boyfriend, Sabrina left him and the hot pink house where Mildred lived in summer 2010. Rony said he didn't know if Sabrina ever worked in adoption. He now runs a pawn shop that advertises gold out of the house's front room.

The Ministerio Público has not charged Marvin Bran, Carla Girón, Dinora Palacios, César Augusto Trujillo, Saul Vinicio García, and Amadeo Guerra with any crime in connection to the Alvarado case. Though three years have passed, prosecutors say that they are still collecting information. Palacios maintains that she did nothing wrong; Vinicio García says Marvin Bran tricked him; and Trujillo repeatedly did not show up for interviews and therefore did not comment. After surprising Amadeo Guerra in person at his parent's home in San José Las Rosas, he said he would answer questions via email. He did not. Marvin Bran said via email that he never had anything to do with Mildred Alvarado or her children. Carla

Girón and Tedi Hedstrom did not respond to repeated requests for comment.

Judge Mario Fernando Peralta of Escuintla was stripped of judicial immunity in November 3, 2010 by the Guatemalan Supreme Court and is under investigation by the Ministerio Público's Organized Crime Unit for the charges of human trafficking, abuse of authority, malfeasance, and dereliction of duty in relation to the adoption and attempted adoption of two other children, "Karen Abigail López García" and "Yahaira Naomi Muyus." The International Commission Against Impunity in Guatemala is acting as complementary prosecutor on the case. According to reports in the Guatemalan press, Judge Peralta's role in twenty other cases of allegedly fraudulent adoptions is also being examined. As of August 2011, Peralta remains in his position presiding over the Minor's Court in Escuintla. He maintains that he did nothing illegal or wrong.

On March 29, 2011, CICIG announced that formal charges of human trafficking and illegal association were being brought against Marvin Bran and eight others for their participation in the adoption network involved in the "Karen Abigail" case. At the time of this book's printing, he remains physically at-large, though he maintains a presence on Facebook, Hi5, and other social networking sites.

Carla Girón, the adoption facilitator who had brought the Alvarado children to Hogar Luz de María, married the former director of the Christian adoption agency World Partners Adoption, Inc, in 2008 and now goes by the name Carla Harding. The couple opened a new business together in 2009 called Surrogacy Partners, which is based in Georgia. The company self-defines as a "pioneer in international surrogacy" and advertises the services of Guatemalan women who are willing to be paid to carry and give birth to a child for American clients.

Fundación Sobrevivientes continues to provide pro-bono legal support and advocate for female victims of violence in Guatemala, including women whose children appear to have been abducted for adoption. Amnesty International held letter-writing campaigns on behalf of Norma Cruz in 2008, 2009, and 2010 after repeated death threats were made against her. According to a memo from the U.S. Embassy on the incident, Guatemala authorities believe one 2009 kidnapping and assault on a member of Cruz's family was carried out in retaliation for her work on cases that "implicates state security agents in a trafficking in persons network." In 2009, Cruz received an "International Woman of Courage" award from U.S. Secretary of State Hilary Clinton on behalf of her work at Sobrevivientes. Cruz, her family, and her staff continue to receive threats.

Jennifer Yasmin Velásquez López is now thirteen years old. The Board of Directors at Fundaniñas, including founder Isabel de Bosch, deny that Sue Hedberg ever visited the child, or delivered presents from the Emanuel family. Fundaniñas refused to confirm whether or not Jennifer is under their care today, citing concerns about the girl's privacy, yet the organization's public Facebook page contains over a hundred photographs of children at their orphanage. Jennifer is among them. Dr. José Venacios Bran González, the pediatrician somehow involved with Jennifer's relinquishment, did not respond to requests for interviews.

The total number of children adopted internationally into the United States has decreased, partially due to implementation of the Hague Convention on Intercountry Adoption as well as trafficking scandals in countries including Vietnam, Haiti, Nepal, India, and Guatemala.

In spring 2011, the Ethiopian government announced that they would be slowing down their processing of adoption applications by 90 percent, saying it was "rather difficult to examine up to 50 files per day," a letter from the Ethiopian Ministry of Women's, Children, and Youth Affairs stated. "…There is also no doubt that taking time to investigate the processes of adoption is highly important to decrease the incidences of adoptions pursued in an illegal manner using falsified documents and leading to violations of the rights and safety of children."

In Guatemala, Raquel Par, Olga López, and Loyda Rodríguez are still searching for their missing daughters. They suspect that their children are living with families in Illinois, Missouri, and Iowa, respectively. Five years have passed. The Ministerio Público's Organized Crime and Trafficking units continue to investigate. On July 29, 2011, Guatemalan judge Angelica Noemi Tellez Hernández of the Juzgado Constituido en Tribunal de Amparo issued orders for the child adopted as "Karen Abigail" to be repatriated to Guatemala within 60 days. As the time of this book's printing in September 2011, the child remains in the United States.

Enma Galicia, one of the three kidnapped sisters featured on the 2008 Dateline special "To Catch a Baby Broker," remains missing.

Mildred and her family, including a new baby named Adriana, are still living with Guillermo. She keeps a framed photograph of Betsy Emanuel's family hanging on her wall.

The International Commission Against Impunity in Guatemala (CICIG) continues helping the Ministerio Público investigate illegal adoption cases. They have signed on as official complementary prosecutor in the Asociacíon Primavera case, which relates to the adoption of "Karen Abigail Lopez García," and two other cases. They provide technical assistance to the Ministerio Público for other adoption and trafficking cases.

Since the conclusion of the Department of Children and Families investigation sparked by Betsy Emanuel's complaint, the state of Florida has investigated Celebrate Children International three additional times. Since 2005, nineteen complaints have been made about the adoption agency. The Department of Children and Families has not substantiated any of them. The Department's file of records, communication, and complaints related to their investigations of Celebrate Children International is over 3,000 pages long. The most recent investigation, from 2010, examined unsubstantiated allegations related to potential trafficking in Ethiopia. The Florida Attorney General's Office has fielded seventeen additional phone calls and emails of inquiry about CCI, eight of which alleged fraud.

In November 2010, the Florida Department of Children and Families sent a letter to the Florida Office of the Inspector General, expressing doubt over their work, saying: "There is no clear policy on who Department personnel should contact or direct clients with concerns outside the licensing scope of the Department, especially with allegations of international human trafficking or harvesting."

At the time of this book's publication, Celebrate Children International's operating license remains in good standing with the state of Florida. The agency has recently started a new pilot adoption program in the Democratic Republic of Congo.

For more information, updates, and detailed citations on this text, please visit www.findingfernanda.com.

Fernanda and Ana Cristina Alvarado at home in Guatemala, August 2010.

ACKNOWLEDGMENTS

This book would have never been possible without one person in particular: Juan Carlos Llorca was at my side almost every day during my time in Guatemala, helping me navigate courts, slums, and hours of challenging interviews with humor, heartfelt dedication, and expert racecar driving. Juan Carlos, may the very best fleas always jump on your mat. Thank you with all of my heart.

Wayne Barrett encouraged me from day one, and his faith, good humor, and advice were sustaining. It's been an honor and privilege to be mentored and supported by Florence George Graves, director and founder of the Schuster Institute for Investigative Journalism at Brandeis University. Fernanda Diaz was invaluable in her varied capacities as a meticulous research assistant, editor, and fact-checker.

The Stabile Center for Investigative Reporting at Columbia University provided the initial funding for my first reporting trip to Guatemala in December 2008; and the Schuster Institute for Investigative Journalism at Brandeis University offered student research assistance, guidance, and some financial support. Investigative Reporters and Editors (IRE) granted me a 2010 Freelance Fellowship Award, and the Journalism and Women Symposium (JAWS) awarded me the 2010 Joan Cook Fellowship. The Newswomen's Club of New York granted me a 2008-2009 McCormick Scholarship from the Anne O'Hare McCormick Memorial Fund, Inc.

Nicole Haff, formerly of Proskauer Rose LLP in New York, offered insightful pro-bono legal counsel regarding federal Freedom of Information Act requests, as did former First Amendment Project lawyers David Greene and Geoff King. Additional in-depth legal consultations were provided by Matthew Morris and Dolores DiBella of Proskauer Rose, and legal counsel was also provided by Bernie Rhodes at Lathrop and Gage LLP.

Thanks also to all of the staff at the Schuster Institute for Investgative Journalism: E.J. Graff, Lindsay J. Markel, Sophie Ellsner, and Claire Pavlik Purgus, as well as the Brandeis University student research assistants who helped with interview transcriptions: Sean Petterson, Jake Yarmus, Theresa Sheehan, Lauren Schloss, Mateo Aceves, Irina Finkel, Jessica Willingham, Carolyn Schweitzer, Jeremy Konar, Scott Evans, and Matthew Kipnis. Thanks also to the literary folks: editor Alexandra Shelley, copyeditor Mel Wohlgemuth, agent Farley Chase, everyone who helped with Cathexis Press, and the editorial team at Beacon Press who first believed in this book.

Certain friends, family, and colleagues read draft chapters and provided feedback: Katharine Brown, Eros Hoagland, Ron and Marcy Klattenberg, Catalina Lobo-Guerrero, Laura McIntyre, Nancy McIntyre, and Malia Politzer. Authors D.W. Gibson, Francisco Goldman, Scott Carney, Kathryn Joyce, and Cathryn Jakobson Ramin generously shared their time, advice, and wisdom, as did private investigator Jim Mintz of the Mintz Group. Writer Michael Shea offered calm aid during a certain turbulent time. Thank you to Heidi Riddle at Half Halt Farms in Martinez, California, and Luis Ballina Pablo and his team of *amazonitas* at the Centro Ecuestre Real del Mar in Baja California, México. The Siegal, McIntyre, and Hoagland families offered love and support, as did my extended family members Alfredo Cruz and Nathaniel Thundering Bear Moore. My sister, the best person in the world, should be thanked for being just that. Heartfelt thanks to Eros Hoagland and "Baby Güey" Siobhan for the daily love, comfort, and "being rad."

When fundraising on Kickstarter to cover expenses for an August 2010 reporting trip to Guatemala, the following people offered support in increments of a single dollar all the way up to five hundred: Sarah Bleviss, Ida C. Benedetto, Audacia Ray, Pearl Gabel, Kathleen Burton McDade, Jennifer Janisch, Brianna Cayo Cotter, Ruth Ann Harnisch, Jen Angel, Amanda Siegal, Kerry Weber, Dale Edmonds, Kelley Bunkers, Brook Cole, Aric Mayer, Juan Carlos Llorca, Renee Feltz, Lisa Jervis, Regina Pollack, C.W. Anderson, Jennifer Hemsley, Patrick Keaney, Caroline Dworin, Allison Harned, Lisa Mancini, Bryan Graham, Arun Gupta, Doug Henwood, J. Bill Chilton, Andrew Boyd, Ananogger, Richard Siegal, Darren Hauck, Michael D. Yates, Mary Cuddehe, Jaime, Angela Tosca, Nicholas

Pinto, Aaron, John Kalonaros, Laura McIntyre, Craig Tyler, Eugenia and Victor Villagra, Nancy Johnson, the Diaz family, Andy Schmid, Anonymous, Aura Bogado, Laura Harris, Hilke Schellmann, S. Alfredo Cruz, Brandon Neubauer, Nathaniel Moore, Jasmine DeFoore, Jennifer MacFarlane, Claire Galli, Brett, Myles, Claire Pavlik Purgus, Kristina Puga, Ken Hawkins, Julie Mack, Eunice Lipton, Beth Barany, Carlos Pareja, Anita Kissee, Kelly Truax, Jordan Flaherty, Mik Kinkead, Zoe Holmes, Michael Au, Renee Dumas, Holly Wilmeth, Bonnie Castellani, Erin Lockward, Melanie Light, Emi Kane, Mikaela Conley, Anonymous, Jake Lawrence, Megan, Mac McClelland, Roninja, Michael Shaw, Tara Cook, Mike Dunshee, Te-Ping Chen, Suzanne Ma, Michael Fox, Lianne Milton, Teru Kuwayama, Sunny Bates, Marcy Klattenberg, Max Moraga, E.J. Graff, Rolando Sandor, Kate Bradley, Susan Sawyers, Jane Isay, Matthew Cassel, Tim Martens, Carolyn Toll Oppenheim, Jane Stevens, Jackie Bischof, Sharon Torres, Cathryn Ramin, Poco a Poco, Seth Herman, Jan Paschal, Mark Renehan, Krista Kennell, Bob Black, Carl Mastandrea, and Sapana Sakya. The Diaz family was especially generous.

Hundreds of sources helped build this book. Various prosecutors within Guatemala's Ministerio Público, especially the Trafficking and Organized Crime units, helped me every time I dropped into their offices, unannounced and full of questions. I'd like to especially thank one prosecutor, "El Casco," for helping. Certain individuals in Guatemala leaked troves of documents that were extremely helpful to the construction of this narrative; thank you all.

Finally, both Mildred Alvarado and Betsy Emanuel spent countless hours detailing their experiences to me, a process that was often difficult and wrought with emotion. Thank you both for your trust and faith.

ADDITIONAL NOTES ON SOURCES

1. The reporting from this chapter is drawn from trips to Amplificación Solano, Villalobos, Villa Nueva, Villa Canales, Villa Sur, Antigua, and Guatemala City. I've personally visited many of the places I describe, including where Mildred lived with Romelio, Marjorie's lot in Villalobos, Sabrina's house, the Pío Lindo foot bridge, and the Bosque de San Nicólas shopping plaza. Reporting here is also based on interviews with Mildred Alvarado, Patricia Alvarado, Marjorie Areola Tomas, Sabrina Donis, Rony de Bautista, Elvira Cruz (Rony's mother), Norma Cruz, Olga Lopéz, Sue Kuyper, Claudia Palencias, Rootman Perez, Mynor Pinto, and Claudia Rodríguez. Archival photographs of Sabrina Donis, Rony de Bautista, Karina Donis, and Coni Galindo Bran from Ministerio Público files helped with visual descriptions. MP files also contained automobile registration for Coni Galindo Bran's white Nissan truck and copies of cédulas, or ID cards, for Coni Galindo Bran, her husband Oscar Bran Herrera, Mildred Alvarado, and Patricia Alvarado.

2. Betsy Emanuel provided digital .mp4 files of the videos of children provided to her in the spring of 2006 by Celebrate Children International. Emanuel also provided copies of correspondence between herself and Sue Hedberg from 2006 onward, which were backed up by correspondence between the Emanuel family and Sue Hedberg/ Celebrate Children International obtained from the Florida Department of Children and Families via Freedom of Information Act request. Emanuel also provided additional adoption documents, including various power-of-attorney forms and photographs of Jennifer Yasmin Velásquez Lopéz. Information on Gallatin, Tennessee came from various photos, local newspapers *The Gallatin News Examiner*, *The Tennessean*, and *The Gallatin Newspaper*, the Gallatin City Hall website, city-data.com, mainstreetmediaonline.com, and archived weather data from 2005.

Additional information is from the websites of Journey Family Fellowship church in Illinois, and LIFE International. I used information from the current incarnations of Rainbowkids.com and Precious. org. Web caches and archival documentation of both sites, and also from Celebrate Children International's website, celebratechildren.org, provided by Archive.org's Wayback Machine. Additional information on CCI from 2003, 2004, 2005, 2006, 2007, 2008, and 2009 tax returns downloaded from Guidestar.org.

Sources who helped illuminate this chapter are: Jason Damkoehler, Robyn Spangler, Alfonso Sandoval Close, Karla Ordoñez, Betsy Emanuel, Leslie Emanuel, and six anonymous Guatemalan adoption lawyers. The U.S. State Department's current website at www.adoption.state.gov provided information on various country's adoption restrictions, as did caches of web pages with adoption information from 2006, accessed via archive.org. Bible references to adoption include Exodus 2:1-10, Esther 2:7, Matthew 1:20, Ephesians 1:5, Galatians 3:26, Psalm 68:5-6, Galatians 4:4-5, Isaiah 1:17, Exodus 22:22, Proverbs 31:8,9, Matthew 18:5, and James 1:27. Additional information on Celebrate Children International's reputation was obtained from adoption.com forums, GuatAdopt.com comments, adoption agency review websites, and interviews with CCI clients including Jane Doe 1, Mike Bius, Jane Doe 2, Rob and Amy Carr, Laura Conk, Jane Doe 5, Sharon Douhitt, Jane Doe 6, Margo Engberg, Dawn Michelle Garland, Sarah Grandstaff, Jane Doe 7, Leslie Harmoning, Jane Doe 8, Beth Hunt, Jane Doe 9, Jane Doe 10, Kim Kennedy, Jane Doe 11, Jane Doe 12, Jane Doe 13, Jane Doe 14, Jane Doe 15, Carolyn Pringle, Jane Doe 16, Jessica Richter, Jane Doe 17, Karen Salemme, Laynah Sheets, Jane Doe 18, Jane Doe 19, Charissa Urban, and others. Interviews with other adoptive parents included but are not limited to Jane Doe 20, Jane Doe 21, Lisa Riegler, Jane Doe 22, David Kruchev, Karen Moline, and Brian Spence.

3. Data on Guatemala GNI per capita income from the World Bank's 2008 Development Data sheet "Guatemala at a Glance" calculated in U.S. dollars using the Atlas method with data from the Development Economics LDB database. Decree 106 of Guatemala's 1963 Civil Code, in conjunction with a 1976 law known as the Programa de Adopciones, provided a legal framework for adoption processes through 1989. See bilbiography for reports, articles, and books related to history of adoption in Guatemala and general Guatemalan history. Additional details from both email and in-person interviews with Marco Tulio Alvárez, Director of Los Archivos de la Paz. Guatemalan adoption numbers provided by the U.S. Department of State. Information on Rios Montt from articles by Raymond Bonner and Larry Rohter in the New York Times and Rios Montt's March 25, 1982 address to Guatemala.

Email between Sue Hedberg and Betsy Emanuel provided by both Emanuel and the Florida Department of Children and Families. Email correspondence also provided by the Thompson family, detailing some of their interactions with the agency. Conversations that were particularly helpful to this chapter include those with Thelma "Thelmy" de Saravía, Isabel Bosch and the Fundaniñas board of directors, Laura Beauvais-Godwin, Donna Wheeler, Mike Bius, Kim Kennedy, Debbie Mignemi, Rudy Rivera, and Gilma Lemus. Information on Cheraya Bor obtained from public records, including bankruptcy documents and web caches of the original Celebrate Children International website which include the Celebrate Children International Country Program Guide 2006. Holt International adoption contract downloaded from www.holtinternational.org in 2010. Visual descriptions were drawn from a visit to Alfonso Close's office, a visit to Fundaninas, photos posted to the Fundaninas public Facebook fan page, in-person interviews with Mayra Estrada and her daughter Adriana, and photographs of Maria Josefa Velasquez Lopéz and her daughter Jennifer provided by Betsy Emanuel.

Information about Tedi Bear Adoptions comes from former Tedi Bear clients, including Jane Doe 1, Jane Doe 2, Jane Doe 3, Jane Doe 4, Jennifer Hemsley, Dawn Stark, and Katie Tuel, and an extensive public records request made to the Florida Department of Children and Families.

Email from Sue Hedberg to the CCI Guatemala listserve provided by a former CCI client. Additional information about Celebrate Children International is from archived caches of the agency's current and former website, celebratechildren.org and cc-intl.org, accessed via Archive.org and saved in .pdf form. Sue Hedberg's salary and other financial information was drawn from Celebrate Children International's tax returns and budget statements provided to the state of Florida and acquired via public records request.

Basic background information related to the Hedberg family comes from Sue Hedberg's online bio (current and cached) and a 2009 phone conversation with Dave Hedberg. Information on Columbia International University comes from the university's website, related articles, a conversation with a university spokesperson, and the 2005-2006 CIU Student Life Catalog, accessed at http://www.ciu.edu/graduate/catalog/2005-2006/studentlife.php. Additional reporting is drawn from public property records, company tax returns, the FISH website, and various other blogs. Sue Hedberg's friendship with Alfonso Close and his vacations in Florida were mentioned in official statements made by Sue Hedberg to the Florida Department of Children and Families during an investigation, which were obtained in a document obtained via public records request entitled "Knowledge of Guatemalan Contacts," July 2008.

4. Much of this chapter is based on Mildred Alvarado's personal history and recollections of childhood, and drawn from in-person interviews with Mildred and her sister Patricia, as well as visits to various places mentioned,

including Finca San Juan Bosco; further reporting from the website of the Guatemala City Nueva Hacienda Country Club. Patricia Hernandez, chief of personnel at the Inlacsa Milk Factory in Villalobos, helped us finally speak to Marjorie Tomas Arreola. Background information was drawn from United Nations Development Programme reports and various other sources mentioned in this book's bibliography.

The childhood and personal history of Betsy Emanuel was told to me by Betsy herself, in person, via phone, and by email. Additional reporting included research into various specific topics, events, and places, including but not limited to the Cottage Hill Baptist Church and Airport Boulevard Baptist Church in Mobile, Alabama, Greystone Academy, and general reporting about Mobile, Alabama in the 1960's and 1970's.

5. Emails between CCI and Betsy Emanuel were provided by Betsy Emanuel and were also obtained via public records request from the state of Florida. Recollection of conversations provided by Betsy Emanuel; Angela Vance, Sue Hedberg, and Dr. Jose Bran González refused to participate. Advertisement for Maria Fernanda Alvarado saved by Betsy's mother Bette, and provided by Betsy.

Details about Sue Hedberg's July 2006 visit to Guatemala, the number of adoptions CCI handled, and quotes from Hedberg herself were drawn from emails posted to the CCI Guatemala listserve. Information about Josefina Arellano, her work style, and her role at the PGN provided by Ministerio Público officials, former colleagues, news reports, and others who interacted with her. Additional information about PGN provided by people who worked in the institution, U.S. Embassy memos obtained via public records request, caches of online adoption bulletins from the U.S. Department of State, private investigators, and various Guatemalan adoption lawyers and facilitators.

Email between Marvin Bran and Sue Hedberg about Fernanda Alvarado obtained via public records requests made to the Florida Department of Children and Families. Adoption documentation, including a Power of Attorney form and pediatric medical records provided by the Emanuel family; additional set of corroborating pediatric medical records obtained from Dr. Napóleon Castillo Mollinedo. Video of Sue Hedberg, Marvin Bran, Kimberly Bran, unknown children, other unknown adults, and Fernanda provided by Betsy Emanuel. The address on Fernanda's DNA test was visited in Guatemala City, where Angela Herrera de Bran lived. She said that she did not work as a cuidadora, but that someone had been threatening her.

6. This chapter is based largely on information obtained through Freedom of Information Act (FOIA) requests made to the Department of State and from archived versions of various websites, including the Department of State's Intercountry Adoption, U.S. Citizen and Immigration Services, GuatAdopt.com, Families Without Borders, and jointcouncil.org. The reports mentioned in this chapter are listed in the bibliography. Further information provided by Kevin Kreutner, various State Department officials, former Consul General Kay Anske at the U.S. Embassy in Guatemala, various Guatemalan lawyers and adoption facilitators, and cuidadoras.

Reports with information were compiled by the International Commission Against Impunity in Guatemala (CICIG), Comisión Presidencial Coordinadora de la Política del Ejecutivo en materia de Derechos Humanos (COPREDEH), UNICEF, Casa Alianza Fundación, Fundación Myrna Mack, Fundación Sobrevivientes, Movimiento Social por los Derechos de la Niñez y la Adolescencia, Oficina de Derechos Humanos del Arzobispado de Guatemala (ODHAG), Secretaría de Bienestar Social de la Presidencia de la República (SBS), Human Rights Watch, the Guttmacher Institute, and a 2006 survey conducted by the Human Rights Institute of San Carlos University of Guatemala (IDHUSAC). Interviews with Judge Mario Peralta, Shyrel Osborn, Stephen Osborn, Judge Ricardo Damman Gomez, Norma Cruz, Vilma Castillo de Bendfeldt, Flory Herrera, Gary Cooper, Rootman Perez, Jennifer Hemsley, Ellora DeCarlo, Diana Perez, Nancy Bailey, Erin Stoy and various officials at the PGN, Ministerio Público, and Office of the Human Rights Ombudsman also helped. So did a few pediatricians, who each requested confidentiality. Advertisements for abandoned children from Guatemalan newspapers provided by Judge Peralta. Additional information was obtained from UNICEF position papers, writing by Susana Luarca on GuatAdopt.com, board meeting minutes and conference call notes from the Joint Council on International Children's Services, November 2006 testimony from the House Subcommittee on Africa, Global Human Rights and International Operations, Department of State table of orphan immigration statistics for 1999, and binders containing paper cutout news clips from the personal archive of attorney Fernando Linares Beltranena, photographed in person in Guatemala City.

7. Some of the visual depictions contained in this chapter were made possible by visits to Dr. Paniagua and the Sanatorio San Antonio de San Miguel, as well as Coni Galindo Bran's home and the house where Mildred Alvarado and her family lived with Sabrina Donis and Rony Cruz de Bautista. Also especially helpful to this chapter were complaint and penal files, receipts, and criminal evidence shared by the Ministerio Público in

Guatemala and Mildred Alvarado's lawyers at Fundacion Sobrevivientes. Betsy Emanuel shared photos of Fernanda and Ana Cristina, as well as an email sent by Sue Hedberg after the child's birth. The Thompson family and other CCI clients also shared email. Please see bibliography for supporting reports, articles, and books.

Additional general information was provided by conversations and communications with the following sources: Kelley Bunkers, Tom DiFilipo, Kathleen Strottman, Steve and Rozlyn Olson, Manuel Manrique, Judith Gibbons, César R. Monterroso Monzón, Luvia de Cabrera, Nancy Bailey, Don Kovak, Carrie Kerskie, Ilse Chambers, Amanda Welch, EJ Graff, two anonymous pediatricians in Guatemala City, Karen Smith Rotabi, Diego Alvarez, Sara Payes, and Armando Ajín.

8. Email related to Fernanda and Ana Cristina Alvarado's adoptions provided by the Emanuel and Thompson families, including copies of U.S. Embassy pre-approval notice. Additional information on CCI client cases drawn from documents obtained via public records requests to the Florida Department of Children and Families and the Office of the Florida Attorney General. Information also drawn from interviews with Janey Brooks, Carrie McFarland, Tammy Grega, Jillian Richman, and Rachel Robinson. Additional information obtained via FOIA request from the Department of Homeland Security, U.S. Citizenship and Immigration Services, and the U.S. Embassy in Guatemala.

Information on Francisco García Gudiel obtained from Guatemalan press clips, and information on Roberto Echeverría from blog posts by Tom DiFilipo, message boards on adoption.com forums, and Guatemalan press clips. A December 4, 2006 Congressional Briefing in Washington, DC sponsored by the Congressional Coalition on Adoption Institute included Echeverría, DiFilipo, a DOS rep, and a CIS rep on a panel together. Wasatch International Adoptions, Guatemala Newsletter and Update, December 2006, and also minutes from the December 13, 2006 JCICS Board Meeting Conference Call. Extensive email communications between Rachel Robinson and Betsy Emanuel provided by Betsy Emanuel. Mike the tattoo artist in Antigua helped with some investigative legwork.

Additional documentation from the Florida Department of Children and Families investigation files related to Sue Hedberg and Tammy Grega of CCI provided by Janey Brooks, and additional documentation from the Florida Department of Children and Families investigation files. "Failure to complete the required additional measures will result in the termination of adoption proceedings," CCI told them in a certified letter sent to the Brooks' home. "CCI reserves the right to instruct in-country adoption officials to temporarily cease proceedings with your case. You would be responsible for any costs (including foster care fees) incurred during this cessation."

Emails between Sue Hedberg and Olga Sullivan of Adopt, Intl. in Texas provided in a batch of documents obtained from Florida DCF via FOIA request. Additional information from interviews with Betsy Emanuel and from Sue Hedberg's explanation of the lost referral for Maria Fernanda Alvarado Yac provided to Florida DCF, which was obtained via FOIA request. Copies of Sue Hedberg's email to and from the email address marvinbran77@hotmail.com, which as of February 2011, is Marvin Bran's working email, provided by sources in Guatemala. The pre-approval email, dated 11-1-2006, was sent from U.S. Embassy in Guatemala to Betsy Emanuel, Sue Hedberg, and Marvin Bran; a copy was forwarded to me by Betsy Emanual.

9. Much of this chapter is based on court documents, including statements by Consuelo Galindo Bran, Sabrina Donis, Marvin Bran, Mildred Alvarado, and Patricia Alvarado. Documents originated in the Villa Canales, Villa Nueva, and Guatemala City branches of the Ministerio Público, as well as the PGN's denuncia unit, the Guatemala City Office of the Human Rights Ombudsman, the Twelfth Penal Court of Guatemala City, the Second Penal Court of Mixco, the Camera Penal Court of Guatemala City, the Juzgado de la Niñez y de Adolescencia y Adolescentes en Conflicto de La Ley Penal, and the Third Minor's Court of Guatemala City. Email from Carla Girón to adoptive American families provided by a confidential source. Interviews with Ministerio Public prosecutors include Álexander Colop, Julio Barrios, Claudia Rodríguez, Mynor Pinto, Dawn Stark, and informal conversations with other investigators/prosecutors. In-person conversations with an anonymous police detective, Victor Hugo Mejicanos, Elfego Orozco, Sabrina Donis, Coni Galindo Bran, Judge Mario Fernando Peralta, Dinora Palacios, Josefina Arellano, Ninette Guevara, PGN investigators, and Mario Gordillo also helped to inform this chapter, as did copies of email correspondence from the DWTD Yahoo listserve. Members of Carla Girón's former adoption network confidentially spoke about Girón. All information on Adoption Supervisors Guatemala and Marco Tulio Merida is from interviews with his clients, email provided by ASG clients, and the Desprosa, BioFamilyTrace, and AdoptionSupervisorsGuatemala websites (current and cached).

Betsy Emanuel provided emails to and from Rachel Robinson, and additional information about the Robinson's adoption was obtained via a public records request to the Florida Department of Children and Families and through web caches of Robinson's adoption blogs.

Information about the raid on Casa Quivira obtained from U.S. Embassy and Department of State press releases and announcements, comments and blog posts on GuatAdopt.com, email from Sue Hedberg to CCI Guatemala clients, U.S. and Guatemalan media clips, and web caches from jcics.org and ccainstitute.org. Rossy Farnes from the Secretaria de Bienestar Social de la Presidencia helped facilitate public records requests from the SBS in Guatemala City.

10. Descriptions of Fundacion Sobrevivientes based on visits to the foundation and in-person interviews with Mildred Alvarado, Olga Lopéz, Loyda Rodríguez, Norma Cruz, Claudia Palencias, Mynor Pinto, Rootman Perez, and Pilar Ramírez, as well as annual organizational reports, studies, and Guatemalan press clips. Additional information obtained from the U.S. Embassy in Guatemala via Freedom of Information Act Request and Prensa Libre reporter Lorena Seijo.

Betsy Emanuel's trip to Guatemala was recreated using information from email between her and Marco Tulio, caches of Betsy's personal blog and photos from October and November 2007, Betsy's own descriptions, and a visit to the Westin hotel.

Information about the Trafficking Unit at the Ministerio Público is drawn from documents obtained from the U.S. Embassy in Guatemala via Freedom of Information Act Request, and interviews with prosecutors and investigators in the unit.

11. Parts of this chapter are based on email between the Emanuel family and Sue Hedberg, as well as interviews with Joni Fixel and other CCI clients who were considering joining into a lawsuit. It was also created from investigation files from the Florida Department of Children and Families, tax returns from Celebrate Children International, and interviews and/or communications with the following Florida DCF staff: Carrie Hoeppner, Amy Hammett, Maria Nistri, Elizabeth Arenas, Alan Abramowitz, Sallie Bond, and Stacey Cleveland. Transcript from the November 16, 2007 CCI Friday night chat provided by an anonymous CCI client; notes from the Hague review of CCI supplied in public records from the Florida Department of Children and Families, as well as interviews with Department of State officials including Mikiko Stebbing and Julie Furuta-Toy.

Information on the quintuple murder of the Girón family and orphan "Jhossy" obtained from news clips, emails provided by anonymous adoptive parents to, from, and about Carla Azhderian and Carla Girón, Guatemalan adoption facilitators, and Carla Azhderian's blog.

12. Some of this chapter is based on interviews and communications with Sue Kuyper, Olga Lopéz, Pilar Ramírez, Mildred Alvarado, Norma Cruz, lawyers at Sobrevivientes, Kelly Caldwell, Kevin Kreutner, Rodolfo "Rudy" Rivera, Lorena Seijo, Kay Anske, Scott Smith, Carrie McFarland, Pablo Hernéndez, Victor Hugo Mejicanos, Ninette Guevara, Laynah Sheets, Carolyn Pringle, Beth Hunt, Susannah Marbutt, and Phil Neff. Additional reporting drawn from the Network in Solidarity with the People of Guatemala (NISGUA). Copies of email correspondence from Benita Noel, Kevin Kreutner, John Lowell, Marco Tulio Mérida Cifuentes, Janey Brooks, Rachel Robinson, and others provided by Betsy Emanuel. Information also provided by archived caches of the Children of the World and GuatAdopt websites. Various public records obtained from the U.S. Embassy in Guatemala reference Norma Cruz and Sobrevivientes. See bibliography for additional reporting attribution.

Julie Erwin, four former CCI staffers who requested confidentiality, Jennifer Crist, Lana Carson, and Karon Dedolchow helped illuminate Celebrate Children International as a workplace. Emails between Lowell and Betsy are on file, as are email from "Carrie Smith" to Betsy. Reporting drawn from emails in CCI archive (archive leaked to me), a copy of Exhibición Personal order, and other documents provided by the Ministerio Público. Reporting also drawn from email provided by CCI clients; archived web caches from jcics.org.

13. This chapter's beginning was comprised based on visits to Hogar Luz de María and an in-person interview with Dinora Palacios. Additional reporting drawn from the hogarluzdemaria.org website, website caches, online adoption forums, public Facebook pages, and adoption blogs. Website caches for the companies Wide Horizons for Children, Open Door Adoption, and Adoption Blessings Worldwide were also helpful. Relinquishment documents, paperwork, and deposition from various authorities, including multiple courts, mention the Alvarado children, Hogar Luz de María, and Carla Girón; documents provided by Ministerio Público and lawyers for Mildred Alvarado.

Photos of Fernanda Alvaro and Carla Girón provided by a confidential source; additional information about Tedi Hedstrom's involvement with the child evidenced by emails provided by multiple confidential sources and interviews with Guatemalan adoption facilitators.

Email communication between Betsy Emanuel and John Lowell provided by Betsy. Reporting on the "raid" in San José Las Rosas drawn from interviews with various Adoption Blessings Worldwide clients in the process of adopting children through Girón at the time of the raid, cuidadoras, and adoption facilitators. Copies of pediatric medical records for children brought in by Bran Galindo organization provided by Dr. Castillo; additional information obtained from visiting Castillo's clinic. Diana Perez spoke to me in person multiple times, and various accounts from adoptive parents, adoption forums and blogs corroborate pieces of her account.

Other key sources for this chapter include Pilar Ramírez, Shyrel and Steve Osborn, various Ministerio Público investigators, and court documents from the Third Court of Minor's in Guatemala City.

Judge Mario Fernando Peralta was interviewed in person, and further reporting came from various source accounts and clips from the Guatemalan media. Multiple Adoption Blessings Worldwide clients say Tedi Hedstrom have said about adopting Fernanda; and some provided corroborating emails sent by Hedstrom to them.

14. Details about the day of the custody hearing were drawn from interviews with Mildred Alvarado, Pilar Ramírez, Rootman Perez, Norma Cruz, Sue Kuyper, Loyda Rodríguez, Olga Lopéz, Betsy Emanuel, Judge Gomez, Shyrel Osborn, Lorena Seijo, Victor Hugo Mejicanos, and were based on various emails, photos and media clips.

Copies of email correspondence to U.S. authorities provided by Betsy Emanuel; also obtained via public records requests to FL-DCF. Communications from the U.S. Embassy obtained through FOIA request.

Deposition from Marvin Bran to the Ministerio Público provided by lawyer Fernando Linares Beltranena. Interviews with the following key sources helped this chapter: Julio Barrios, Mynor Pinto, Claudia Rodríguez, Oscar Rivas, Álexander Colop, Jaime Técu, and Fernando Linares Beltranena.

Information about the "Karen Abigail" adoption drawn from various documents originating from the Ministerio Público, the PGN, copies of DNA test results, the blog of Susana Luarca, interviews with prosecutors, Judge Mario Fernando Peralta, deposition from Marvin Bran, and more.

Details about CICIG drawn from visits to the CICIG compound, interviews, the CICIG website, the Ministerio Público, and various press clips.

15. Statistics reported to DCF during licensing review, documents accessed via FOIA request. Communications between Betsy Emanuel and Miki Stebbing, John Ballif, and Maria Nistri, Amy Hammett, and Stacy Cleveland provided by Emanuel. Additional and supporting communications provided via public records request.

Additional information about the Ministerio Público's Trafficking Unit provided by MP prosecutors, investigators, the U.S. Embassy, PGN officials, CAN officials, Guatemalan press clips, and the International

Commission Against Impunity in Guatemala (CICIG). Hunger strike information gleaned from video clips, press clips, and interviews with participants and observers.

Lester Porras provided help fulfilling lengthy public records requests at the Archivo General de Protocolos in Guatemala City.

16. Much of this chapter is based on interviews with Mildred Alvarado and Betsy Emanuel, staff at Florida DCF, and Richard Klarberg, as well as documents from Florida DCF, the Division of Consumer Services at the Florida Department of Agriculture and Consumer Services, Celebrate Children International's tax returns, public Facebook pages, and various adoption websites, both current and page caches. CICIG information drawn from in-person interviews and CICIG publications.

Information about adoption in Ethiopia provided by a 2009 interview with a high-ranking official at the U.S. Embassy in Ethiopia; the U.S. State Department, adoption forums, adoption blogs, public records requests made to Florida DCF, the March-April 2010 PEAR survey of adoption service providers in Ethiopia, and interviews with Americans adopting Ethiopian children.

REFERENCES

"Abogado que tramitaba adopciones recupero su libertad." Telediario Newscast. July 28, 2009. http://telediario.com.gt.

Acuña, Claudia. "Hogares incumplen requisitos ante CNA." *La Prensa Libre*, April 6, 2009. Accessed May 13, 2011. http://replay.web. archive.org/20090410151219/http://www.prensalibre.com/pl/2009/abril/06/305516.html.

------. "Capacitarán a personal de hogares que abrigan niños y adolescentes." *La Prensa Libre*, April 12, 2009. Accessed May 11, 2011. http://www.prensalibre.com/pl/2009/abril/12/307434.html.

------. "Activista Norma Cruz denuncia amenazas de muerte." *La Prensa Libre*, May 15, 2009. Accessed May 13, 2011. http://replay.web. archive.org/20090523095029/http://www.prensalibre.com/pl/2009/mayo/15/314789.html.

------. "Ligan a proceso a presunto autor de amenazas contra activista Norma Cruz." *La Prensa Libre*, October 23, 2009. Accessed May 11, 2011 http://www.prensalibre.com/pl/2009/octubre/23/351267.html.

------."Abogada de Asociación Primavera, paga fianza de Q50 mil." *La Prensa Libre*, December 16, 2009, Accessed May 11, 2011. http://www.prensalibre.com/pl/2009/diciembre/17/363455.html.

Aho, Barbara. "Antipas: A CIA Front." *Watch Unto Prayer*, Accessed May 10, 2011. http://watch.pair.com/antipas.html.

Aizenman, N.C. "Guatemalan Children In Limbo of Orphanages: Parents Push U.S. Officials to Help." *Washington Post*, June 18, 2009.

Allen, Kevin Minh. "The Price We All Pay: Human Trafficking in International Adoption." *CONDUCIVE Magazine,* August/September 2009. Accessed May 11, 2011. http://www.conducivemag.com/?option=com_content&view=artic%E2%80%A6n-international-adoption902&catid=38:innovative-thinking&Itemid=6.

Alvarado, Hugo and Raúl Barreno. "Mujeres demandan justicia." *La Prensa Libre*, March 19, 2011. Accessed May 10, 2011. http://www.prensalibre.com/noticias/justicia/Mujeres-demandan-justicia_0_446955314.html.

Álvarez, Marco Tulio Bobadilla. "Las Adopciones y Los Derechos Humanos de la Niñez Guatemalteca, 1977-89." Guatemala: Secretaría de la Paz (SEPAZ), September 2009. Accessed May 13, 2011. http://www.sobrevivientes.org/docs/informe-adopciones_cpaz.pdf.

"Ambassadors & Diplomacy." *Talk of the Nation*, Neal Cohen; featuring guests Prudence Bushnell, former U.S. ambassador to the Republic of Guatemala; Ambassador Thomas Simons; Ambassador James Lilly. NPR, Chicago, January 7, 2003.

Amnesty International. "Still no Justice for Guatemala Massacre Victims after 26 Years." Last Modified December 5, 2008. http://www.amnesty.org/en/news-and-updates/news/still-justice-guatemala-massacre-victims-after-26-years-20081205.

Amnesty International. "Guatemala: Amnesty International Report 2007, Human Rights in the Republic of Guatemala." Accessed May 11, 2011. http://www.amnesty.org/en/region/guatemala/report-2007.

Amnesty International. "Guatemala: No protection, no justice: killings of women (an update)." Last Modified July 18, 2006. http://www.amnesty.org/en/library/asset/AMR34/019/2006/en/970f9ee4-d423-11dd-8743-d305bea2b2c7/amr340192006en.pdf.

Arrazola, Carlos. "Guatemala Ring Selling Children On Internet; Journalists Google 'babies for sale.'" *Latin American Herald Tribune*, Accessed May 10, 2011. http://laht.com/article.asp?CategoryId=23558&ArticleId=321843.

Asamblea Permanente por los Derechos Humanos. "Guatemala." Accessed May 13, 2011. http://www.apdh-argentina.org.ar/piajal/relator/summary_guatemala_2007.pdf.

Avendaño, Maco. "Golpe a Robaniños: Hallan Otra Casa Cuña." *Al Dia*, August 4, 1998

Avila, Oscar. "Guatemala seeks domestic fix to troubled overseas adoptions: Central American nation recruiting adoptive and foster parents internally." *The Chicago Tribune*, October 26, 2008

Avilés, Karina. "La Jornada de México, publicado comprometedor reportaje sobre tráfico de niños en Guatemala." *Siglo XXI*, September 23, 1997

Barker, Michael. "The Religious Right And World Vision's 'Charitable' Evangelism." *Swans Online Magazine,* December 28, 2009. Accessed May 10, 2011. www.swans.com/library/art15/barker39.html.

Barnard, Jackelyn. "Embattled Adoption Agency Gives Up Its License." *First Coast News*, July 18, 2008. Accessed May 10, 2011. http://www.firstcoastnews.com/printfullstory.aspx?storyid=11403

Blas, Ana Lucía. „Familia teme por su vida." *La Prensa Libre,* June 20, 2007. Accessed May 10, 2011. http://www.prensalibre.com/noticias/Familia-teme-vida_0_148187026.html.

Bonillo, Cristina. "Internet une familias con adoptados." *La Prensa Libre,*

June 6, 2010. Accessed May 10, 2011. http://www.prensalibre.com/noticias/Internet-une-familias-adoptados_0_275372465.html.

Bonner, Raymond. "Guatemala Leader Reports Aid Plan." *The New York Times*, May 20, 1982.

------. "Guatemala Enlists Religion in Battle." *The New York Times*, July 18, 1982.

Booth, William. "WITCH HUNT; Babies Are Disappearing. Ugly Rumors Abound, And a Tourist's Life Is at Stake." *The Washington Post*, May 17, 1994

Briggs, Billy. "Violence and secrets: Guatemala bares its soul." *The Scotland Herald/ Sunday Herald*, March 29, 2009. Accessed May 13, 2011. http://replay.web.archive.org/20090415172920/http://www.sundayherald.com/misc/print.php?artid=2498500.

Briggs, Laura. "Mother, Child, Race, Nation: The Visual Iconography of Rescue and the Politics of Transnational and Transracial Adoption." *Gender & History*, Vol. 15, No.2, August 2003.

------. "Making American Families: Transnational Adoption and U.S. Latin America Policy." *Haunted by Empire*, edited by Ann Laura Stoler. Duke, 2006.

Bush, Elizabeth. "The Joys of Adoption: A Daniel Island couple celebrates their ,forever family.'" *The Daniel Island News*, November 5, 2008. Accessed May 10, 2011. http://www.thedanielislandnews.com/artman2/publish/Top_Stories_69/The_joys_of_adoption_printer.php.

"Capturan a hijo de médico asesinado junto a su familia." *La Prensa Libre*, December 9, 2008. Accessed May 11, 2011. http://www.prensalibre.com.gt/pl/2008/diciembre/09/282190.html.

Cardona, Karen. "Al menos 500 habrían sido robados: Tres mil niños están pendientes de adopción." *La Hora*, February 6, 2008. Accessed May 10, 2011. http://www.lahora.com.gt/notas.php?key=25627&fch=2008-02-06.

"Carlos Castresana, el látigo de la corrupción judicial en Guatemala." *La Hora*, June 7, 2010. Accessed May 10, 2011. http://www.lahora.com.gt/notas.php?key=68088&fch=2010-06-07.

"Caso de niña robada deja dudas sobre infantes adoptados por parejas de EE. UU." *Associated Press, La Prensa Libre*, January 8, 2008. Accessed May 10, 2011 http://www.prensalibre.com/pl/2008/agosto/01/254441.html.

Castillo, Juan Manuel. "Los casos en contra de Susana Luarca." *El Periódico*, December 19, 2009. Accessed May 10, 2011. http://www.elperiodico.com.gt/es/20091219/pais/129680.

Cereser, Leonardo. „Camotán extraña a su princesa." *La Prensa Libre*, October 14, 2007. Accessed May 10, 2011. http://www.prensalibre.

com/noticias/Camotan-extrana-princesa_0_150585398.html.

Chadwick, John. "Gospel Outreach: Church or cult?" *The Bergen Record*, December 18, 2004. Accessed May 10, 2011. http://www.rickross. com/reference/gospel_outreach/gospel_outreach1.html.

Chang, Lester. "Hundreds of Marhallese babies adopted on Kaua'i and O'ahu." *The Garden Isle*, August 10, 2003. Accessed August 10, 2011. http://thegardenisland.com/news/article_333db369-04c3-5f53-859a-6018c173c0f9.html.

CICIG report. "Informe sobre actors involucrados en el proceso de adopciones irregulares en Guatemala a partir de la entrada en vigor de la Ley de Adopciones." December 1, 2010.

"CICIG responsabiliza a jueces y abogados en adopciones ilegales." *ACAN-EFE*

News Agency. La Prensa Libre, December 1, 2010. Accessed May 10, 2011. http://www.prensalibre.com/noticias/CICIG-responsabiliza-guatemaltecos-adopciones-ilegales_0_382162020.html.

Clemetson, Lynette. "Adoptions From Guatemala Face an Uncertain Future." *The New York Times*, May 16, 2007.

Cochran, Jeff. "Attorney General sues Tucson adoption agency for fraud." November 18, 2008. Accessed May 13, 2011. http://www.abc15. com/content/news/centralsouthernarizona/story/Att...eneral-sues-Tucson-adoption-agency-for/hF6w76rnz0WY5YtNHquL8Q. cspx, http://www.abcadoptions.com/hotline/index. php?showtopic=213&pid=239&mode=threaded&show=&st=0.

Comisión Presidencial Coordinadora de la Política del Ejecutivo en materia de Derechos Humanos, Fundación Myrna Mack, Fundación Sobrevivientes, Movimiento Social por los Derechos de la Niñez y la Adolescencia, Oficina de Derechos Humanos del Arzobispado de Guatemala, and the Secretaría de Bienestar Social de la Presidencia de la República. "ADOPCIONES en guatemala ¿protección o mercado?" Guatemala, 2007.

Committee on Hemispheric Security, Permanent Council of the Organization of American States. Working Group to Prepare a Regional Strategy to Promote Inter-American Cooperation in Dealing with Criminal Gangs. "U.S. Strategy to Combat the Threat of Criminal Gangs from Central America and Mexico: Inputs for the Development of a Regional Strategy to Promote Inter-American Cooperation in Dealing with Criminal Gangs." February 23, 2010.

Connolly, Kate. "Romania lifts lid on babies for sale racket." *The Guardian*, October 31, 2001. Accessed May 10, 2011. http://www. guardian.co.uk/world/2001/oct/31/internationalcrime.

Corbett, Sarah. "Where Do Babies Come From?" *The New*

York Times Magazine, June 16, 2002. Accessed May 10, 2011. http://query.nytimes.com/gst/fullpage. html?res=9C00EEDE113DF935A25755C0A9649C8B63.

Corderi, Victoria. "To catch a baby broker." *Dateline NBC*, January 20, 2008.

"Corrupt Police Purged In Guatemala As Femicide Soars." *NotiCen: Central American & Caribbean Affairs*, February 10, 2005. Accessed May 10, 2011. http://findarticles.com/p/articles/mi_go1655/ is_2005_Feb_10/ai_n29158451/.

Covenant House/Casa Alianza. *Trafficking in Children in Latin America and the Caribbean*, July 2004. Accessed May 10, 2011. http://www. casa-alianza.org.

Danner, Mark. *The Massacre at El Mozote*. United States: Vintage Books, 1993.

Darling, Juanita. "Little Bundles of Cash." *The Los Angeles Times*, January 17, 2001.

Davenport, Dawn. *The Complete Book of International Adoption: A Step by Step Guide to Finding Your Child*. New York: Broadway Books, 2006.

Davidson, Joe. "Guatemalan matriarch is mother to girls in need." RotaryClub of Covington. No date. http://bit.ly/p6QiSW

De Leon, Sergio. "Adoption regulations targeted." *Associated Press*, February 9, 2005.

Diamond, Sara. *Spiritual Warfare: The Politics of the Christian Right*. Boston: South End Press, 1989.

Díaz, Wendy and Acuña, Claudia. "Identifican en México red de tráfico de niños que opera en Guatemala." *La Prensa Libre*, October 10, 2010. Accessed May 10, 2011. http://www.prensalibre.com/noticias/ Identifican-Mexico-trafico-Guatemala-paises_0_350965015.html.

Duarte, Carlos. "Se venden bebés: REQUISITOS: NO TENER ESCRÚPULOS Y 30 MIL DÓLARES." *La Hora*, November 24, 2007. Accessed May 10, 2011. http://www.lahora.com.gt/notas. php?key=18590&fch=2007-11-24.

Dudley, Steven. "Parents protest delays in adopting Guatemalan kids: Frustrated by delays in Guatemala's adoption process, American parents protested in Washington." *The Miami Herald*, June 18, 2009.

"Estadounidenses demandan agilizar antejuicio contra jueza de menores." *La Prensa Libre*, March 12, 2008. Accessed May 10, 2011. http:// www.prensalibre.com/pl/2008/marzo/12/226198.html.

"Expertos debaten sobre adopciones irregulares en Latinoamérica." *AFP News Agency*. Printed in *La Prensa Libre*, September 9, 2009. Accessed May 11, 2011 http://www.prensalibre.com/pl/2009/ septiembre/07/340491.html.

Farbman, Madeline. "Adoption across an ocean: Ethiopian orphans finding homes with American families." *The Post-Star*, February 22, 2007.

Fernández, Marcela. "Consejo Nacional de Adopciones aún funciona sin reglamento." *La Prensa Libre*, August 5, 2009. Accessed May 11, 2011. http://www.prensalibre.com/pl/2009/agosto/05/333053.html.

Fieser, Ezra. "Guatemala slowly confronts widespread rape of women." *The Christian Science Monitor*, November 20, 2009. http://www. csmonitor.com/2009/1120/p90s01-woam.html. Accessed May 10, 2011.

Frosch, Dan. "New Rules and Economy Strain Adoption Agencies." *The New York Times*, May 11, 2008.

Fundación Myrna Mack. "Informe de Situación Sobre la Fiscália Especial de Delitos Contra Operadores de Justicia: La persecución penal frente al fenómeno de la violencia en el Sistema de Justicia." Guatemala, September 2005.

Fundación Sobrevivientes. "Estudio Juridico-Social Sobre Trate de Personas en Guatemala-Con Estudio de Casos Atendidos por la Fundación Sobrevivientes." August 2009.

------. "Informe Anual de Trabajo Periodo Julio 2006-Junio 2007." 2007.

Gill, Lesley. "The School of the Americas: Military Training and Political Violence in the Americas." United States: Duke University Press, 2004.

Gillespie, Natalie Nichols. "Successful Adoption: A Guide for Christian Families." United States: Integrity Publishers, 2006.

Godoy, Emilio. "Five Million Women Have Fallen Prey to Trafficking Networks." *IPS News Service (Mexico)*, September 22, 2010. Accessed May 13, 2011. http://www.ipsnews.net/news.asp?idnews=52940.

Goicoechea, Ignacio and Jennifer Degeling. "Report of a Fact-Finding Mission to Guatemala in Relation to Intercountry Adoption February 26 – March 9, 2007." Hague Conference on International Private Law. May, 2007.

Goldman, Francisco. "The Long Night of White Chickens." United States: Grove Press, 1992.

------. "The Art of Political Murder: Who Killed the Bishop?" United States: Grove Press, 2007.

Goodman, Peter S. "Stealing Babies for Adoption: With U.S. Couples Eager to Adopt, Some Infants Are Abducted and Sold in China." *Washington Post*, March 12, 2006. Accessed May 13, 2011. http:// www.washingtonpost.com/wp-dyn/content/article/2006/03/11/ AR2006031100942.html.

Gosier, Chris. "Parsippany couple lose funds, but not hope." *The Daily*

Record of Morristown, New Jersey, February 4, 2004.

Graff, E.J. "The Lie We Love." *Foreign Policy*, November/ December 2008.

Grainger, Sarah. "Guatemala pushes for DNA test of kids adopted in U.S." *Reuters*, December 8, 2009. Accessed May 10, 2011. http://www.reuters.com/article/idUSTRE5B741820091208.

Greene, Melissa Fay. "There Is No Me Without You: One Woman's Odyssey to Rescue Africa's Children." United States: Bloomsbury, 2006.

Grobman, Linda May. "Days in The Lives Of Social Workers: 54 Professionals Tell 'Real-life' Stories from Social Work Practice". United States: White Hat Communications, 2004.

Grossman, Robert. "Interpreting the Development of the Evangelical Church in Guatemala: 2002." Doctor of Ministry diss., Southeastern Baptist Theological Seminary, Wake Forest, North Carolina, September 2002. Accessed May 13, 2011. http://www.prolades.com/cra/regions/cam/gte/grossmann/grossmann.htm

Guatadopt Blog. http://www.guatadopt.com/archives/000060.html.

Guatemala. El Congreso de la Republica de Guatemala. "Ley contra la Violencia Sexual, Explotación y Trata de Personas." March 2009. Accessed May 11, 2011. http://www.scribd.com/doc/17542534/Ley-contra-la-violencia-sexual-explotacion-y-trata-de-personas-Decreto-92009.

"Guatemala y EE. UU. acuerdan transparentar adopciones de niños." *AFP News Agency, La Prensa Libre*, December 9, 2010. Accessed May 13, 2011. http://www.prensalibre.com/noticias/Guatemala-EE-UU-transparentar-adopciones_0_386961525.html.

"Guatemalan army stole children for adoption, report says." CNN World Desk. CNN.com. September 12, 2009.

Guatemalan Human Rights Commission USA. "Femicide and Feminicide." 2009. www.ghrc-usa.org.

Guatemalan Human Rights Commission USA. "Gangs in Guatemala: Villa Nueva: Crime Prevention Laboratory." Fact Sheet.

"Guatemalan Scandals Over Adoption Procedures." *Inside Costa Rica Daily*, May 11, 2008. Accessed May 11, 2011. http://www.insidecostarica.com/dailynews/2008/may/11/reg02.htm.

Guttmacher Institute. "Early Maternity in Guatemala: an Ongoing Challenge." 2006.

Harbury, Jennifer K. *Searching for Everardo: A Story of Love, War, and the CIA in Guatemala*. New York: Warner Books, 1997.

Harlow, Summer. "Adoptive parents visit Guatemala to give back." *The Christian Science Monitor*, January 2, 2009.

"Hawaii Resident Pleads Guilty in Cambodian Adoption Conspiracy." US

Department of Justice Press Release. June 24, 2004.

"Head of UN anti-impunity panel in Guatemala resigns." *BBC News Latin American and Caribbean*, June 8, 2010. Accessed May 13, 2011. http://www.bbc.co.uk/news/10263494.

Herman, Ken. "Guatemala Under Scrutiny For Abuses In Adoptions." *Cox News Service*, March 1, 2007.

Hernández, Sandra and Megan O'Matz. „Officials: 3 Moms Sold Their Babies." *Florida Sun Sentinel,* December 19, 2003. Accessed August 11, 2011. http://articles.sun-sentinel.com/2003-12-19/news/0312190231_1_costa-rica-adoption-agency-iar.

"Hilda Morales refuta a la Fundación Sobrevivientes." *La Prensa Libre.* August 16, 2009. Accessed May 10, 2011 http://www.prensalibre.com/pl/2009/agosto/27/337805.html.

"Homicidios en Guatemala superan las muertes de civiles en Irak y Afganistán." *La Prensa Libre*, December 31, 2010. Accessed May 13, 2011. http://prensalibre.com/noticias/Violencia-Guatemala-Guerra_0_400160144.html.

Human Rights Office of the Archbishopric (ODHA). "The REMHI Report: Guatemala, nunca más (Guatemala never again)." Guatemala.

Huitz, Dalila. "PGN denuncia a 21 notarios." *Siglo XXI*, November 11, 2006. Accessed May 11, 2011. http://www.sigloxxi.com/index.php?link=noticias&noticiaid=6910.

Human Rights Watch /Americas, Human Rights Watch Children's Rights Project. "Guatemala's Forgotten Children: Police Violence and Abuses in Detention." July 1997. Accessed May 10, 2011. http://www.hrw.org/reports/1997/guat1/.

Huntenberg, Bettina. "Guatemalan Adoptions Suspended by Overseas Crack-Down." Council on Hemispheric Affairs. March 13, 2008. Accessed May 11. http://www.coha.org/guatemalan-adoptions-suspended-by-overseas-crack-down/. 2011.

IDHUSAC. "Derechos humanos de la juventud guatemalteca. (Human Rights of Young Guatemalans)." Guatemala.

ILPEC Guatemala report for UNICEF. "Adoption and the Rights of the Child in Guatemala." Guatemala, 2000.

"Indagaran a abogado por adopciones ilegales." *Siglo XX*, July 6, 1998.

"Instan a Clinton a resolver adopciones." *EFE News Agency, La Prensa Libre*, February 9, 2009. Accessed May 13, 2011. http://www.prensalibre.com/pl/2009/septiembre/03/339443.html.

Interiano, Elder. "Condena de 20 años para Arnoldo Noriega: Sentencia: Ex guerrillero, culpable de abusos deshonestos." *La Prensa Libre*, August 14, 2002. Accessed May 10, 2011. http://www.prensalibre.com/noticias/Condena-anos-Arnoldo-Noriega_0_57594553.html.

Investigation Team. "Investigación: Abogados acusados de participar en actividades ilícitas, encabezan trámites de adopciones." *El Periódico*, May 26, 2008. Accessed May 10, 2011. http://www.elperiodico.com.gt/es/20080526/investigacion/55928.

Keller, Amy. "Whose Standards?" *Florida Trend Magazine*, November 1, 2010.

Kerbs, Scott. "Residents call for support of orphans abroad." *The Southern Utah Spectrum*, December 1, 2008. Accessed May 10, 2011. http://www.thespectrum.com/apps/pbcs.dll/article?AID=/20081201/NEWS01/81201001&template=printart.

Koch, Wendy. "Cuts in foreign adoptions causing anxiety in USA; Rules protecting kids create barriers for some." *USA Today*, August 13, 2008.

Kolbay, Brendan. Columbia University School of International and Public Affairs and Association Nuestros Derechos Guatemala City. *Guatemala's Ley de Proteccion Integral de la Niñez y Adolescencia: One Year On*. January 2005. Accessed May 13, 2011. http://www.juvenilejusticepanel.org/resource/items/G/u/GuatemalaBrendanKolbayReportJan05.pdf.

Lacey, Marc. "Guatemala System Is Scrutinized as Americans Rush In to Adopt." *The New York Times*, November 5, 2006.

------. "Abuse Trails Central American Girls Into Gangs." *The New York Times*, April 11, 2008. Accessed May 10, 2011. http://www.nytimes.com/2008/04/11/world/americas/11guatemala.html?scp=1&sq=Abuse%20Trails%20Central%20American%20Girls%20Into%20Gangs%20&st=cse.

"La Cifra: Adopciones 2006." *Siglo XX*, May 19, 2007.

Lakshmanan, Indira A. R. "Unsolved killings terrorize women in Guatemala; Culture of impunity seen." *The Boston Globe*, March 30, 2006. Accessed May 10, 2011. http://www.boston.com/news/world/articles/2006/03/30/unsolved_killings_terrorize_women_in_guatemala/.

Lanchin, Mike. "El Salvador families seek adoption answers." *BBC News*, San Salvador. January 31, 2010. Accessed May 11, 2011. http://newsvote.bbc.co.uk/mpapps/pagetools/print/news.bbc.co.uk/2/hi/americas/8484887.stm?ad=1.

Llana, Sara Miller. "Why adopting in Guatemala is getting harder." *Christian Science Monitor*, September 12, 2007. Accessed May 11, 2011. http://www.csmonitor.com/2007/0912/p01s03-woam.html.

Llorca, Juan Carlos and Watson, Julie. Llorca, "Guatemalan adoption raid riles parents." *Associated Press*, *USA Today*, August 16, 2007.

Llorca, Juan Carlos. "Treaty Likely to Slow Guatemala Adoptions." *The

Associated Press, July 29, 2006.

------. "Guatemala Adoption Fraud May Hit U.S." *Associated Press, CBS News*, March 11, 2007.

------. "Officials rescue 46 children at alleged illegal adoption agency." *The Associated Press*, August 12, 2007.

------. "Empty cradles protest against adoptions." *Associated Press*, November 15, 2007.

------. "Guatemala adoption lawyers charged." *Associated Press, USA Today*, March 25, 2008. Accessed May 13, 2011. http://www.usatoday.com/news/topstories/2008-03-25-492777574_x.htm.

------. "Guatemala: Dirty war orphans put up for adoption." *Associated Press, Washington Post*, March 23, 2009. Accessed May 11, 2011. http://www.washingtonpost.com/wp-dyn/content/article/2009/03/23/AR2009032302381.html.

------. "Guatemala reopening international adoptions." *Associated Press*, November 20, 2009.

------. "Guatemala arrests show how drug cartels target weak nations, threaten global security." *Associated Press*, March 3, 2010.

------. "UN finds irregularities in Guatemalan adoptions." *The Associated Press, Washington Post*, December 1, 2010.

López, Olga O. "Alarma por el robo de niños." *La Prensa Libre*, July 1, 2006. Accessed May 13, 2011 http://web.archive.org/web/20060716201124/www.prensalibre.com/pl/2006/julio/01/145715.html.

------. "Señalan a jueza por autorización anómala: Operadora de justicia habría obviado dictamen de PGN." *La Prensa Libre*, September 3, 2007. Accessed May 11, 2011. http://web.archive.org/web/20071029023707/http://www.prensalibre.com/pl/2007/septiembre/03/181373.html.

------. "Darán recompensa por datos de niña robada." *La Prensa Libre*, March 24, 2009. Accessed May 13, 2011. http://replay.web.archive.org/20090327073441/http://www.prensalibre.com/pl/2009/marzo/24/303566.html.

------. "Madre descubre que su hija fue adoptada por extranjeros." *La Prensa Libre*, May 25, 2009. Accessed May 13, 2011. http://replay.web.archive.org/20090528200323/http://www.prensalibre.com/pl/2009/mayo/25/312319.html.

------. "Intimidan a madre de tres niñas asesinadas." *La Prensa Libre*, June 15, 2009. Accessed May 13, 2011. http://replay.web.archive.org/20090619202025/http://prensalibre.com/pl/2009/junio/16/321595.html.

López, Olga, Claudia Munaiz, and Carlos Menocal. "Guatemala, país exportador de bebés." *La Prensa Libre*, July 9, 2006. Accessed May 10, 2011. http://web.archive.org/web/20060816041318/www. prensalibre.com/pl/2006/julio/09/146417.html.

Loudis, Richard, Christina del Castillo, Anu Rajaraman, and Marco Castillo. "Central America and Mexico Gang Assessment, Annex 2: Guatemala Profile." USAID, April 2006. Accessed May 13, 2011. http://www.usaid.gov/gt/docs/guatemala_profile.pdf.

Lundy, Sarah. "Adoptive dad gets probation on son-abuse charge." *Orlando Sentinel*, March 31, 2009. Accessed May 10, 2011. orlandosentinel. com/news/local/orl-locdadabuse31033109mar31,0,1114189.story.

Ma, Kelvin. "Adoption Crackdown Puts Valrico Family In Limbo." *The Tampa Tribune*, October 11, 2007.

Manson, Pamela and Rosetta, Lisa. "Adoption scam defendants cut no-jail-time deal." *The Salt Lake Tribune*, January 7, 2009. Accessed May 10, 2011. http://www.sltrib.com/portlet/article/html/ fragments/print_article.jsp?articleId=11386108&siteId=297, http:// poundpuplegacy.org/node/24204

Marroquin, Ericka. "Vacío legal frena adopciones: Rechazan 74% de Trámites de Adopción." *Siglo XXI*. February 10, 2007.

Martínez, Ángeles Cruz. "Trámites y vacíos legales impiden la adopción de niños en el país." *La Jornana (Mexico)*. October 4, 2007. Accessed May 10, 2011. http://www.jornada.unam.mx/2007/10/04/index. php?section=sociedad&article=045n1soc.

Martinic, Sergio. *EFA Global Monitoring Report 2003/4, The Leap to Equality*. "Educational progress and problems in Guatemala, Honduras and Mexico." November, 2003.

Meier, Patricia J. and Xiaole Zhang. „SOLD INTO ADOPTION: THE HUNAN BABY TRAFFICKING SCANDAL EXPOSES VULNERABILITIES IN CHINESE ADOPTIONS TO THE UNITED STATES." *Cumberland Law Review,* October 25, 2008. http://www.ethicanet.org/MeierZhang.pdf Accessed August 10, 2011.

Melville, Kathleen. Guatemala Human Rights Commission. "Confronting Femicide in Guatemala." September 7, 2006. Accessed May 10, 2011. http://www.ghrc-usa.org/.

Miller, Carol Marbin. „State goes after records of adoptions." *The Miami Herald.*, December 25, 2003. Accessed August 11, 2011. http://sites. google.com/site/internationaladoptionfacts/costa-rica---state-goes-after-records-of-adoptions.

Miller, Talea. "From the Field: Violence Against Women in Guatemala." The Rundown on PBS NewsHour. February 7, 2011.

Ministerio Público of the República de Guatemala. "Memoria de Labores Ano 2006. Memoria de Labores Ano 2007. Memoria de Labores Ano

2009." Accessed May 10, 2011. http://www.mp.gob.gt/.

Montt, José Efraín Ríos. "Guatemala coup leader's broadcast to the nation." *BBC*, March 25, 1982.

Moore, Russell D. *Adopted for Life: The Priority of Adoption for Christian Families & Churches.* United States: Crossway Books, 2009.

Morales, Mario. "Una oficial abatida: Trabajaba en la Fiscalía." *Nuestro Diaria*, Accessed May 11, 2011. http://digital.nuestrodiario. com/Olive/ODE/NuestroDiario/LandingPage/LandingPage. aspx?href=R05ELzIwMDgvMDMvMTI.&pageno=Ng..&entity=QX IwMDYwMA..&view=ZW50aXR5.

"MP Fiscal General reacciona contra acusaciones de Castresana." *La Hora*, June 7, 2010. Accessed May 10, 2011. http://www.lahora.com.gt/ notas.php?key=68090&fch=2010-06-07.

"Muere en accidente ex abogado de militares condenados por el asesinato de Gerardi." *Noticias de Guatemala*, July 9, 2010. Accessed May 13, 2011. http://noticias.com.gt/nacionales/20100709-muere-en-accidente-ex-abogado-de-militares-condenados-por-el-asesinato-de-gerardi.html.

Municipality of Villa Nueva. "General Data." Fact Sheet. Accessed May 11, 2011. http://www.villanueva.gob.gt/home/mi-municipio/datos. html.

"National Geographic: Ambassador - Inside the Embassy." Prod. Robin Goldman, John B Bredar, Writ. Alex Chadwick. November 26, 2002. National Geographic Video. DVD.

Nelson, Diane M. *A Finger in the Wound: Body Politics in Quincentennial Guatemala.* Los Angeles: University of California Press, 1999.

Nelson-Erichsen, Jean. *Inside the Adoption Agency: Understanding Intercountry Adoption in the Era of the Hague Convention.* United States: iUniverse, 2007.

Network in Solidarity with Guatemala (NISGUA). "The School of the Americas and Guatemala." Accessed May 10, 2011. http://www. nisgua.org/themes_campaigns/impunity/The%20School%20of%20 the%20Americas%20and%20Guatemala.pdf.

"Nine Tots Rescued From Illegal Adoption in Guatemala." *EFE wire service, The Latin American Herald Tribune*, April 8, 2009. Accessed May 13, 2011. http://www.laht.com/article. asp?ArticleId=331425&CategoryId=23558.

"Niños para adoptar serán sometidos a pruebas ADN." *ACAN-EFE News Agency, La Prensa Libre*, May 24, 2010. Accessed May 10, 2011. http://www.prensalibre.com/noticias/justicia/Ninos-adoptar-sometidos-pruebas-ADN_0_267573504.html.

Noel, Benita. "Kidnapped kids reunite with family in Guatemala."

Dateline NBC, Accessed May 10, 2011. http://insidedateline.msnbc.
msn.com/_news/2008/01/17/4374303-kidnapped-kids-reunite-with-
family-in-guatemala.

"Notariales." *El Periódico*, December 12, 2007. Accessed May 10, 2011.
http://www.elperiodico.com.gt/es/20071212/pais/46605.

O'Dwyer, Jennifer. *Mamalita: An Adoption Memoir.* United States: Seal
Press, 2010.

Oficina de Democracia y Gobernabilidad, Programa de Transparencia
y Anticorrupción de la Agencia de los Estados Unidos para el
Desarrollo Internacional (USAID). "Indicadores de Percepción y
Experiencias de Corrupción en Guatemala." July 2006. Accessed May
10, 2011. http://accionciudadana.org.gt/index.php?option=com_
content&task=view&id=40&Itemid=50.

Olkon, Sara. "Baby selling is a major business in Guatemala." *The Miami
Herald*, June 4, 2000.

Operation Blessing International. "Blessings." August 2009. Accessed May
10, 2011. http://www.operationblessing.org.

Orantes, Coralia. "Bebé robada iba a ser dada en adopción." *La
Prensa Libre*, July 23, 2008. Accessed August 26, 2011. http://
www.prensalibre.com.gt/noticias/Bebe-robada-iba-dada-
adopcion_0_166785822.html

------. "Detienen a médico, por adopción ilegal." *La Prensa Libre*, July
27, 2008. Accessed August 26, 2011. http://replay.web.archive.
org/20090327073441/http://www.prensalibre.com/pl/2009/
marzo/24/303566.html.

------. "Capturan a dos abogados por caso de adopción ilegal." *La Prensa
Libre*, May 14, 2009. Accessed August 26, 2011. http://www.
prensalibre.com.gt/noticias/Capturan-abogados-caso-adopcion-
ilegal_0_42595773.html.

------. "Deportan de EE. UU. a mujer vinculada a adopciones ilegales."
La Prensa Libre, April 22, 2010. Accessed May 10, 2011. http://
www.prensalibre.com/noticias/justicia/Llega-EE-UU-vinculada-
adopciones_0_247775465.html.

Ordóñez, Antonio. "Empieza a funcionar el RENAP." *La Prensa Libre*,
April 12, 2007. Accessed May 11, 2011. http://www.prensalibre.com/
noticias/Empieza-funcionar-Renap_0_151785113.html.

Ortiz, Gerson. "Acciones legales contra adopciones ilegales." *La Hora*,
November 21, 2007. Accessed May 13, 2011. http://www.lahora.
com.gt/notas.php?key=18556.

------. "Capturan a abogada sindicada de ser cabecilla de red de adopciones
anómalas." *La Hora*, December 16, 2009. Accessed May 10, 2011.
http://www.lahora.com.gt/notas.php?key=59930&fch=2009-12-16.

------. "Débil situación penal para la trata de personas en el país." *La Hora*, March 1, 2010. Accessed May 10, 2011. http://www.lahora.com.gt/notas.php?key=63313&fch=2010-03-01.

Ovando, Olga Lopez. "Cicig revela un complot para apoderarse del MP." *La Prensa Libre*, June 15, 2010. Accessed May 10, 2011. http://www.prensalibre.com/noticias/Cicig-revela-complot-apoderarse-MP_0_280771944.html.

Palencia, Gema. „Adopciones: Piden intervención de PDH." *La Prensa Libre*, July 5, 2008. Accessed August 20, 2011. http://www.prensalibre.com.gt/noticias/Adopciones-Piden-intervencion-PDH_0_165584155.html.

Palma, C. and Estrada, R. "Se aprueba ley que elimina las adopciones notariales." *El Periódico*, December 12, 2007. Accessed May 10, 2011. http://www.elperiodico.com.gt/es/20071212/pais/46605.

Paxtor, Edwin. „Piden 50 años para sindicadas por muerte de niña." *La Prensa Libre*, June 6, 2011. Accessed August 20, 2011. http://www.prensalibre.com/noticias/justicia/Piden-prision-sindicadas-muerte-nino_0_494950770.html.

PEAR (Parents for Ethical Adoption Reform). "Ethiopia: Best Practices Survey." March 16-April 16, 2010.

Perera, Victor. *Unfinished Conquest: The Guatemalan Tragedy.* United States: University of California Press, 1995.

Pérez, Sonia. "Incertidumbre por destino de menor: Niño supuestamente secuestrado está en casa hogar." *La Prensa Libre*, April 17, 2004. Accessed May 10, 2011. http://www.prensalibre.com/noticias/Incertidumbre-destino-menor_0_91791814.html.

Permanent Bureau of the Hague. "Guide to Good Practice Under the Hague Convention of May 1993 on Protection of Children and Co-Operation in Respect of Intercountry Adoption Implementation." Hague Conference on International Private Law. August, 2005.

Pertman, Adam. *Adoption Nation: How the Adoption Revolution Is Transforming America.* United States: Basic Books, 2000.

Poe, Andrea C. "Not home for the holidays: A story of adoption in Guatemala." *The Washington Times*, January 3, 2011.

Porter, Claire. "Norma Cruz Aims to Stop Femicide in Guatemala." *UPIP, News Wire*, March 29, 2010. Accessed May 11, 2011. http://www.upiu.com/articles/norma-cruz-aims-to-stop-femicide-in-guatemala.

Priest, Dana. "U.S. Instructed Latins on Executions, Torture." *The Washington Post*, September 21, 1996.

"Programan indagatoria por tercera vez." *Siglo XII*, July 4, 1998.

"Protestan por cierre de caso de adopción anómala." *La Prensa Libre*, March 3, 2009. Accessed May 13, 2011. http://replay.web.archive.

org/20090326075529/http://www.prensalibre.com/pl/2009/
marzo/23/303676.html.

"Retiran inmunidad a juez vinculado a adopciones ilegales." *La Hora*,
May 27, 2010. May 11, 2011. http://www.lahora.com.gt/notas.
php?key=67538&fch=2010-05-27.

Reynoso, Conié. "Se desploman las adopciones." *La Prensa Libre*,
September 9, 2009. http://www.prensalibre.com/pl/2009/
septiembre/28/341040.html.

Riben, Mirah. *The Stork Market: America's Multi-Billion Dollar
Unregulated Adoption Industry.* New Jersey: Advocate Publications,
2007.

Rohter, Larry. "Guatemala Election Becomes Vote on Former Dictator."
The New York Times, January 7, 1996.

Roig-Franzia, Manuel. "Killings on the Campaign Trail: 50 Guatemalan
Candidates, Activists Have Died in Run-Up to Vote." *The
Washington Post*, September 9, 2007. Accessed May 10, 2011. http://
www.washingtonpost.com/wp-dyn/content/article/2007/09/08/
AR2007090800704.html.

Rosales, Carlos Castañaza. "Adopciones: 4,270 expedientes desde 1996."
Siglo XXI, June 5, 1998.

Rosenberg, Mica. "Cleaning Up International Adoptions." *TIME
Magazine*, August 29, 2007. Accessed May 10, 2011. http://www.
time.com/time/printout/0,8816,1657355,00.html.

Rotabi, Karen Smith. "Guatemala City: Hunger Protests Amid Allegations
of Child Kidnapping and Adoption Fraud." *SocMag*, August 22,
2009. Accessed May 10, 2011. http://www.socmag.net/?p=540.

------. "From Guatemala to Ethiopia: Shifts in Intercountry Adoption
Leaves Ethiopia Vulnerable for Child Sales and Other Unethical
Practices." *SocMag*, June 8, 2010. Accessed May 11, 2011. www.
socmag.net/?p=615&print=1.

Ruhl, Katharine. "Guatemala's Femicides and the Ongoing Struggle for
Women's Human Rights: Update to CGRS's 2005 Report Getting
Away With Murder." The Center for Gender & Refugee Studies,
University of California, Hastings College of the Law. September,
2006.

Russell, George and James Willwerth. "Guatemala: Surprise in the
Sermon." *TIME Magazine*, May 23, 1983. Accessed May 10, 2011.
http://www.time.com/time/printout/0,8816,953896,00.html.

Sactic, Wálter. "Reconocen avances en proceso de adopciones." *La
Prensa Libre*, March 9, 2009. http://www.prensalibre.com/pl/2009/
septiembre/08/339807.html.

------. "Bajan adopciones." *La Prensa Libre*, August 9, 2009. http://www.

prensalibre.com/pl/2009/septiembre/10/340814.html

Samayoa, Claudia Virginia. „Front Line Guatemala: Ataques en Contra de Defensoras y Defensores de Derechos Humans 2000-2005." Front Line and La Unidad de Protección de Defensores de Derechos Humanos del Movimiento por los Derechos Humanos, Guatemala, 2005.

Sandoval, Marta. "Niños con dos madres." *El Periódico*, June 14, 2009. Accessed May 10, 2011. http://www.elperiodico.com.gt/es/20090614/portada/103825/.

Sanford, Victoria. "Buried Secrets: Truth and Human Rights in Guatemala." United States: Palgrave MacMillan, 2003.

Sas, Ángel and Kenia Reyes. "Salen libres implicados en robo de niño: Fueron beneficiados por una medida sustitutiva legal." *El Periódico*, July 20, 2007. Accessed May 10, 2011. http://www.elperiodico.com.gt/es/20070720/actualidad/41782/.

Satyanarayana, Megha. "Lawsuit accuses adoption agency of racketeering, fraud." *Detroit FREE PRESS*, December 28, 2008.

Schemo, Diana Jean. "THE BABY TRAIL: A special report, Adoptions in Paraguay: Mothers Cry Theft." *The New York Times*, March 19, 1996. Accessed May 11, 2011. http://www.nytimes.com/1996/03/19/world/the-baby-trail-a-special-report-adoptions-in-paraguay-mothers-cry-theft.html?pagewanted=print.

Schirmer, Jennifer. *The Guatemalan Military Project: A Violence Called Democracy.* United States: University of Pennsylvania Press, 1998.

Schlesinger, Stephen, et al. *Bitter Fruit: The Story of the American Coup in Guatemala, Revised and Expanded.* United States: Harvard University David Rockefeller Center for Latin American Studies, 1982.

Schuster Institute for Investigative Journalism's Gender & Justice Project. "Capsule History of International Adoption." Last Modified February 23, 2011. http://www.brandeis.edu/investigate/gender/adoption/history.html.

Seelke, Clare Ribando. "Gangs in Central America." Congressional Research Service Specialist in Latin American Affairs. January 11, 2010.

Seijo, Lorena. "Embajada de EE. UU. "aprobó" adopción de niñas raptadas." *La Prensa Libre*, February 4, 2008.

------. "Where are our children?" ("¿Dónde Están Nuestros Hijos?") *La Prensa Libre*, November 25, 2007. http://www.prensalibre.com/pl/2007/noviembre/25/lectura_nac.html # 188800.

Serrill, Michael S., Constable, Anne, and Ricardo, Chavira. "Going Abroad to Find a Baby." *TIME magazine*, October 21, 1991. Accessed May 11, 2011. http://www.time.com/time/

printout/0,8816,974083,00.html.

Sherwell, Phillip. "Mother reunited with baby stolen for adoption." *The Sunday Telegraph (London)*, July 27, 2008.

Singh, Susheela, Elena Prada, and Edgar Kestler. "Induced Abortion and Unintended Pregnancy in Guatemala." Guttmacher Institute. September 3, 2006. Accessed May 13, 2011. http://replay.web. archive.org/20080820233442/http://www.alanguttmacher.org/pubs/ journals/3213606.html.

Smith, SSA J. Perry and Kim A. Robson. "The Rise of New Religions in Latin America and their Impact on Society." Inter-American Defense College. Washington, D.C. May, 1994.

Solinger, Rickie. *Beggars and Choosers: How the Politics of Choice Shapes Adoption, Abortion, and Welfare in the United States.* United States: Hill and Wang, 2001.

Spar, Debora L. *The Baby Business: How Money, Science, and Politics Drive the Commerce of Conception.* United States: Harvard Business School Press, 2006.

Stanford, Victoria. "Femicide in Guatemala." *Harvard Review of Latin America*, Winter 2008.

Stoll, David. *Is Latin America Turning Protestant? The Politics of Evangelical Growth.* United States: University of California Press, 1990.

Stramwasser, Isabel and Brenda J. Wemp. "GUATEMALA: ATTACKS ON JURISTS 2005-2009." Accessed May 11, 2011. http://www. lrwc.org.

Summerfield, Robin. "The business of global adoption." *The Calgary Herald*, November 10, 2008.

Tayler, Letta. "Adoptions Under Fire in Guatemala." *Newsday*, October 26, 2003.

"The Elders Said Go: Brigadier General José Efraín Ríos Montt." *TIME Magazine.* April 5, 1982. Accessed May 11, 2011. http://www.time. com/time/magazine/article/0,9171,921160,00.html.

"The End does not Justify the Means." *Ethica*, Accessed May 11, 2011. http://www.ethicanet.org/item. php?recordid=Galindo&pagestyle=default.

The International Crisis Group. "Guatemala: Squeezed Between Crime and Impunity." July 2010.

The World Bank. "2010 Country Report: Guatemala 2010." Accessed May 10, 2011. http://data.worldbank.org/country/guatemala.

"Threatened and attacked -- the dangers of opening Guatemala's police files." Amnesty International Bulletin. March 27, 2009. Accessed May 10, 2011. http://www.amnestyusa.org/document. php?id=ENGNAU200903279963&lang=e.

Thomas, Jeffrey. "U.S. Says International Adoption Important for Children in Need." The U.S. Department of State's Bureau of International Information Programs. December 17, 2009. Accessed May 10, 2011. http://www.america.gov/st/peopleplace-english/2009/December/200912171352431CJsamohT0.6776174.html.

Tinsley, Anna M. "Adoptive parents are still waiting on Guatemalan authorities." The Texas Star Telegram, December 8, 2008. Accessed May 13, 2011. http://www.star-telegram.com/804/v-print/story/1079877.html.

Tobik, Amy K.D. "Finding a home." The Voice/ The Seminole Voice, May 16, 2008. Accessed May 13, 2011. http://www.golfest.com/Seminole_Voice/article.asp?ID=475.

Transparency International. "Transparency International Global Corruption Barometer 2007." December 6, 2007.

"U.N. Expert: Majority of International Adoptions in Guatemala Illegal." Casa Alianza. March 31, 2000. http://www.casa-alianza.org/EN/lmn/docs/20000331.00394.htm.

UNESCO EFA Monitoring Report. "Literacy for Life 2006: Latin America and the Caribbean." 2006.

"UNICEF, Guatemalan Adoption, and the Best Interests of the Child: An Informative Study." Families Without Borders. November 2003.

United Nations Development Program. "Human Development Report 2009 Overcoming barriers: Human mobility and development." 2009.

United Nations. UN Special Rapporteur on the Sale of Children, Child Prostitution and Child Pornography. "Report on the Mission to Guatemala." January 27, 2000.

USAID. "Dirty money, Former Gang Member Gets Second Chance." Accessed May 13, 2011 http://www.usaid.gov/stories/guatemala/fp_guatemala_gangs.html

US Department of Justice. "Justice Department Indicts Employee of Adoption Agency on Visa Fraud Charges." January 8, 2004.

US Department of State. "Victims of Trafficking and Violence Protection Act of 2000: Trafficking in Persons Report." 2004. Accessed May 11, 2011. http://classic-web.archive.org/web/20040625213226/http://www.state.gov/documents/organization/33614.pdf.

------. "Trafficking in Persons Report 2008 – Guatemala." UNHCR Refworld. June 4, 2008. Accessed May 10, 2011. http://www.unhcr.org/refworld/docid/484f9a1a9.html.

US Embassy in Guatemala. "2004 Crime Incidents Involving Foreigners." Accessed May 10, 2011. http://guatemala.usembassy.gov/2004_incidents.html.

------. "2005 Crime Incidents Involving Foreigners" Accessed May 10, 2011. http://guatemala.usembassy.gov/2005_incidents.html.

------. "2006 Crime Incidents Involving Foreigners." Accessed May 10, 2011. http://guatemala.usembassy.gov/2006_incidents.html.

Valdez, Sandra. "Emiten reglamento para adopciones." *La Prensa Libre*, July 13, 2010. Accessed May 10, 2011. http://www.prensalibre.com/noticias/Emiten-reglamento-adopciones_0_297570257.html.

------. "Adopciones foráneas siguen en un impasse." *La Prensa Libre*, December 22, 2010. Accessed May 13, 2011. http://www.prensalibre.com/noticias/Adopciones-foraneas-siguen-impasse_0_394760546.html.

------. "Aumentan rescates de niños por medio de Ley Alba-Keneth." *La Prensa Libre*, December 25, 2010.

Valladares, Danilo. "Foreign Adoptions Are Back – Along with the Doubts." *IPS Inter Press Service*, May 11, 2010. Accessed May 11, 2011. http://www.ipsnews.net/print.asp?idnews=51378.

Vásquez, Byron Rolando. "Cuatro supuestos Zetas dejados en libertad De doce delitos que les imputaban, sólo serán procesados por dos." *El Diario de Central América*, June 23, 2009. Accessed May 13, 2011. http://liveweb.web.archive.org/http://dca.gob.gt:85/archivo/090623/nacional4-3.html.

------. "CSJ retira inmunidad a juez de Escuintla." *Siglo XXI*. May 28, 2010. Accessed May 10, 2011. http://www.s21.com.gt/node/11783.

"Violencia contra el sistema de justicia: el aparato estatal sigue postergando la prevención y el combate." Fundación Myrna Mack. July 2005, Guatemala.

Webber, Marlene. *As If Kids Mattered: What's Wrong in the World of Child Protection and Adoption.* Toronto: Key Porter Books, 1998.

Welch, Amanda. "Oviedo agency faces multiple complaints." *The Seminole Chronicle*, December 3, 2008. Accessed May 11, 2011. http://www.seminolechronicle.com/vnews/display.v?TARGET=printable&article_id=4937184fab40b.

Wilkinson, Daniel. "Silence on the Mountain: Stories of Terror, Betrayal, and Forgetting in Guatemala (American Encounters/Global Interactions)." United States: Houghton-Mifflin, 2002.

Wittner, Kelly. „Curbing Child-Trafficking in Intercountry Adoptions: Will International Treaties and Adoption Moratoriums Accomplish the Job in Cambodia?" *Pacific Rim Law and Policy Journal,* March 2003. Accessed August 10, 2011. http://digital.law.washington.edu/dspace-law/bitstream/handle/1773.1/735/12PacRimLPolyJ595.pdf?sequence=1

World Bank. "Guatemala at a Glance." Accessed May 13, 2011. http://

devdata.worldbank.org/AAG/gtm_aag.pdf

Zamora, Juan M. Castillo. "Arlene, Anyelí y Heidy, causa de la lucha de Cruz." *El Periódico*, July 24, 2009. Accessed May 10, 2011. http://www.elperiodico.com.gt/es/20090724/pais/108141/?tpl=54.

------. "MP solicita antejuicio contra Juez de Escuintla por varios delitos." *El Periódico*, June 14, 2009. Accessed May 11, 2011. http://www.elperiodico.com.gt/es/20090714/pais/106846/

Zarembo, Alan. "A Place To Call Home: The Anger, Tears And Frustrating Runarounds Of A Guatemalan Adoption Case." *Newsweek*, July 15, 2002.

Zelada, Rodolfo. "Condenan a cuatro mujeres por robar niño." *Agencia AFP, La Hora*, April 18, 2009. Accessed May 10, 2011. http://www.lahora.com.gt/notas.php?key=47469&fch=2009-04-18.

ABOUT THE AUTHOR

Erin Siegal is a writer and photographer whose work has been publis-hed by various outlets, including the New York Times, Reuters, and Rolling Stone. *Finding Fernanda* is her first book. Siegal is an Ethics and Justice Fellow at the Schuster Institute for Investigative Journalism, and lives in Northern California and Baja California, México. To learn more, please visit www.erinsiegal.com.